International User Interfaces

Edited by

Elisa M. del Galdo

and Jakob Nielsen

WILEY COMPUTER PUBLISHING

John Wiley & Sons, Inc.

New York • Chichester • Brisbane • Toronto • Singapore

I'd like to dedicate this book to my husband in gratitude for his contagious enthusiasm by which I have always been happily infected. But I can't. The truth is, my husband is a miserable old sod (i.e., the British version of a grumpy old man) who always has something negative to say about everything I do. However, he's frequently right and, on the occasions that I can accept the criticism, I always do a better job because of it. So I'll dedicate the book to him anyway in spite of his bad attitude because I love him. Somebody has to. I think of it as a service to the European community.

E. M. del Galdo

Publisher: Katherine Schowalter
Editor: Theresa Hudson
Managing Editor: Angela Murphy
Text Design & Composition: Publishers' Design and Production Services, Inc.

Designations used by companies to distinguish their products are often claimed as trademarks. In all instances where John Wiley & Sons, Inc. is aware of a claim, the product names appear in initial capital or all capital letters. Readers, however, should contact the appropriate companies for more complete information regarding trademarks and registration.

This text is printed on acid-free paper.

This publication is designed to provide accurate and authoritative information in regard to the subject matter covered. It is sold with the understanding that the publisher is not engaged in rendering legal, accounting, or other professional service. If legal advice or other expert assistance is required, the services of a competent professional person should be sought.

Library of Congress Cataloging-in-Publication Data:

ISBN: 0-471-14965-9

Printed in the United States of America
10 9 8 7 6 5 4 3 2 1

Contents

Preface

We all know the world is becoming a global marketplace. This is especially true for producers of computer products. All major companies in the industry have 50 percent or more of their sales outside their native country and it's now common for major software products to be released simultaneously in ten to twenty languages. Customers previously unaccustomed to translated products now expect them. If they aren't available from one vendor, they will go elsewhere. Not surprisingly, within almost all computer companies, there is considerable interest in the design and production of international products and their user interfaces. Presumably this is partly responsible for the recent explosion of books, magazines, videos, journal articles, and a variety of information on the Internet.

Unfortunately, this heightened interest in internationalization and localization has not yet been translated into increased usability for international users. By *international*, we mean users from countries other than the one where the product was designed. A localized product will typically allow international users to use their native character set and see menu commands and possibly error messages and dialog boxes in their own language. Superficially, this may seem sufficient, but the actual usability of the resulting user interfaces often leaves much to be desired. This does not just occur in cases where products are translated from English. You are sure to have experienced bad translations into English, so it should be easy to empathize with a user who is subjected to a poorly translated product. Too often, localization is done without knowledge of usability engineering principles or the context in which the product will be used. For example, documentation may either not be translated or translated in a way that in some cases makes it even harder to understand than the original. The fact is, we have not been doing a complete job.

We believe there are three levels at which to tackle the problem of producing international user interfaces. The first level is being able to process and display the user's native language, character set, notations, and formats. This has been accomplished by most companies. It is the levels beyond this where many companies lack expertise and experience, a fact which is all too often apparent in the quality and usability of the international versions of their products.

The second level concerns producing a user interface and user information that is *understandable* and *usable* in the user's native language. This involves the use of common usability methods that must be adapted for use in different countries or cultures. The third level is the ability to produce systems that accommodate users' cultural characteristics. This means producing designs that go beyond avoiding offensive or nonsensical icons. Designs must address specific cultural models, for example, the way business is conducted and the way people communicate in various countries.

Companies have begun to recognize the need to address the issues included in levels two and three. And that is why we believe it is time to produce a new book that takes a more expansive view of internationalization than has been done in the past. Chapters such as Nielsen's on international usability engineering, and Dray and Mrazek's, which discusses their experiences in tailoring contextual inquiry methods across cultures, address the second level of internationalization. Chapters by Hoft, del Galdo, Krock, and Ito and Nakakoji touch on some of the more abstract cultural issues of level three.

The effect of technology on man and culture is impressive. One has only to look at how computer and communications technology has changed our lives in the last 35 years. Depending on where you live and how old you are, the changes may not be so dramatic, beneficial, or even recognizable, but they are there. Technology is there to serve us and improve the quality of our lives. The thought that technology may force users to lose their language or to make detrimental changes to their culture is contrary to the goals of the user-interface designer. The authors have tried to show how you can accommodate language and culture in your designs, regardless of users' original language. We hope that the information in this book will start people thinking about some of the other concerns beyond just language translation.

ELISA M. DEL GALDO
Opio, Alpes-Maritimes
France

JAKOB NIELSEN
Mountain View, California
USA

List of Contributors

Fethi Amara
LangBox International
Immeuble Space, Bat. B
208-212 Route de Grenoble
06200 NICE France

Lei Chen
Object Systems Integrators
1950 Spectrum Circle, Suite #400
Marietta, GA 30067

John Connolly
Loughborough University of
Technology
Department of Computer Studies
Loughborough, Leicestershire
LE11 3TU United Kingdom

Steven D. Copeland
Schiesser-Copeland Consulting
1507 Wren Road
Bowling Green, OH 43402

Elisa del Galdo
del Galdo Consulting Ltd.
1 chemin du bois d'Opio
Les Tomieres, villa 2
06650 OPIO
France

Susan M. Dray
Dray & Associates
2115 Kenwood Parkway
Minneapolis, MN 55405

Yong Gao
Intelligent Agents Group
FTP Software, Inc.
2 High Street
North Andover, MA 01845

Nancy Hoft
Intl Tech Comm SVCS
RR2 Box 493 Oran Road
Temple, NH 03084-9761

Masao Ito
Nil Software
2-17-7 E-Space 3F
Kinuta, Setagaya
Tokyo 157
Japan

Wanying Jin
Computing Research Laboratory
New Mexico State University
Box 30001/Dept. CRL
Las Cruces, NM 88003

Eric Krock
Interleaf Japan
Takadanobaba 1-31-18-10F
Shinjuku-ku, Tokyo 169
Japan

Aaron Marcus
Aaron Marcus and Associates, Inc.
1144 65th Street, Suite F
Emeryville, CA 94608-6125

Deborah Mrazek
Hewlett-Packard
P.O. Box 8906
Camas, WA 98607

Kumiyo Nakakoji
Department of Computer Science
CB 430
University of Colorado
Boulder, CO 80309-0430

Jakob Nielsen
Sun Microsystems
2550 Garcia Avenue
Mountain View, CA 94043

Frank Portaneri
LangBox International
Immeuble Space, Bat. B
208-212 Route de Grenoble
06200 NICE
France

CHAPTER 1

International Usability Engineering

This is a very pragmatic chapter: it concerns the specific steps you can take to assess the usability of your designs for international customers. The key lesson of the chapter is that there are such steps and that you can take action to improve international usability.

The first rule of Douglas Adams' *The Hitchhiker's Guide to the Galaxy* is "don't panic," and similarly, the first rule of international usability engineering is "don't despair." In principle, there are myriad issues to consider when one wants to serve an international audience, and it is easy for people reading books like the present volume, to despair and give up on international usability because of the many problems. As anecdotal evidence, I can cite one of the reviewers of the manuscript of my earlier book, *Usability Engineering* (Nielsen 1994a): In her comments on the chapter about international user interfaces she wrote, "I despaired pretty early." The *last* section of that earlier chapter was my "don't despair" principle, and to avoid similar problems with this new book, I have moved this advice up to the very beginning here.

If you were an American user of a British color graphics application that had a "Colour" menu you might think "Oh, those crazy Brits forgot to localize the Color menu." Similarly, if you were a British user of an American application with a

"Color" menu, you might think "Oh, those chauvinist Americans didn't bother localizing the Colour menu." In either case, the users would have no problems recognizing the function of the menu, so the usability problem would mainly be an annoyance and a reminder that the software was foreign-made. Consider, though, what would happen if these British and American users had to use a Danish application where the menu was called "Farve." *This* lack of localization would indeed be a usability catastrophe. The point is that major usability problems are often fairly easy to discover with a minimum of usability engineering effort. It would be nice to do a perfect job and study all details, but if you are pressed for time, the so-called "discount usability engineering" approach (Nielsen 1994a) will at least help you avoid the catastrophes, even though some minor problems may go undetected.

Remember: If you do nothing, then for sure your user interface will have horrible international usability and you will suffer condescending reviews in the foreign trade press and lose sales. Even if you only do a small amount of international usability engineering, you will probably avoid the really bad problems and the resulting customer complaints.

All the major user-interface platforms come with a handbook for developing internationalized versions of your code, and the first step toward international usability will certainly be to acquire the appropriate book for your platform and follow its rules about character sets, recommended translations of menu titles, and so forth. If no guidelines are available for your platform, you can still benefit from books about mainstream platforms (e.g., Kano 1995) and you should consider following their recommended terminology translations. Using standard translations is recommended for the sake of external consistency (having your terminology match other terms users may have seen in other products).

The next step after following platform standards is to pay attention to available knowledge about international user interfaces, such as the chapters in this book. There are limits to how much can be achieved by pure planning and thinking, however, no matter how well-intended (Stiff 1995). Therefore, you should also try out one or more of the usability engineering activities described in the following. To a large extent, usability engineering is process, by which I mean that simply *doing* something about it is one of the most important factors in getting a good user interface. It has been said that 80 percent of success is showing up, and even though I am not sure that 80 percent of the quality of a user interface is derived from simply doing something about it, there is no doubt that the difference between doing something and doing nothing is substantial. Of course, it is preferable to combine several usability methods and use each of them as well and thoroughly as possible, but it is paramount not to let lofty ideals prevent you from taking more pragmatic action on those projects that have more modest budgets.

A first method to improve international usability might be called *international inspection*, in analogy with the usability inspection methods (Nielsen and Mack 1994) that have become so popular in recent years. An international inspection simply involves having people from multiple countries look over your user interface and analyze whether they think it would cause any problems in their country. In contrast to international user testing (discussed in the following), international inspection is partly guesswork since it does not involve real users doing real tasks with the system; but at least it results in *educated* guesses.

The inspectors in international inspection should preferably be usability specialists from the various countries in question. Most usability consultants perform heuristic evaluations as part of their everyday practice and should therefore be experienced in receiving a user interface "in the mail" and returning an evaluation within a few days. In some countries it may be difficult to find usability consultants, but North America, most European countries, and the leading countries in Asia all have plenty of available usability consultants who can be contacted through, for example, postings on the comp.human-factors newsgroup on the Internet or on the jobs bulletin board at major user-interface conferences like CHI (Computer-Human Interaction), INTERACT, or the Usability Professionals Association.

If no usability consultants can be found or if you don't have a sufficient budget to hire them, then it is also possible to use people without usability expertise from the various countries. Your local sales offices will often serve as a source of available personnel for an international inspection, and you can simply mail them the design for comments. When using usability professionals for the international inspection, it will be possible to send out a user-interface specification, but when using nonprofessional inspectors it is normally better to send a prototype implementation since they may have difficulty in visualizing the user experience from written specs.

Due to the increased penetration of the Internet, it will often be possible to send out design specs and even executable prototypes by electronic mail to people in other countries, meaning that the turnaround time is essentially the same as when asking for comments from colleagues in the office next door. At Sun, we often circulate design specs to email aliases of people in various branch offices (especially in Japan where internationalization issues are likely to be the most critical) who have indicated an interest in a given project. We also put up prototypes of the software on internal servers that can be accessed through our internal corporate network. It is possible for people overseas to connect to a computer in California via the net and ask it to display the user interface on their own monitor (using the xhost feature of the window system), so they can run the software without having to download and install it (which can be difficult for pre-alpha code!). UNIX is particularly flexible with respect to remote execution and display, but most other platforms have utility software available to allow users to run software on remote servers.

A final possibility is to put designs up on the World Wide Web: Each screendump can be a hypertext page, with the pages connected by links to simulate using a prototype: "If you click on *this* button, we take you to *this* next screen." As a word of caution, it is often hard to keep pages secret on the WWW even if one does not advertise their URL (Universal Resource Locator or a hypertext address). There are many so-called robots and spiders that traverse the web to look for new pages, and companies have been known to sic such spiders on their competition to find out what they are up to. The two most popular solutions are to use access control to only serve the pages to users who can provide an accepted userid and password or to keep the pages off the Internet and place them on an internal corporate network that is protected by a firewall.

A variant of international inspection is to take advantage of the multinational nature of the development group itself, if applicable. On one project I worked on at Sun recently, the development group included engineers from Brazil, Canada, Denmark, Japan, Russia, and Sweden, as well as the United States. Such a diverse set of nationalities may be hard to achieve outside of Silicon Valley, but to the extent that you do have people from different countries on the team, you can ask them to comment on international use aspects of the design even if their primary responsibility on the project is far removed from user-interface design.

The ultimate international usability engineering method is international user testing. As with all user testing (Nielsen 1994a), the two fundamental parts of international user testing is to involve real users and have them do real tasks with the system without getting any help. It is normally possible to have users recruited for a test through your local branch office in the country in question, but it is important to emphasize when asking them for help that you need real users and not necessarily their immediate customer contacts. Often, your sales reps or support engineers will have lots of contacts to customers who work in purchasing or MIS management, or who are the senior system administrators who call for help when they have serious problems with their installation. Unless you happen to be testing a product for senior sysadmins or MIS (Management Information Systems) managers, you will need to get beyond these personnel categories to the employees at the customer site who sit at the keyboard on a day-to-day basis. Usually, this concept is easy to explain, and your local staff's customer contacts can usually find such users quite easily, but unless you are explicit about your needs, you will find that unrepresentative test participants have been recruited when you show up for the test. And by then it will be too late.

A touchy point regarding user recruitment is the possibility of offering the user a gift or payment in return for having participated in the study. It is common practice to do so, but both gift-giving and appropriate levels of payment are highly culturally dependent, so you will be wise to discuss these issues in advance with representatives of your local branch office. Consulting advice can also be had from companies that specialize in organizing focus groups or other market research (your advertising agency may have a local contact, or your branch office may have a company on contract already). Sometimes it is preferable to have a professional recruiting firm find test participants for you, though you will have to be very explicit about the user profile you need for your study since these companies often know more about consumer products than about software testing.

There are four main ways to conduct international user testing: Go to the foreign country yourself, run the test remotely, hire a local usability consultant to run the test for you, and have staff from your local branch office run the test even though they are not trained in usability. A fifth possibility is only open to the largest companies: Build additional usability groups in your major markets. This last option may be the best, but it is usually beyond the available budget. Also, even if you do have local usability groups in major foreign markets, you may still want to do additional testing in some of the smaller markets, in which case you face the same problem over again.

In many ways, the ideal approach to international usability testing is for you to go to the foreign country and conduct the test yourself. This is because the experiences of visiting local customers in the various countries give a much stronger impression than simply reading even the most well-written report. There are always many small (but important) details you will observe when you go there yourself. Because of the benefits from observing the customers in their own environment, I recommend trying to set up the test at the customer's premises, though that is not always possible because of the need to use special equipment, hard-to-install software, or having to access data that is only available on your internal corporate network (which only works inside your branch office). If you do visit customer locations, try to get permission to bring a still camera and snap a good deal of pictures of their installation and working conditions. Pasting several such photos on a wall back in your development lab will often be a good way to remind everybody on the project team about the different needs in different countries.

If you do travel yourself, you will need to worry about jet lag in the case of intercontinental trips. Do not plan any user tests for the first two days after your arrival since it is a very intense experience to conduct a user test: You have to pay attention to the user, the user interface, the test tasks, your notes, any additional observers, and any video equipment you may be using—all at the same time. Also, the test may be conducted in a foreign language, meaning that it will be additionally hard for you to concentrate on the test. The first two days after your arrival should be used for visiting your branch office and for checking all of the equipment and software to make sure that the tests will run smoothly. Also, you will need to meet with any interpreters who are going to be involved in the test. The main issue to discuss with interpreters is that they should not provide any help to the test user during the test.

An added benefit of traveling yourself is that you get to meet people in the branch office who can be interviewed about their experience from working with many additional customers. Also, you will sometimes be able to get press coverage in local newspapers and thus improve your company's image ("they really care about our country").

You can eliminate many travel costs by using remote user testing (Hammontree et al. 1994). This method involves having the user run prototype software (or a screen-by-screen mockup) on his or her own computer while you observe over the Internet (or some other network connection). There are many utilities that allow one user to see what is on another user's screen, and these utilities are perfect for remote user testing. You can communicate with the user over an audio link that *might* run over the Internet but would normally be a telephone call (which you should definitely initiate and pay for). The three main downsides of remote testing are the need for you to be in your office at horrible hours due to the time difference, the lack of visual feedback as to what the user is doing (unless you can hook up a camera over, say, an ISDN link), and the need for the user to install and operate possibly quite unfamiliar utilities for remote access.

Whether you travel yourself or conduct the test remotely, you will normally have a language problem. One solution is to recruit users who speak your language, even if they don't speak it fluently. This solution is not perfect, but is often pragmatically the easiest to implement. The key issue is to make sure that you don't get too unrepresentative users who, for example, have spent years at college in your country and thus have been acclimated to the possible linguistic and cultural peculiarities you hope to smoke out during the test. Alternatively, you can conduct the test in the local language. This may be possible if you speak it at least reasonably well, but you will often have to rely on an interpreter. You can normally understand what is happening on the screen (since you have to know the product very well before embarking on an international test), but the user's comments will normally lose a lot in translation.

The final option is to have local people conduct the test: either a local usability consultant or staff from your own branch office. You will definitely get the highest-quality report from a usability professional, but there are also some benefits to involving your local staff: Not only is it cheaper, but they will feel very positive about having influence over product development at headquarters and they will learn a great deal from the test itself. As always, much additional information is gained from actually carrying out a usability study as opposed to simply reading the report, and this added information might as well benefit your own employees as a consultant.

When you are not conducting the test yourself, the selection of appropriate test users becomes particularly critical, so you will have to emphasize the need to recruit representative users in your earliest communications with the people who will be running the test. In spite of the reduced amount of data communicated through a report as opposed to first-hand experience, I have found tests conducted by local representatives to be very useful. Even when the test is conducted by company representatives (normally support engineers or sales staff) there is often much to be learned from reading the reports. As long as it is an infrequent experience for branch office staff to be asked to contribute to product development they will be highly motivated to do a good job and write thorough test reports.

If the test is conducted by foreign usability consultants you can assume that they know the basic principles of usability testing and it will be better in any case to have the foreign experts run the test in the way they are comfortable with. Thus, you should concentrate your discussions with the usability consultants on explaining the goals of the test and the scope of the test tasks. It may be better to have the consultants develop the detailed tasks to make them match the needs of the country in question, even though some billable hours can be saved by providing an initial set of test tasks from your domestic testing. If the test is conducted by staff from your local office, you will have to assume that they know nothing about usability and that your test will be their first user test. Thus, you will have to design the test and the test tasks yourself and give detailed instructions on how to run the test and what you want to see in the report. The appendix to this chapter gives an example of test instructions that have worked well for me.

Usability tests are often conducted in special usability laboratories that are equipped with cameras to record the user's comments and facial expressions as well as events on the computer screen. Usability labs almost always also have one-way mirrors to allow additional observers to monitor the test from an observation room without distracting the test participant. For international usability testing, usability labs will often not be available since only a handful of the very largest computer companies have usability laboratories in multiple countries. The simplest approach is to do without the usability lab and rely solely on initial impressions, notes, and written reports. Doing so will almost certainly be necessary for tests conducted by your branch office since it will not be reasonable to expect them to set up new equipment and learn how to use it.

There are many difficulties involved in using a usability lab for international user testing, so it may be the best solution to skip the lab even for tests you conduct yourself. Often, the main usability problems are obvious from simply observing the user and there is no need to spend time reviewing a videotape anyway. On the other hand, international user testing has two characteristics that make it desirable to have a formal record of the type generated in a lab: First, the user may be speaking a foreign language, meaning that it may be necessary to replay the tape to understand what the user was saying. Indeed, if it is desired to get a full translation in order to know exactly what happened then it may be necessary to provide the translator with a recording of the user's comments. Second, financial constraints normally dictate that only a very small number of people actually get to travel to the foreign country to conduct the test. Normally, other team members have the opportunity to sit in on as many or as few tests as they like, thus gaining a good impression of the way users use their product. Since most team members will not have the chance to sit in on the international tests, showing them a video is the next best thing and a much more vivid way of communicating the international user experience than a written report. If videotaping is infeasible then still photographs can sometimes help make the report more approachable and memorable.

If you are having foreign usability consultants conduct the test then they may have their own lab or they may have local contacts that allow them to easily rent a lab. If so, pricing considerations will obviously influence whether you should request use of a lab for the test. If you do decide to pay for a lab I would advise also paying for the editing of a highlights tape (again, of course, depending on the price). Realistically, you will probably be reluctant to sit and watch many hours of video of users talking in a foreign language when you already have a report that shows the main findings. It is much better to watch selected shorter segments of those events that relate to the key findings. Also, if you are getting a highlights tape it is normally feasible to have the narrative translated and added as subtitles, meaning that the tape can be shown to management and other members of the project team. A practical consideration is that the highlights tape may be in a different video format than the one used in your country. The typical problem is PAL (video format for most of Europe) versus NTSC (video format for North America and Japan), and since these two formats are very widely used you may have a multiformat video player available that can show the tape. If not, it is possible to have a video service bureau convert the tape into your local format for a small fee. It is advisable to use a professional service rather than a cheap corner store since you will want to retain as much of the signal quality as possible to be able to see what is happening on the screen.

If you travel yourself, the two main options (besides not using a lab) are to rent a local lab or to bring a portable lab. Since usability engineering is becoming an integral part of the development process in more and more countries, you will often find local companies that have usability labs. These labs may not always be highly sophisticated but they do have the advantage that somebody else is responsible for the equipment and for making sure it works under local conditions. In a few cases, foreign usability labs are advertised for rent in various user-interface publications or at major conferences. It is more common that you have to do the legwork yourself and approach a company that is known (or suspected) to have a lab and ask them whether they would rent it. In addition to real usability labs, it may also be an option to rent a focus group lab from a market research company, though you will then have to worry about setting up the computer and making sure that the cameras are suited for recording events on the screen. If you are renting a lab in a country with a different video format than your own, then the lab will presumably be equipped to support the local format and it is probably best to rent their editing equipment if you want to construct the (recommended) highlights video since you will otherwise have to get a very large pile of tapes converted when you get home.

Bringing a portable lab is only feasible if you either already have one or if you are willing to invest $10,000 or more to buy the necessary equipment. There are several vendors of portable usability labs and they normally exhibit at conferences like the Usability Professionals Association's (UPA) annual meeting and the ACM CHI (Association of Computing Machinery, Computer Human Interaction) conference. Physically, a portable usability lab is one or more large reinforced cases with plenty of padding and an assortment of video, audio, editing, and event-logging equipment. It is recommended to include a scan converter to allow direct capture of the computer monitor image to videotape. There are three benefits of portable labs: You can bring them to customer sites and to remote locations, whereas renting a lab normally means being restricted to the capital or other big cities; you will be experienced in using the equipment since you will presumably use the same lab for multiple tests; and the lab will use your own country's videotape format. A downside of using your own videotape format is that you have to bring all the tapes you will need since you may not be able to buy any locally.

If you are bringing a portable lab you will have to ensure that it can run on local electricity in the countries you will be visiting. You can bring (or buy) power converters, but doing so is very awkward and it is much better to buy equipment that is rated for international power to begin with. Whether you ship the equipment separately or bring it with you as luggage, you should get the necessary customs forms made out to allow the equipment to cross borders without paying import duty. If your company is used to participating in international tradeshows or has other frequent international dealings, then there will probably be a person in the shipping department, the export department, or the tradeshow department who knows how to deal with customs forms. If not, it may be easiest to use an experienced shipping company rather than trying to figure out the formalities yourself. Before shipping the equipment to a new test site make sure to remove any shipping labels from the previous trip: Alan Asper from Andersen Consulting told a story at the UPA'95 conference about how he once forgot to remove a label only to have his equipment show up at the previous site since the shipping company had read the old label when routing the case.

A final question is how many foreign countries to cover in international usability engineering. The optimal solution will obviously be to cover all countries in which you have nonnegligible sales (or where you hope to expand). Doing so is normally unrealistic unless you are a rather small company that only exports to one or two other countries. The normal solution is to evaluate international usability in a small number of countries with at least one country in each of the main areas of the world: Asia, Europe, and North America. Since you will normally be located in one of these areas to begin with, your local usability engineering efforts (which I hope you have!) will have covered that area already, meaning that you will need two countries as the minimum for international usability engineering. If you only have the resources to cover a single foreign country, then I encourage you to go ahead and do that: There is so much to be gained from going the initial step from *no* international usability to *some* that the largest payoff comes from the very first foreign country you include. It would be nice to cover three or four foreign countries since both Europe and Asia are quite heterogeneous regions. Also, some companies have sufficient sales in other parts of the world that they need to cover them too.

The key point remains, though: Don't despair! Don't overplan; don't give up because you cannot implement the ideal international usability study the first time. Maybe you will have to start with a single country: Do it! Normally what happens is that management gets so encouraged by the initial results of even a small-scale pilot project that more resources are made available for future projects.

REFERENCES

Hammontree, M., P. Weiler, and N. Nayak. 1994. Remote usability testing. *ACM Interactions Magazine* **1**, 3 (July), 21–25.

Kano, N. 1995. *Developing International Software for Windows 95 and Windows NT*. Redmond, WA: Microsoft Press.

Nielsen, J. 1994a. *Usability Engineering*, paperback edition. Boston: AP Professional.

Nielsen, J. 1994b. Heuristic evaluation. In Nielsen, J., and R. L. Mack, (eds.), *Usability Inspection Methods*. New York: Wiley, 25–76.

Nielsen, J. 1995. *User Interface Design for Sun's WWW Site*. Hypertext available on the World Wide Web at http://www.sun.com/sun-on-net/uidesign.

Nielsen, J., and R. L. Mack, 1994. *Usability Inspection Methods*. New York: Wiley.

Stiff, P. 1995. Design methods, cultural diversity, and the limits of designing. *Information Design Journal* **8**, 1:36–47.

Appendix

The following are the instructions we gave to the people at various Sun branch offices in Europe and Asia for their user testing of a new design for the company's web pages. In a few places, these instructions refer to web-specific issues, so they will have to be modified slightly for use in other projects. These instructions were sent by electronic mail to those local Sun reps who had volunteered to lead a test.

INSTRUCTIONS FOR BRANCH OFFICE TESTING

Thank you again for volunteering to help perform international usability testing on Sun's new WWW pages. A prototype of the redesigned pages will be available on the following URL:

```
http://hugin.eng/sun.categories/
```

Some info is there now, but the graphics will not be available until Monday, May 1. You can try out the information structure now and you should schedule your user for as soon as possible after May 1.

Step 1. Getting a Customer

Using your contacts to customers in your location, call around and recruit a person who is a typical user for the kind of accounts you expect to be most important in the future. The user should be average for WWW users in that organization and not a super expert or high-level manager (unless they are the only ones using the WWW). The user should have some ability to read written English since the pages will not be translated, but the user should not be uncommonly good at English (and will not need any skills in spoken English). In recruiting the user, you should explicitly ask how much he or she has used the WWW (or use terms like "Mosaic" or "Netscape" if they don't know what WWW means). For the WWW test, the user should have had previous experience with the WWW, though he or she need not have visited Sun's home page. Since you will be accessing files inside Sun's internal network, you will need to ask the user to come to your office. Set up an appointment for a specific date and time and tell the user that the test will last about an hour but might go a little bit longer or might be over faster, depending on what happens.

Tell the user that volunteering for the test will help Sun make a better user interface for people in your country and that the results of the test will be communicated back to headquarters without revealing the identity of the user or his or her company. That is, all results will be kept confidential.

Step 2. Preparing the Test

Make sure that you have a room with a workstation reserved for the test and that you will have no interruptions during the test: Shortly before the test you should put a sign on the door reading something like USER TESTING, DO NOT ENTER and unplug the telephone. Also, shortly before the test you should make a last check that you have your WWW software (e.g., Mosaic) running so that there are no surprises once the user gets there. The last part of setting up the test is to make the browser software forget the navigation history so that all link anchors are blue (usually, the ones the user has already seen are purple).

At least a day before the test you should translate the test tasks into your local language (the test tasks are described below). Go through the test tasks yourself to make sure they can be done and that the instructions make sense. While doing so, you may observe some aspects of the user interface that seem poorly suited to users from your country, and you should make a note of any such problems.

Step 3. Running the Test

When the user arrives, explain once again that you are doing a usability study to see how easy it is to use Sun's new WWW pages. Explain that you are going to be trying a prototype and that not everything has been completed yet, meaning that errors may occur during the test.

Ask the user to "think out loud" during the test: The user should keep up a running monologue, saying anything that comes to mind and not hold back anything. Say that you are interested in all the user's thoughts, comments, and interpretations of the design, even the ones that may seem minor at the time. Since thinking aloud is somewhat unnatural, many users stop doing so and need to get prompted to speak. If the user sits quietly for an extended period of time, a good prompt is "what are you thinking about now?"

Other than prompting the user to keep talking, you should not say anything yourself during the test. If the user asks about the meaning of some element of the user interface, you should not answer, but instead ask the user "what do *you* think it might be?" Encourage the user to make a wild guess if necessary. Also, you should neither agree nor disagree with the user's comments. Just make a sound to confirm that you have heard the user's comment without indicating your personal opinion and then write down the user's comment. Actually, you can't write down everything the user says, but try to make as extensive notes as possible as that will help you write the report.

Step 4. The Test Tasks

There are two tasks: exploratory and directed. Of the one-hour test time, you should spend about 30 minutes on exploratory tasks, about 20 minutes on directed tasks, and about 10 minutes on debriefing (see the next section).

Exploratory Tasks Bring up the new home page and ask the user to begin by giving his or her general comments on the page before starting to click. When the user has finished commenting on the page, you tell the user to do anything he or she would normally want to do on that page. You just let the user navigate the system freely for the rest of the exploratory test time. You may need to help the user get back to the home page if the user gets hopelessly lost, but don't offer help too soon since it is often very valuable to see how users get out of trouble on their own.

At the end of the exploratory time, you make sure that the user has seen and commented on the following new features in the system:

a. The "What's Happening" page
b. The news story about network security
c. The column (under What's Happening) called User Interface Alert Box
d. The "About this Server" page

It is likely that the user will have visited some of these pages during the free exploration, and if so, you need not return to them.

Finally, give the user these tasks (translated):

You have heard that Sun recently introduced a new, low-cost desktop workstation. Can you find the product specification information for it in the Web site?

You have recently acquired some Sun systems, and you are now looking for a good word processor to run on them. Can you find what word processing programs are available for the Sun platform?

These tasks should be given in writing. Give the test tasks to the user one page at a time (you want them to concentrate on one task at a time). If you come to the end of the scheduled test time or if the user starts feeling uncomfortable, you should stop the test and not give out any remaining test tasks.

Step 5. Debriefing the User

After the test tasks (and while sitting at the computer), you tell the user that this completes the test. You should then ask the user for his or her general comments about the design. Use two questions: "What did you particularly like about this system?" and "What did you particularly dislike about this system?" If the user does not have enough comments, you can often elicit additional comments by asking the question: "If we now compare with other sites you have visited on the Web, what things have you seen that you liked and would want us to do, and what things do you want to warn us against doing?"

After the test, you should thank the user for helping and mention how you have made a lot of interesting notes that you will now send back to the development team at Sun's headquarters. If doing so is appropriate for your culture, you should also give the user a gift to thank him or her for participating. You can use the Multimedia and Hypertext book we sent you for this purpose.

Step 6. Reporting the Results

Please respect the anonymity of the user and his or her company and do not mention them in the report. We only need to know the general type of work done by the user and the general type of company.

In writing the report, you should refer both to usability problems experienced by the test participant and to issues you observed yourself while preparing for the test. Please distinguish between these two kinds of data: We want to know what issues are your personal critiques of the user interface and what issues refer to actual events during the usability test. Both are valuable information, but we should treat them differently. When reporting data from the user, please also distinguish between cases where the user said that something *might* be confusing or problematic to other people in your country and where that specific user *actually* was confused or had problems.

As a guideline, a typical report would be maybe two pages long, but of course you should write as much or as little as needed to describe the major findings of your specific study.

Please email the report to me at jakob@eng.sun.com as soon as possible since we are on a tight deadline to finish the redesign effort.

For Further Reference

Read the following sections in Jakob Nielsen: *Usability Engineering* (paperback edition: AP Professional 1994, ISBN 0-12-518406-9):

6.4: Ethical aspects of tests with human subjects
6.6: Stages of a test
6.8: Thinking aloud

For a discussion of the types of usability problems you might find and ways of conceptualizing them according to established usability principles, read Chapter 5, Usability Heuristics.

ABOUT THE AUTHOR

Jakob Nielsen is a Sun Microsystems Distinguished Engineer working on strategic user-interface issues, including next-generation user interfaces and World Wide Web designs. He is Danish but moved to the United States in 1990. He has worked in both academia (Technical University of Denmark and Aarhus University) and industry (Sun, Bellcore, IBM) and participated in European Union projects. He was papers co-chair for the ACM/IFIP INTERCHI'93 international conference on computer-human interaction in Amsterdam, April 1993.

CHAPTER 2

Problems in Designing the User Interface for Systems Supporting International Human-Human Communication

INTRODUCTION

Whereas most of the other contributions to this book relate primarily to human-*computer* interaction, the focus of attention within the present chapter is upon human-*human* communication via computer networks. That is to say, we are concerned here with systems whose purpose is to support computer-mediated communication (CMC), and more specifically, CMC at the international level.

Not surprisingly, in situations where CMC takes place across national borders, issues arise which can, at the very least, cause the familiar problems of user-interface design to be seen in a fresh light, and may even raise new questions which would not otherwise have been discussed within the field of international user-interface design (IUID). The purpose of this chapter, therefore, is to discuss some of the salient issues that affect IUID at the present time. We shall start by considering some of the basic characteristics of CMC, and then proceed to discuss the particular problems that may arise when CMC takes place across national or cultural boundaries. In the light of this, we shall move to a consideration of IUID itself, and end with some conclusions as to possible future developments.

COMPUTER-MEDIATED COMMUNICATION

Certain recent developments in computing have served to lend particular currency to the subject of international CMC. Particularly notable has been the burgeoning growth of the Internet, which supports a huge volume of CMC traffic generated through the widespread use of such communication methods as email messages and contributions to Usenet newsgroups. In addition, the emergence of the field of computer-supported cooperative working (CSCW) provides an important potential source of international CMC. (For an introduction to CSCW, see Wilson 1991.)

CMC may take various forms. To begin with, it may be private, as is the case with email or with teleconferencing, or it may be public, as when communications are posted to bulletin boards, conferences, or Usenet newsgroups, or when information is deposited on ftp, gopher, or World Wide Web (WWW) archive sites for others to peruse.

Furthermore, CMC may be either spoken or (type-)written. For example, the written language is used in email and bulletin board postings, while the spoken language is used in voicemail (which is now a widely used facility). Messages may also include nonlinguistic material in the form of visual images (still or moving) or auditory data such as music. Consequently, CMC potentially entails use of the full range of multimedia technology. In addition, it may involve the use of hypermedia, as with WWW and its associated tools such as Mosaic.

Another well-established distinction is that between synchronous and asynchronous CMC. In the former case the interlocutors (i.e., the participants in the communicative activity) all have to be on-line at the same time, for example, when "chatting," whereas in the latter case they need not be, for example, when interacting via email. (It should be noted that the terms *synchronous* and *asynchronous* ,when used in this context, are being employed in a different sense from that which is common in telecommunications to describe methods of data transmission, and that "synchronous" or "asynchronous" in the one sense does not in any way imply "synchronous" or "asynchronous" at the other level.)

In the preceding paragraphs we have had cause to mention

a number of different activities involving CMC: email, voice-mail, the use of bulletin boards and archives, chatting, and tele-conferencing. However, despite the variety seen here, all these activities have at least one common characteristic which is of central importance in the present context. They all involve communicating simultaneously both with a human addressee (who may be an individual or a group) and with a computer system which mediates the human-human communication. This fact is clearly a fundamental consideration in the design of user interfaces for such systems.

INTERNATIONAL AND INTERNATIONAL COMPUTER-MEDIATED COMMUNICATION

Even when communication takes place between people of the same nationality, cultural tradition, and tongue, success is not guaranteed, and misunderstanding or bafflement can result. How much more likely, then, must the danger of miscommunication be when one or more of these commonalities is absent. Of course, the presence or absence of such commonalities does not correlate perfectly with the distinction between intranational and international communication, but nevertheless, national, cultural, and linguistic differences are especially likely to be encountered in the conduct of international communication, and systems which support international CMC need to be designed with this fact very much in mind. It is, therefore, appropriate at this juncture to consider the question of what additional problems are entailed when CMC takes on an international dimension.

Among the problems that may affect the success of international CMC are the following:

1. The interlocutors may not share a common language. If they do not, then they will require support in the form of automatic translation. Where the written language is used, it is possible that different alphabets may be required, perhaps mixed together in the same piece of text.
2. There may be any of a number of cultural differences between the societies in which the respective interlocutors are situated. These may include:

a. Institutional matters such as time zones or currencies, which will in certain circumstances require automatic conversion to the interlocutor's equivalents.

b. Environmental factors, for example, the architecture of buildings and the appearance of artifacts, which may impact upon the design of visual representations such as icons on computer screens.

c. Social conventions, such as what is regarded as polite or otherwise.

We shall now consider these problems in turn.

Differences of Language

Let us first consider the situation where two individuals with different native languages wish to communicate electronically. It is possible that at least one of them will have sufficient knowledge of the other's language to enable the latter to be used as the means of interaction, or alternatively that they will both have sufficient knowledge of some other language which, although it is not the mother tongue of either interlocutor, can nevertheless serve them as a vehicle of communication in the relevant context. English, of course, often serves such a purpose, and it is an important consideration that many users of IT systems throughout the world have either a native or at least an adequate command of English. However, access to networked computer systems, including connection to the global Internet, is increasingly becoming available to the general population of countries around the world, and not just to scientists and technologists who may be more likely than the average individual to be competent in English in lands where this is not one of the official languages. Consequently, it is likely that the coming years will see an increasing demand for language translation support in the context of CMC.

We therefore need to consider what degree of support we can expect automatic translation systems to offer, either now or in the foreseeable future. Of course, machine translation (MT) is an extremely challenging area of technology. This is not surprising, given the complexity of human language itself, together with the fact that the translation of utterances depends upon a knowledge not only of the languages involved but also of all manner of facts or assumptions about the world in general. For example, the German word *Stadt* may be translated as either "town" or "city," and the selection of the appropriate alternative depends on extralinguistic, real-world information about the place concerned (particularly its size, and also, in some instances, whether it has, or used to have, a cathedral). The implication of this, many would argue, is that effective MT requires the engineering of massive knowledge-based systems (KBS), encompassing a large amount of both linguistic and extralinguistic information. It is natural, therefore, to ask how realistic a proposition such systems may be in the present state of MT technology.

Certainly, as is clear from recent texts on the subject of MT, such as Hutchins and Somers (1992), Nirenburg et al. (1992), and Arnold et al. (1994), computer-based MT is an active area of research and development. Furthermore, the field has quite a long history for a computer-related subject, dating as it does from the middle of the twentieth century. The earliest attempts at MT were founded upon a relatively direct approach to the process of translation. The essence of this approach may be outlined as follows. The text in the source language is input to the system and undergoes a morphological analysis, whose purpose is, where appropriate, to break words down into their component parts. For example, the word *watched* can be analyzed into *watch* (the base form of the verb concerned) and the suffix *-ed* (which indicates either the past tense or the past participle). The next stage is to look up the base of each word in a bilingual dictionary, which supplies the equivalent base in the target language, and to convert this base, if necessary, into a modified form such as (in the case of a verb) the past tense. Finally, some syntactic adjustments are made. For example, in an English-to-French translation it is often necessary to change the order adjective + noun into noun + adjective. However, this direct approach obviously has its limitations, and as a result, more indirect approaches have been tried.

There are two main types of indirect approach to MT: the *interlingua* strategy and the *transfer* strategy. The idea behind the interlingua strategy is that each sentence in the source text be analyzed linguistically into an abstract representation which is independent of any particular human language, rather as first-order predicate calculus (FOPC) is intended to be, although of course a richer form of representation than FOPC is necessary in this case. On the basis of this intermediate, abstract representation, the text in the target language is then generated. As for the transfer strategy, each sentence in the source text is again analyzed into an abstract representation, but the latter is specific to that particular source language and can therefore afford to be less abstract, since it is not expected to serve as a means of representing the structure and content of all the languages served by the system in the way that an interlingua would. The next stage is to transform the abstract representation of the source language text into the corresponding representation pertaining to the target language, and then the final step is to convert the latter representation into actual target language text.

Some measure of success has been achieved on the basis of all three strategies. Although early direct-translation systems were a failure, versions of the Systran system, first developed in the 1960s, have been employed by a number of organizations, including (more recently) the Commission of the European Union. It must be said, however, that although it began as a direct-translation system, later versions of Systran have incorporated superior methods of linguistic analysis of a kind more typically associated with the indirect strategy. Several transfer-style systems have also been employed to advantage, for example, the METAL system, which performs German-to-English translation and has enjoyed some commercial success since its introduction to the market by the Siemens company. On the other hand, interlingua-oriented systems have been developed at a number of academic and industrial centers, the latter including the Fujitsu company. Most current research in MT is directed toward indirect translation, with particular interest being shown in the interlingua strategy.

In general, a certain amount of human intervention is needed in order to obtain high-quality MT. Usually, this involves an expert in postediting the translation to correct whatever errors or infelicities the system has committed. This naturally adds both expense and delay to the process. However, in some cases a medium-quality translation for private use can be obtained completely automatically and prove adequate for the user's purposes, for example, in determining the gist of a scientific paper in a foreign language. However, the Météo-2 system, which emerged from the work of a team at the University of Montreal and which translates weather reports between English and French, produces acceptable quality output with comparatively little postediting. Météo-2 employs the direct strategy, but because it was developed by a team that was also very interested in transfer-oriented MT research, it is more linguistically sophisticated than direct translation systems in general. An important factor in its considerable success is that it deals with a restricted subject domain. General-purpose MT systems have yet to achieve a comparable level of performance.

Most MT research and development to date has pertained to the written rather than the spoken language. As has already been mentioned, in the MT of the written language the problem of multiple character sets is often involved. The same problem can also arise in the context of computer-supported collaborative writing (an established branch of CSCW; see further Sharples 1993), particularly in international contexts. However, this problem has already been addressed with some success in the context of the internationalization of computer systems; see for example Martin O'Donnell (1994). It will therefore not be further discussed in the present chapter.

The MT of the spoken language has not yet reached a level of development compared with that of the written language. Probably the main reason is that the speech technology on which it relies poses a difficult challenge in itself. Although speech synthesis of reasonable quality is offered by commercially available systems, high quality tends to require fine tuning, which is not always feasible. As for automatic speech recognition (ASR), this has proved to be a very tough problem to crack, and while it is the case that some reasonably usable systems have now reached the marketplace, nevertheless there still remains plenty of scope for improvement. In both synthesis and recognition, KBS has an important part to play; see, for example, Allen, Hunnicutt, and Klatt (1987) and Hayes-Roth (1980).

Whatever the current limitations of speech technology, however, some work has been done on speech-to-speech translation, for example, in the laboratories of British Telecom, ATR, and Carnegie-Mellon University. However, at present it appears that MT of spoken language is most likely to be effective in highly restricted domains.

For the time being, therefore, it would appear that it is written rather than spoken CMC that is better placed to benefit from MT. An additional consideration is that because MT is a complex process, it is in general unrealistic to expect near-instantaneous performance of MT systems. Consequently, at the moment it is asynchronous rather than synchronous forms of CMC which are the more amenable to enhancement by the addition of MT facilities.

Thus, asynchronous written means of communication like email, bulletin boards, and archives are currently the best candidates for MT facilities. On the other hand, asynchronous spoken methods like voicemail, and synchronous written methods like chatting, present a higher level of difficulty for the application of MT, and indeed are likely to continue to do so for some time, while synchronous spoken communication, such as takes place during teleconferencing, offers an even greater challenge.

However, even in contexts where automatic translation is not currently feasible, other forms of computer support are worth considering. For example, an individual with a moderately good knowledge of a foreign language may well be able to understand and compose material in that language with the help of a bilingual dictionary and perhaps also a thesaurus and a grammar. It is possible to provide such resources on-line, with the advantage of fast lookup that a computer system can offer.

Other Cultural Differences

Let us now consider some of the other cultural factors which can interfere with communication. Differences in institutional conventions such as time zones or currencies can give rise to a need for adjustment for the benefit of the addressee of a message in which reference is made to these. It is not difficult for the requisite conversion to be carried out by the system, which may well be made to display both the original and the adjusted values, appropriately labeled.

Environmental differences, on the other hand, are not so

simple to deal with. An example of a well-known problem is the difficulty of choosing a suitable icon for an electronic mailer (del Galdo 1990). An obvious metaphor lies in a conventional mail-box, but these artifacts have such different designs around the world that they do not make a good basis for the design of an icon. Del Galdo suggests, in fact, that an envelope would make a better choice. In addition, all kinds of mistaken assumptions may be made by an individual in one country about the situation in another. One slightly amusing example is reported by Scrivener et al. (1993), who describe some experiments in computer-supported cooperative product design. One of these experiments involved a person living in England and another living in Australia, and their brief was to design a leaf mulching machine. For understandable reasons, the kind of leaves which came immediately to the Australian's mind were dry, while those which the Englishman pictured were wet! As this difference clearly affected the task to be performed, it had to be cleared up before the designers could proceed. No amount of computer-based information could hope to forestall all such discrepancies of interpretation!

The different social conventions of different cultures also constitute an area where there is plenty of potential for misunderstanding; see, for example, Loveday (1983), Wierzbicka (1991), and Scollon and Scollon (1995). For instance, in British society, although self-praise is deprecated, praise of others is quite acceptable, whereas in Japanese society it is viewed negatively, being seen as rather presumptuous. To take another example, in English, requests and offers are often expressed as interrogatives (e.g., "Why don't you tell me what you would like to do today?"), whereas in Polish, interrogatives really do sound like questions.

Plainly, if individuals with different social backgrounds engage in communication with one another, there is a real danger that sooner or later ignorance of the social conventions to which the other is accustomed will give rise to misunderstanding, awkwardness, or even offense. Consequently, the more one knows about the cultural assumptions of one's interlocutor, the more chance one has of avoiding inadvertently causing embarrassments of this kind. However, the problem is more complex than this. Individuals who communicate with others from different backgrounds are often aware of some of the different cultural assumptions that they can expect the other to hold. Consequently, it can be hard to know whether or not the other person is making allowances for one's own expectations, and vice versa. This can result in even greater difficulties and uncertainties than if one could simply assume a predictable set of habits and attitudes on the part of one's interlocutor.

It is clear that computers cannot obviate communication problems of the kind just outlined. Nevertheless, if the greatest danger of intercultural miscommunication lies in ignorance, then the provision of an information system detailing the communication conventions of different cultures would be a real help to anyone planning to engage in CMC with people from other cultural backgrounds. As Uren, Howard, and Perinotti (1993, 81) note, information on matters such as the sensitivities and taboos that exist in other cultures is never irrelevant or useless in the context of international communication.

USER-INTERFACE DESIGN

Support for Interaction

The human-computer interface may be thought of as being the point of contact between the individuals or groups of people who use a computer-based system and the software-hardware amalgam with which they interact. The purpose of the human-computer interface is to act as one end of the communication channel between user and processor, but of course in CMC it also serves as a terminal to a communication channel between/among human users, the two channels sharing common facilities.

In previous writings on human-computer interaction (HCI), a large number of guidelines have been proposed with the aim of assisting designers of interactive systems. See, for example, Shneiderman (1987), Sutcliffe (1988), Preece (1993), and works cited therein. Insofar as a CMC system is bound to involve HCI, these guidelines are no less applicable to CMC-oriented systems than to other types of system. We shall therefore briefly review some of the most widely accepted guidelines at this point, taking the opportunity to add comments with particular reference to systems supporting international CMC.

3a. Make users feel in command rather than at the mercy of the system. In particular:

    i. Keep them informed. This means: Provide them with feedback about the actions carried out by the system, and also, when they are navigating through an environment with a complex structure, give them an indication of their whereabouts.

    ii. At every step, make it clear what they are expected to do next. If they wish to escape from the current process, enable them to do so quickly and easily.

    iii. Offer help facilities, allowing for varying levels of user knowledge and experience.

  b. Spare users as much effort as possible. Hence:

    i. Minimize the number of actions required to accomplish a given task. In furtherance of this aim, enable defaults to be set where appropriate.

    ii. Minimize the burden upon users' memories. To this end, make the interface as consistent as possible.

    iii. Make error handling as simple and graceful as possible. Enable user actions to be easily undone, in circumstances where this is feasible.

In CMC systems the need for feedback extends not only to the machine with which the user is directly interacting but also to the network over which the communication is taking place. Network breakdowns are by no means uncommon, and in the context of international communication there is often additional scope for such occurrences, in view of the relatively high likelihood that more than one network will be involved in the link. Moreover, the setting up of connections across a network can take some time and, what is worse, the amount of time taken may vary considerably from one occasion to another. Consequently, it is important for the user to be reassured that matters are proceeding according to plan when this is true, or else to be notified as quickly as possible that a problem has arisen. For example, as matters stand currently, it is often impossible to be certain whether or not an email message has been delivered. It is true that if a failure occurs, one can expect a notification, but it is not prudent to rely completely on the arrival of the latter, and so the absence of a failure message does not constitute a guarantee of success. Of course, if notifications of successful delivery messages were generated automatically on every occasion, this would increase congestion on the network, but nevertheless the addition of a facility to enquire after the safe delivery of selected messages would in many cases represent an improvement in the level of feedback compared with what is currently available.

When CMC involves navigating through the Internet using a search tool such as Gopher or a WWW browser, and/or navigating through a complex database or hypertext document, there is an obvious danger of losing track of where one is, and therefore there is a need for a means whereby the system can provide the user with an indication of the point reached. However, in highly complex environments the problem of satisfactorily answering this need has not so far been totally overcome. If the navigation is taking place within a foreign-language environment, of course, the problem is correspondingly magnified.

Although the succession of steps through a human-computer dialogue may be precisely specifiable in advance, the same is not generally true of human-human communication. Nor do we normally expect escape-hatches from interpersonal conversation to be provided, although there might well be occasions when we wished that they existed! However, if one party does decide to perform a rapid exit from a synchronous interpersonal communication session, then at the very least the other person or persons should receive feedback from the system, explaining what has happened.

The usefulness of help facilities is self-evident, particularly if they do not require users already to know the names of the commands or functions which they need to use in order to achieve their goals! In CMC the scope for help facilities extends both to the groupware involved and to the international dimension of the communication. Thus, the help provision might well include MT facilities or translation aids. It might also incorporate useful information on intercultural differences affecting communication (see above), this information being dispensed either by a database or by an expert system.

The incorporation of default settings into software also runs into complications in the context of international CMC. Different interlocutors in a given interaction may have different personal preferences, and they may also be operating in different locales. If the choice of defaults by one interlocutor not only differs from those of another but also impinges upon the other person, as in the choice of date format, then a discrepancy arises which may call either for negotiation or for automatic adjustment by the system during the process of communication.

The implication here is that consistency of the user interfaces at different terminals to an international groupware system is not necessarily a desideratum, as long as each terminal allows the selection of the preferred version of the interface by its local users. On the other hand, systemwide consistency should prevail insofar as there is no overriding reason to violate it, in order that, for example, users should have a minimum of adjustment to make if they interact with the system at different sites on different occasions.

In CMC it is possible for errors to arise not only within the HCI activity but also within the interpersonal communication process (a simple example being the inclusion of typing errors in an email message). Such errors call for a facility to allow easy and quick correction. In addition, as far as asynchronous CMC is concerned, there is room for an "undo" function which enables the user to retrieve (for instance) an ill-judged or erroneous email message, as long as it has not yet been opened by the recipient.

Screen Display

Another aspect of HCI where a number of guidelines have been proposed in the past is the display of material on the screen. However, here again additional complications arise in the context of international CMC. Let us begin by summarizing some of the guidelines presented by authors such as Shneiderman (1987), Sutcliffe (1988), and Preece (1993):

4a. Tread a judicious middle path between a cluttered and an oversparse screen display, and include only what is necessary to the user. Highlight especially important information.

b. Organize the display in a helpful manner, by ensuring that the grouping and sequencing of information is well-motivated. Maintain neatness and consistency in the format of displays, and provide clear navigation aids between one display and another.

c. Keep abbreviations and codes to a minimum, and keep them consistent.

d. Adopt appropriate and consistent formats for dates, and so on.

As before, we shall now comment on these guidelines from the point of view of international CMC. To begin with, although the avoidance of clutter or excessive spareness is a laudable aim, its accomplishment is not helped by the fact that the information requirements of all users of an item of groupware will not necessarily be the same. For example, recipients of messages may require additional annotations (e.g., local currency equivalents of sums expressed in foreign currencies, alongside the original amounts). Again, in cases where translations are required, this may significantly affect the display space requirements (del Galdo 1990), and if the translations need to be shown alongside the originals, then the potential disparity is even greater. Indeed, the whole organization of the display can be affected in such circumstances. As for the highlighting of important information, the means for achieving this include the use of color or of different fonts. However, fonts available for one language may have no counterpart in another language, while the existence of intercultural differences in the significance of particular colors is well known; again, see del Galdo (1990). Minimizing the use of abbreviations is more important than ever in international communication, where they may baffle a person from a different country. However, as has already been noted, systemwide rigidity in matters such as date format is not necessarily appropriate.

This last point again illustrates the need to exercise caution in the application of the principle of *consistency* in the context of international CMC groupware. A strict application of this principle would lead to the adoption of the approach commonly known in CSCW circles as WYSIWIS ("What you see is what I see"). However, it is clear that WYSIWIS can be quite impractical in international CMC.

In teleconferencing applications, an additional complication may well arise from a requirement for the participants to see one another. This requires the installation of video cameras and the provision of suitable display facilities. The latter could simply be a screen window, but because of the danger of clutter, a separate screen may need to be provided.

In the light of a study of this subject area, Sasse, Handley, and Ismail (1994) propose a number of design guidelines relating to multimedia teleconferencing. Some of the salient points here are as follows:

5a. Users should be notified by the system of significant events of which they might not otherwise be aware, for example, the fact that an additional participant has joined the conference. However, only the most important events should be notified in an attention-grabbing manner.

  b. A system of floor control needs to be adopted. The larger the group, the simpler this needs to be.

  c. In the absence of WYSIWIS, users need to be given some means of synchronizing their respective views of a given screen-displayed object (e.g., a 2D graphical representation of a 3D object). In particular, they need to be able to share the view seen by the current floor holder.

These guidelines are all applicable to international teleconferencing. However, differing conventions of floor control could be an issue in intercultural contexts, and this should be borne in mind by the designers of such systems.

Tools or Agents?   The user interfaces which are most familiar today are the GUIs (graphical user interfaces) based on the idea of direct manipulation, where (for instance) moving a file into another directory involves selecting the file icon and dragging it into the directory icon, using a mouse to select and move the file icon across the screen. Such interfaces have been characterized as tool-based, inasmuch as they make available instruments (in the form of objects and processes) which users can manipulate in order to accomplish tasks. However, a good deal of interest has been shown recently in the development of alternative types of human-computer interface, based on the idea of *agents*. See, for example, the contributions to Connolly and Edmonds (1994) and volume 37, part 7, of the *Communications of the ACM* (1994).

An agent is considered to be an intelligent entity, possessing a capacity for independent action. Such a definition allows, in principle, for an agent to be either a human being or a software process endowed with the appropriate characteristics. Agents of this latter type, that is, "software agents," can be designed to perform functions required of a human-computer interface (e.g., organizing the contents of an electronic mailbox into subdirectories). The user would be required to apprise the agent of his or her intentions, possibly by means of a natural-language dialogue, and the agent would then carry out the task on behalf of the user, who would be free to start attending to the next task.

According to Wooldridge and Jennings (1995), software agents are characterized by the following properties:

6a. *Autonomy*. They can operate without waiting for a human user to launch them into action.
  b. *Social Ability*. They can communicate with other agents and, if appropriate, with human users.
  c. *Reactivity*. They detect and respond to changes in the environment in which they operate.
  d. *Proactiveness*. Besides reacting to events, they can themselves take initiatives.

Clearly, such processes may fulfill any of a wide range of possible functions. However, those which serve the specific purposes of the human-computer interface are (naturally enough) termed "interface agents."

Some successful interface agents, performing such functions as email handling and electronic news filtering, have already been described in the literature; see, for instance, Maes (1994). Nevertheless, it is true that fully fledged agent-based interfaces may appear somewhat futuristic at the moment. On the other hand, as far as international CMC is concerned, they would surely offer certain attractions. First of all, they would enable a new kind of homogeneity to be attained in CMC. All one's interlocutors, human or electronic, would now be agents. Nor would this necessarily mean replacing direct manipulation as a means of human-computer communication, should users wish to retain this. Rather, the difference would be that the effect of the user's actions would not be to launch a process directly, but instead to inform the relevant agent of the user's wishes. The agent could then either comply without hesitation or else engage in an interaction with the user if (for example) it noticed some potentially undesirable consequence of the action which might have eluded the user's own attention. The user could then decide how to proceed in the light of the agent's initiative.

An agent which acted in the way just described would be exhibiting intelligent behavior and, as is generally the case in AI, would need to be designed as a knowledge-based entity. By virtue of its reactivity, it would also be classed as an adaptive entity. As Norcio and Stanley (1989, 401) argue, the provision of an adaptive user interface imposes a necessity for the system to maintain internal models of:

7a. The user.
  b. The system itself.
  c. The user-system dialogue.
  d. The task.

An agent-based interface endowed with this kind of knowledge would also offer the possibility of providing better help facilities than are generally available at present. Thinking somewhat along the lines suggested by Chin (1990), we might imagine a situation where a user named Sam, who is not very experienced in the use of computers, has just received an email message containing an attachment from a friend in another country. Unfortunately, the attachment has arrived in uuencoded form! Baffled, Sam stares at the screen for a moment, and then calls upon the help agent, asking:

```
What is this gibberish?
```

The agent examines the text and infers that the message has been encoded. Its internal models indicate that Sam is attempting to read the attachment (task model), that Sam is inexperienced (user model), that the system has access to a decoding program (system model), and that Sam has asked for help (dialogue model). Accordingly it replies:

```
The text seems to have been encoded.
I will attempt to decode it for you.
```

It then passes the attachment through the decoder and restores it to its original, human-readable form, much to Sam's relief. Would not a cooperative help agent like this make the lives of many users easier?

There are other functions, too, which interface agents might usefully perform in the context of international CMC. Among others, these include:

8a. Finding email addresses, especially of people in foreign countries.
   b. Following up mail delivery errors without waiting to be instructed to do so.
   c. Translating data and/or system messages from foreign languages into that of a particular user.
   d. Reconfiguring screen displays when necessary.
   e. Converting times between time zones, currencies between countries, and so on.
   f. Advising on intercultural matters and/or finding sources of information on such topics.

Of course, an agent-based interface of the kind suggested here would be likely to have a rather complex architecture. There would be a number of distinct, intercommunicating agents, and some of these, such as a natural-language translation agent, could be very large. This could well mean that they could not all be stored on the same computer, but would instead need to be distributed over several nodes of a network. However, since the systems that form the subject of this chapter are networked in any case, there is no reason why they should not support distributed AI as an intrinsic part of their function, provided that the actual distribution of the agents was sensibly designed.

CONCLUSION

Clearly, there are many issues in international CMC which merit further investigation. As we have seen, standard HCI guidelines may require modification when applied in this context. In some cases they may need to be extended (e.g., with regard to the provision of error-correction facilities and feedback), while in others there may be a call for judicious restriction (as with the application of the principle of consistency). In addition, the need to support interpersonal communication between people with no common language and/or with other cultural differences that affect communication imposes additional demands on the user interface which are not normally even considered under this heading. However, at present we are unfortunately not in a position to propose a comprehensive and reasonably definitive set of IUID guidelines for CMC systems, and a good deal of research will be required before this becomes feasible.

One area of technology whose relevance to the improvement of the user interface to CMC systems has come repeatedly to our attention during the course of this chapter is that of knowledge-based systems (KBS). This is highly pertinent both to the provision of MT facilities and to the construction of agent-based interfaces of the type suggested here as being a promising line of development for IUID.

International CMC on a global scale is already a reality (virtual and actual!). Moreover, its use continues to increase sharply, both for the purposes of industry and commerce and for the purposes of leisure and entertainment. The economic, social, cultural, and perhaps political consequences of this are considerable. Therefore, the investment of substantial efforts directed toward the design of good user interfaces for international CMC systems seems amply justifiable.

REFERENCES

Allen, J., M. S. Hunnicutt, and D. Klatt. 1987. *From Text to Speech: The MITALK System*. Cambridge: Cambridge University Press.

Arnold, D., L. Balkan, R. Lee Humphreys, S. Meijer, and L. Sadler. 1994. *Machine Translation: An Introductory Guide*. Oxford: NCC Blackwell.

Chin, D.N. 1990. Intelligent interfaces as agents. In Sullivan, J. W., and S. W. Tyler (eds.), *Intelligent User Interfaces*. New York: ACM Press.

Connolly, J. H. 1994. Artificial intelligence and computer-supported cooperative working in international contexts. In Connolly and Edmonds (1994), 141-159.

Connolly, J. H. and E. A. Edmonds (eds.) 1994. *CSCW and Artificial Intelligence*. London: Springer-Verlag.

del Galdo, E. 1990. Internationalisation and translation: Some guidelines for the design of human-computer interfaces. In Nielsen, J. (ed.), *Designing User Interfaces for International Use*. Amsterdam: Elsevier, 1-10.

Hayes-Roth, F. 1980. Syntax, semantics and pragmatics in speech understanding systems. In Lea, W. A. (ed.), *Trends in Speech Recognition*. Englewood Cliffs, NJ: Prentice-Hall, 206-233.

Hutchins, W. J., and H. L. Somers. 1992. *An Introduction to Machine Translation*. London: Academic Press.

Loveday, L. 1983. Rhetoric patterns in conflict: The sociocultural relativity of discourse-organizing processes. *Journal of Pragmatics* **7**:169-190.

Maes, P. 1994. Agents that reduce work and information overload. *Communications of the ACM* **37,** 7:31-40.

Martin O'Donnell, S. 1994. *Programming for the World: A Guide to Internationalisation*. Englewood Cliffs, NJ: PTR Prentice-Hall.

Nirenburg, S., J. Carbonell, M. Tomita, and K. Goodman. 1992. *Machine Translation: A Knowledge-Based Approach*. San Mateo: Morgan Kaufmann.

Norcio, A. F. and J. Stanley. 1989. Adaptive human-computer interfaces: A literature survey and perspective. *IEEE Transactions on Systems, Man and Cybernetics* **19**:399-408.

Preece, J. (ed.). 1993. *A Guide to Usability: Human Factors in Computing*. Wokingham: Addison-Wesley.

Sasse, M. A., M. J. Handley, and N. M. Ismail. 1994. Coping with complexity and interference: Design issues in multimedia conferencing systems. In Rosenberg, D., and C. Hutchison (eds.), *Design Issues in CSCW*. London: Springer-Verlag, 179-195.

Scollon, R., and S. Wong Scollon. 1995. *Intercultural Communication: A Discourse Approach*. Oxford: Blackwell.

Scrivener, S. A. R., S. M. Clark, A. A. Clarke, J. H. Connolly, S. W. Garner, H. K. Palmén, M. G. Smyth, and A. Schappo. 1993. Real-time communication between dispersed work groups via speech and drawing. *Wirtschaftsinformatik* **35**:149-156.

Sharples, M. (ed.). 1993. *Computer Supported Collaborative Writing*. London: Springer-Verlag.

Shneiderman, B. 1987. *Designing the User Interface: Strategies for Effective Human-Computer Interaction*. Reading, MA: Addison-Wesley.

Sutcliffe, A. 1988. *Human-Computer Interface Design*. Basingstoke: Macmillan.

Uren, E., R. Howard, and T. Perinotti. 1993. *Software Internationalisation and Localisation: An Introduction*. New York: Van Nostrand Reinhold.

Wierzbicka, A. 1991. *Cross-cultural Pragmatics: The Semantics of Human Interaction*. Berlin: Mouton de Gruyter.

Wilson, P. 1991. *Computer Supported Cooperative Work*. Oxford: Intellect.

Wooldridge, M.J. and N. R. Jennings. 1995. Agent theories, architectures and languages: A survey. In Wooldridge, M. J. and N. R. Jennings (eds.), *Intelligent Agents*. Berlin: Springer-Verlag, 1–39.

ABOUT THE AUTHOR

Dr. John Connolly is a senior lecturer in the Department of Computer Studies at Loughborough University of Technology, England. He has over twenty years' experience of academic research (conducted in the UK, of which he is a native), and his main interests relate to natural language and human-computer interaction. He has written or co-edited three books, and is also the author of a number of research-related papers. Among his particular current interests are computer-supported cooperative work and the internationalization of computing systems. These topics are brought together within his contribution to the present volume.

CHAPTER 3

Developing a
Cultural Model

There is no denying that culture influences human-product interaction. Culture is, after all, learned behavior consisting of thoughts, feelings, and actions.[1] But how do you study culture, compare the data you gather, and apply it in a meaningful way to your product's design and implementation?

Using the approach taken by some leading cultural anthropologists and international business consultants, you develop a *cultural model*. A cultural model compares the similarities and differences of two or more cultures by using *international variables*.[2] International variables are categories that organize cultural data. Cultural data can reflect national cultures, corporate cultures, the cultural diversity of groups of users, international markets, and so on as is appropriate for your international user interface.

International variables can focus on objective, easy-to-research cultural differences like political and economic contexts, text directionality in writing systems, and differences in the way that you format the time of day, dates, and numbers.

Note: The material in this paper is adapted in large part from *International Technical Communication: How to Export Information about High Technology*, by Nancy L. Hoft, copyright 1995, John Wiley & Sons, and is reprinted with permission from John Wiley & Sons.

International variables can also focus on subjective information, like the value systems, behavioral systems, and intellectual systems of one or more cultural groupings of users. Examples of these more complex international variables include attitudes toward authority and technology and concepts of time and space.

The remainder of this chapter takes you through the process of developing a cultural model by showing you some popular and tested cultural models that are in use today. Each of these cultural models has its own purpose, which most likely will be different from your own. This suggests that they cannot be used "as is" for your needs; however, the cultural models and the stories behind how they were developed should suggest a methodology for creating a cultural model that is unique and meaningful for your company, its family of products, and its global user community.

The final sections of this chapter offer suggestions for how to gather cultural data for your cultural model and then how to apply the data. The goal for any cultural model, of course, is to gather data that lets you design products more closely addressing the cultural needs of your user community worldwide. In order to do so, you must understand the cultural context of your users and how it is similar and how it differs around the world.

THE USES OF A CULTURAL MODEL

- A cultural model can be used to identify *global information* (information that is relevant or appropriate in many cultural contexts without modification of any kind) for *internationalization*.
- A cultural model can be used to identify *cultural bias*. You do this by applying the cultural model to your own culture.
- A cultural model can be used to identify effective *cultural metaphors*.
- A cultural model can be used to assess the *degree of localization* that is necessary.
- A cultural model can be used to avoid making *cultural mistakes* that can offend or mislead.
- A cultural model can be used to *evaluate the effectiveness of an international user interface*.

SELECTING MEANINGFUL INTERNATIONAL VARIABLES

To be able to select meaningful international variables you must first understand how and where culture comes to influence our lives in such a profound way. To do so, you identify which layer or layers of culture you want to study.

Some Metamodels

To study layers of culture, we review four *metamodels* of culture:

- Objective culture and subjective culture
- The Iceberg model
- The Pyramid model
- The Onion model

The Objective Culture and Subjective Culture Edward C. Stewart and Milton J. Bennett, both professors in the United States of psychology and communication, respectively, introduce two layers of culture, objective culture and subjective culture, in their now-classic work *American Cultural Patterns: A Cross-Cultural Perspective* (Yarmouth, Maine: Intercultural Press, 1991). Both layers of culture are illustrated in Figure 3.1.

- *Objective culture* is "the institutions and artifacts of a culture, such as its economic system, social customs, political structures and processes, arts, crafts and literature."[3] Objective culture is visible, easy to examine, and tangible.
- *Subjective culture* is "the psychological features of a culture, including assumptions, values, and patterns of thinking." Subjective culture is difficult to examine because it operates outside of conscious awareness.

Stewart and Bennett point out an interesting irony about the relationship between objective and subjective culture and how we perceive them. Objective culture, because it is the externalization of subjective culture, is therefore abstract. Subjective culture is what is real and concrete. However, we tend to treat objective culture as more real and concrete than its source, subjective culture.

values

assumptions

patterns of thinking

FIGURE 3.1   Objective and subjective culture.

The Iceberg Model   The Iceberg model is a popular metamodel
that is often used by cross-cultural communication consultants,
since it provides a useful metaphor for describing the layers of
culture and how aware we are of their influence in our lives.[4]
The analogy drawn in the Iceberg model is that just as 10 percent of an iceberg is visible above the surface of the water, only
10 percent of the cultural characteristics of a target audience is
easily visible to an observer (us). It follows that just as the
remaining 90 percent of an iceberg is below the surface and not
visible, the remaining 90 percent of our cultural characteristics
are hidden from view and are therefore easier to ignore and
more difficult to identify and study.

The Iceberg model identifies three metaphorical layers of
culture, which are illustrated in Figure 3.2:

FIGURE 3.2   The Iceberg model. (*International Technical Communication: How to Export Information about High Technology*, Nancy Hoft, copyright 1995, John Wiley & Sons. Reprinted by permission of John Wiley & Sons, Inc.)

- *Surface*. The cultural characteristics at this level are visible, obvious, and easy to research. They include: number, currency, time, and date formats, language, and so on. This layer of culture is similar to Bennett and Stewart's objective layer of culture.
- *Unspoken Rules*. The cultural characteristics at this level are somewhat obscured. You generally need to identify the context of situation first in order to understand what the unspoken rules are. Examples include business etiquette and protocol.
- *Unconscious Rules*. The cultural characteristics are out of conscious awareness and difficult to study for this reason. Examples include nonverbal communication, a sense of time and physical distances, the rate and intensity of speech, and so on.

The Pyramid Model   Geert Hofstede, best known for his book *Culture's Consequences* (Sage, 1980) and currently a professor of Organizational Anthropology and International Management at the University of Limburg in the Netherlands, introduces three layers of culture in the Pyramid model. The three layers of culture in this metamodel, which are illustrated in Figure 3.3, attempt to show the origin of culture and why it is unique in "human mental programming."[5]

- *Personality*. Personality is specific to an individual and is both learned and inherited.
- *Culture*. Culture is specific to a group or category of people. It is learned and not inherited. "Culture should be distinguished from human nature on one side, and from an individual's personality on the other . . . although exactly where the borders lie between human nature and culture, and between culture and personality, is a matter of discussion among social scientists."[6]
- *Human Nature*. Human nature is what is common to all human beings. It is universal and it is inherited, not learned. It is passed down through the generations via DNA.

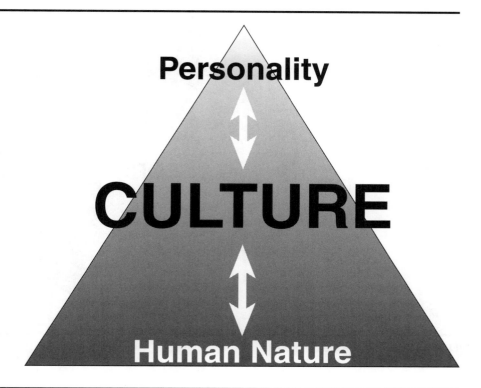

FIGURE 3.3   The Pyramid model.

The Onion Model   Another three-layer metamodel is the Onion model, introduced by Fons Trompenaars, the managing director of the Centre for International Business Studies in The Netherlands.[7] The three layers of culture in the Onion model are illustrated in Figure 3.4.

- *Outer Layer.* The outer layer of culture is again very similar to the concept of objective culture introduced in Bennett and Stewart's metamodel. The outer layer consists of explicit products and artifacts of culture. Trompenaars suggests that the outer layer consists of the first things we encounter at a cultural level. "Explicit culture is the observable reality of the language, food, buildings, houses, monuments, agri-

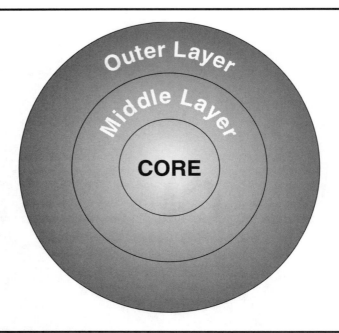

FIGURE 3.4   The Onion model.

culture, shrines, markets, fashions and art. They are the
symbols of a deeper level of culture."[8]
- *Middle Layer*. The middle layer of culture defines norms
  and values. Norms are principles of right and wrong that
  are shared among a group of people. Values define what is
  good and bad, desirable and undesirable, among a group of
  people. In some respects values are ideals.
- *Core*. The core of culture is implicit and consists of how people adapt to their environments. The core consists of the
  basic assumptions of human existence.

Some Known and Tested Models of Culture

Metamodels provide a useful backdrop for models of culture and
their international variables. They offer some perspective for
how deep into a group's cultural context we actually peer when
we identify and study international variables. As all metamod-

TABLE 3.1   The Focus of the Four Models of Culture

Author	Focus of Model of Culture
Edward T. Hall	Determining what releases the right response rather than what sends the right message.
David A. Victor	Determining the aspects of culture most likely to affect communication specifically in a business setting.
Geert Hofstede	Determining the patterns of thinking, feeling, and acting that form a culture's mental programming.
Fons Trompenaars	Determining the way in which a group of people solves problems.

els suggest, most culture is "below the surface," buried in unconscious reality.

Here we review four known and tested models of culture. Table 3.1 compares the data that each model attempts to collect.

Each model of culture identifies international variables that look below the surface and focus on the unconscious level of culture. Culture is learned and not inherited. These models offer ways to analyze people's cultural contexts.

Each model is authored by a particular individual who has written extensively on his model. This section summarizes the international variables in these models of culture to provide some incentive and ideas for creating international variables for your own model of culture. You should refer to the original works of each author to learn more about any particular international variable.

The authors introduced here developed these models of culture as a result of questionnaires, surveys, extensive interviews, focus groups, and years of experience and observation. As mentioned previously, these models of culture are not necessarily applicable to your corporate setting and business needs. Your international team can develop a model of culture that is particularly well suited to your business arena and target audiences by applying the same methods as these authors. Hofstede's model, for example, developed out of an initial multinational study he did of IBM Corporation.

These models of culture offer you a place to begin creating and selecting meaningful international variables. Note too that there are other models of culture that this chapter does not cover. Review the literature of intercultural communication for other models.

Edward T. Hall   Edward T. Hall, is a well respected anthropologist and intercultural communication consultant. His model of culture is based on years of observation and extensive interviewing throughout the world. To Hall, culture is a program for behavior. Effective cross-cultural communication "has more to do with releasing the right response than with sending the 'right' messages."[9]

Note that the following international variables do not form a nice, neat cultural model. Hall never created a cultural model per se. His international variables, however, have greatly influenced the study of culture and of how people from different countries tend to respond to various situations.

Speed of Messages   Hall talks about the message velocity continuum, which refers to the speed with which people decode and act on messages. Some cultures are more comfortable with fast messages in many instances, while other cultures are more comfortable with slow messages.

- Examples of slow messages include:
  - deep relationships
  - works of art
  - television documentaries
  - poetry
  - books
- Examples of fast messages include:
  - headlines
  - cartoons
  - television commercials
  - manners
  - propaganda

Context   Hall articulated the idea of *contexting* in his book *Beyond Culture*. Contexting offers product designers a way of assessing the amount and kind of detail they should include in a product for maximum effectiveness. Hall defines two kinds of contexting, *high context* and *low context*. Here is his definition of both:

> High context or low context refers to the amount of information that is in a given communication as a function of the context in which it occurs. A highly contexted communication is one in which most of the meaning is in the context while very little is in the transmitted message. A low context communication is similar to interacting with a computer—if the information is not explicitly stated, and the program followed religiously, the meaning is distorted. In the Western world, the law is low context, in comparison with daily transactions of an informal nature. People who know each other over a long period of years will tend to use high context communication.[10]

Hall offers several examples of problems that arise when people of low context communicate with people of high-context cultures. His "favorite" examples seem to be of Americans interacting with the Japanese; America is a low-context culture, and Japan is a high-context culture. Hall describes the legal systems of both countries. In America, we remove the context of the crime and rely on the plain, hard facts to decide a case. In Japan, they reenact the crime publicly, deliberately making its context literal for all to see, not the least of whom is the criminal.

Hall created a Context Square to illustrate communication, which consists of context, information, and meaning. The Context Square, shown in the background of Figure 3.5, uses two right triangles and a rectangle to show the relationship among context, information, and meaning. "[A]s context is lost, information must be added if the meaning is to remain constant. . . .There can be no meaning without both information and context."[11]

Hall's writings are taken a bit further in David Victor's LESCANT model, explained next. Victor, though, provides an interesting diagram of high- and low-context cultures, which is superimposed on Hall's Context Square in Figure 3.5. Victor diagrams the context ranking of ten cultures on a continuum. First in the continuum for high-context cultures is Japan, where

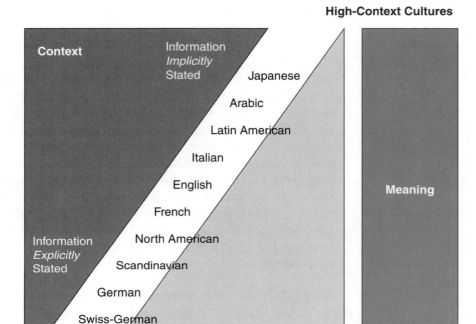

FIGURE 3.5   Hall's Context Square and Victor's diagram of the Context Ranking of Cultures (author's interpretation). (*International Technical Communication: How to Export Information about High Technology*, Nancy Hoft, Copyright 1995, John Wiley & Sons. Reprinted by permission of John Wiley & Sons, Inc.)

information is implicitly stated. Last in the low-context cultures are the Swiss-Germans, for whom information must be explicitly stated. The French and the British fall in the middle of the continuum.[12]

Space   All cultures have difference senses of space, or invisible boundaries. (Note here how objective and subjective culture, to borrow Stewart and Bennett's metamodel again, overlap such that the one disguises the other.) Hall qualifies these invisible boundaries in the following ways:

- *Territoriality*. This cultural trait includes "ownership" and extends to communicate power. The layout of the floors in an office building in Japan, for example, is very different from that in the United States. In Japan, it is often difficult to identify who has power and authority based on the layout of a floor or even of a building. In the United States, those with power typically have the largest and most lavish offices, which are often located on the top floors of a building.
- *Personal Space*. Cultures have different expectations of personal space and therefore have unspoken and unconscious rules about when personal space is violated. Hall cites an example of how in northern Europe you do not touch others, and even brushing the overcoat sleeve of another in passing is enough to warrant an apology.
- *Multisensory Space*. Invisible boundaries extend to all the five senses. Cultures have unconscious rules about what is too loud and intrusive, for example. In low-context cultures, like Germany, a loud conversation is perceived as infringing on another's private space. In high-context cultures, as in Italy, loud conversations are expected to take place and are not perceived as infringing on invisible boundaries.
- *Unconscious Reactions to Spatial Differences*. The distance you keep when having a conversation can influence the response the person has to you and your conversation. For example, if you have a conversation with someone from a culture where maintaining a close physical distance during conversation is expected, and yet you converse at a greater distance than this, you send an unconscious and negative message to the other person.

Time   Time is an important and complex international variable in Hall's model of culture, and it figures in the other three models of culture as well.

In its simplest form, time, as an international variable in Hall's model of culture, is of two types, *polychronic time* and *monochronic time*.

- Polychronic time (P-time) is characterized as simultaneous and concurrent. "Many-things-at-once" is the phrase Hall uses to define polychronic time.

- Monochronic time (M-time) is characterized as being sequential and linear. "One-thing-at-a-time" is the phrase Hall uses to define monochronic time.

Hall applies these definitions to cultures and speaks of polychronic and monochronic people. Table 3.2 identifies the characteristics of both.

Examples of monochronic people include Northern European cultures. Examples of polychronic people include Middle Eastern, Latin American, and Mediterranean cultures. (Notice the geography at work here; warmer climates tend to be polychronic, while colder or erratic climates tend to be monochronic. Victor discusses this in his *environment* international variable.)

Successful communication with these cultures is often attributed to a respect for their concept of time. Note that cultures are not exclusively polychronic or monochronic. The Japanese, for example, are polychronic in their dealings with other people, but monochronic in their approach to official business dealings. The relationship with a client and a rigid schedule for accomplishing goals are closely entwined.

TABLE 3.2   Monochronic and Polychronic People[13]

Monochronic People	Polychronic People
• Do one thing at a time	• Do many things at once
• Concentrate on the job	• Are highly distractible and subject to interruptions
• View time commitments as critical	• View time commitments as objectives
• Are low-context and need information	• Are high-context and already have information
• Are committed to the job	• Are committed to people and human relationships
• Adhere strictly to plans	• Change plans often and easily
• Emphasize promptness	• Base promptness on the importance of and significance of the relationship
• Are accustomed to short-term relationships	• Have a strong tendency to build lifetime relationships

Hall also talks of past- and future-oriented cultures. For example, he frequently speaks of Germans as very past-oriented, and of the fact that their information needs are closely tied to this. "German time and German consciousness are steeped in the past. When they explain something, they often find it necessary to lay a proper foundation and as a result are apt to go back to Charlemagne."[14]

He notes an odd contrast to the Japanese, whose culture is also "steeped in history," but because of the high-context nature of their culture, they tend to plan far ahead into the future due to the value they place on long-term business.

Information Flow   Information flow is defined as the measure of "how long it takes for a message intended to produce an action to travel from one part of an organization to another and for that message to release the desired response."[15]

Hall states that in high-context cultures, which value relationships and information more than schedules, the information flow tends to be very fast and free. Knowing the right people is highly valued. In low-context cultures, where everything tends to be compartmentalized and where bureaucracies flourish, the information flow tends to be slow. Following procedure is highly valued.

Action Chains   An action chain is a sequence of events that lead to the accomplishment of a goal. Action chains are central to technical communication. Tasks, procedures, methods for performance, are all examples of action chains. "There are important rules governing the structure, though not the content, of action chains. . . . All planning must take into account the elaborate hierarchy of action chains." Action chains should be considered when we do task analyses, for example.

David A. Victor   David A. Victor's LESCANT model provides yet another view of culture and offers a rich array of variables that you can explore when creating your model of culture. Victor's work is based mostly on extensive academic research, and thus pulls together a large collection of independent research and findings from throughout the world. Therefore, the following information provides merely an outline of his model.

A central theme in Victor's work is that cultural differences and similarities are essential to and inseparable from effective international business communication. His LESCANT model identifies the international variables where cultural differences and similarities are manifest. The following quotation summarizes his logic:

> First, as global demands for products grow and international trade barriers decrease, the need of business people to communicate with their counterparts from other cultures increases. At the same time, as pressures for global conformity in such areas as consumer preference mount with the expanded volume of world trade, cultural differences will intensify as a defensive mechanism. Since the area over which people have the most individual control is their manner of communication, business communication in an integrated world economy will reflect an increase in cross-cultural differences in direct proportion to the decrease in other international barriers.[16]

LESCANT is an acronym based on words in English, each of which is an international variable that is briefly described here:

Language Victor offers some interesting discussion about degrees of fluency, accents, and regional dialects and how they affect business communication, and about linguistic determinism. He also discusses the pros, cons, and misperceptions of English as the international language of business.

Environment and Technology This international variable considers larger issues such as the ways in which geography, population, concepts of physical space, and perceptions of technology affect business communication. (Compare to Trompenaars's concept of the core in his Onion model.) Victor offers the radical example of Switzerland, where its mountain ranges have contributed to the development of very distinct cultures within the same country.

Social Organization This variable explores educational, economic, social, political, and religious systems as they affect business communication. Clearly a huge and important collection of topics, but perhaps it is a bit too broad a category for an international variable.

Contexting Victor expands on Hall's model of contexting, and includes the research of Martin Rosch and Kay Segler, who ranked cultures using Hall's context square. This is illustrated in Figure 3.5.

Authority Conception This international variable considers differences and similarities in power, authority, and leadership; how they are perceived differently in cultures; and how this perception affects business communication.

Nonverbal Behavior This is a broad category for many types of nonverbal behavior, which Victor divides into two categories, active and passive.

He reviews six facets of active nonverbal behavior. These facets study how people communicate through:

1. Movement
2. Appearance
3. Eye behavior
4. Touching behavior
5. Space usage
6. Sound

He reviews four facets of passive nonverbal behavior:

1. Colors
2. Numbers and counting indicators
3. Symbols
4. Smells

Temporal Conception In a word, time: Victor explores various perspectives of time, highlighting Hall's P-time and M-time, and how they can affect business communication, particularly with respect to scheduling.

Geert Hofstede Geert Hofstede founded and managed the Personnel Research Department of IBM Europe from 1965-1971. While at IBM, he developed a multinational survey that "dealt mainly with the employees' personal *values* related to the work situation. . . ."[17] The results of this survey greatly influenced the development of his model of culture, and led him to develop or refer to other multinational surveys that validated these initial findings. It is interesting to note the scope of the IBM survey, since it reflects what is possible to pursue in your own corporate environment by creating your own model of culture:

> The database was unusually extensive, covering employees in 72 national subsidiaries, 38 occupations, 20 languages, and at two points in time: around 1968 and around 1972. Altogether, there were more than 116,000 questionnaires with over 100 standardized questions each.[18]

Of equal importance is being familiar with Hofstede's definition of *culture*.

> Every person carries within him or herself patterns of thinking, feeling, and potential acting which were learned throughout their lifetime. . . . Using the analogy of the way in which computers are programmed, [Hofstede calls] such patterns of thinking, feeling, and acting *mental programs, or . . . "software of the mind".* . . . Mental programs vary as much as the social environments in which they were acquired. . . . Culture is always a collective phenomenon, because it is at least partly shared with people who live or lived within the same social environment, which is where it is learned. It is the *collective programming of the mind which distinguishes the members of one group or category of people from another."*[19]

The following international variables identify differences in mental programming.

Power Distance   Power distance measures how subordinates (employees, staff members) respond to power and authority (leaders, managers), which Hofstede summarizes as how subordinates value (respond to and perceive) inequality.

He created an index to measure this in his IBM surveys. What he found was that high power distances tend to exist in

Latin American countries, France, Spain, and in Asia and Africa. In these countries, subordinates tend to be afraid of their bosses, bosses tend not to confer with their subordinates, and bosses tend to be paternalistic or autocratic.

Low-power-distance countries include the United States, Great Britain, much of the rest of Europe (Sweden, Germany, Norway, the Netherlands, Denmark), New Zealand, and Israel. In these countries, subordinates are more likely to challenge bosses and bosses tend to use a consultative management style.

Collectivism versus Individualism   These polar values measure the ties among individuals in a society.

- In *individualistic cultures*, people are expected to look out for themselves. There is little social cohesion. Examples of countries that value individualism include the United States, France, Germany, South Africa, and Canada. Some values include personal time, freedom, and challenge.
- In *collectivist cultures*, individuals develop strong personal and protective ties and are also expected to provide unquestioning loyalty to the group during their lifetimes and sometimes beyond. Examples of countries that value collectivism include Japan, Costa Rica, Mexico, Korea, and Greece. Some values include training, physical conditions, and use of skills.

Femininity versus Masculinity   Hofstede's IBM survey found men's work goals were markedly different from women's work goals, and that these differences could be expressed on a masculine pole and a feminine pole. Table 3.3 summarizes some of these findings.

Examples of countries where the feminine index is more valued include Sweden, Israel, Spain, Korea, France, Denmark, Finland, and Indonesia. The masculine index is more valued in the United States, Japan, Mexico, Great Britain, Hong Kong, Italy, Germany, and New Zealand.

Uncertainty Avoidance   This international variable focuses on "the extent to which people feel threatened by uncertain or unknown situations." It is an attempt to plot on a continuum people's

TABLE 3.3   Masculine and Feminine Work Goals Index

Masculine Index	Feminine Index
Have a high opportunity for earnings	Have a good working relationship with your direct supervisor
Get the recognition you deserve	Work with people who cooperate well with one another
Have an opportunity for advancement to higher-level jobs	Live in an area desirable to you and your family
Have challenging work to do to derive a sense of accomplishment	Have the security that you will be able to work for your company as long as you want to

response to unknown situations. Hofstede characterizes uncertainty avoidance as "what is different, is dangerous." Uncertainty avoidance is measured using the units *strong* and *weak*.

Strong uncertainty avoidance indicates that a culture tends to perceive unknown situations as threatening and that people, therefore, tend to avoid these situations. Here are some of the characteristics that Hofstede outlines for cultures that measure low on the uncertainty avoidance scale: [20]

- Uncertainty is a continuous threat that must be fought.
- There is acceptance of familiar risks, but fear of ambiguous situations and of unfamiliar risks.
- What is different is dangerous.
- Students are comfortable in structured learning situations and concerned with the right answers.
- Teachers are expected to have all the answers.
- Precision comes naturally.
- There is suppression of deviant ideas and behavior.
- There is a resistance to innovation.
- Motivation is by security and esteem or belongingness.

Examples of countries where this is so include Latin American countries, Japan, and South Korea.

Weak uncertainty avoidance indicates that a culture is less threatened by unknown situations. Here are some of the characteristics that Hofstede lists for cultures measuring low on the uncertainty avoidance scale:[21]

- Uncertainty is a normal feature of life.
- People feel comfortable with ambiguous situations and un-familiar risks.
- What is different is curious.
- Students are comfortable with open-ended learning situations and concerned with good discussions.
- Teachers may say "I don't know."
- Precision has to be learned.
- Motivation is by achievement and esteem or belongingness.
- There is tolerance of deviant and innovative ideas.

Examples of countries where this is so include the Netherlands, West Germany, the United States, Singapore, Hong Kong, and Great Britain.

Long-term versus Short-term This international variable came about after Hofstede performed his IBM surveys. It is the result of a long process of weeding out what he discovered to be cultural bias inherent in the original surveys; that is, the IBM surveys had a Western bias. The surveys did not consider non-Western values, particularly those of China and relating to the teaching of Confucius. An index measuring cultures' long-term versus short-term orientation toward life resulted.

The values for *long-term orientation* (concern about the future) are:

- persistence and perseverance
- respect for a hierarchy of the status of relationships
- thrift
- having a sense of shame

Examples of countries that have a long-term orientation toward life include China, Hong Kong, Taiwan, Japan, and India.

The values for *short-term orientation* (concern with the past and the present) are:

- sense of security and stability
- protecting your reputation
- respect for tradition
- reciprocation of greetings, favors, and gifts

Examples of countries that have a short-term orientation toward life include: Pakistan, the Philippines, Canada, Great Britain, Germany, Australia, and the United States.

Fons Trompenaars   Fons Trompenaars studied under Hofstede, so it is no wonder that there are artifacts from Hofstede's model in Trompenaars's seven dimensions of corporate culture, although their models are quite different. Trompenaars, like Hofstede, has quantified his model with data from an extensive multinational survey, the results of which are printed in *Riding the Waves of Culture: Understanding Cultural Diversity* (Nicholas Brealey, London, 1993).[22] This survey posed 16 questions across 30 companies and 50 countries. The respondents were 15,000 managers in operations, sales, and marketing (75 percent) and general administrative staff (25 percent). The result is the Trompenaars Data Bank, a rich collection of cultural data that Trompenaars sells to corporations worldwide. Note the obvious value here in owning cultural data.

Trompenaars defines culture as the way in which a group of people solve problems.[23] He groups the problems into three headings, and then identifies seven dimensions of culture (value orientations) that typify the solutions that cultures apply when they solve these problems. They are:

1. Problems that arise from our relationships with other people
   - universalism versus particularism
   - individualism versus collectivism
   - neutral or emotional
   - specific versus diffuse
   - achievement versus ascription
2. Problems that come from the passage of time
   - attitudes to time
3. Problems that relate to the environment
   - attitudes to the environment

Universalism versus Particularism *Universalists* are rules-based. Rules define morality, ethics, or what is good and right. In a serious situation involving another person (what is becoming commonly referred to as an ethical dilemma), universalists tend to apply these rules regardless of their relationship with the other person. Examples of countries where universalism is the value orientation include Canada, the United States, Sweden, Great Britain, and the Netherlands.

Particularists are relationship-based. In a serious situation involving another person, particularists base their solution to the problem on the relationship that they have with the other person and "break the rules" if necessary. Countries where particularism is the value orientation include South Korea, Russia, China, France, Japan, and Hong Kong.

Individualism versus Collectivism Individualism and collectivism relate to self-perception: Do people perceive themselves primarily as individuals or as members of a group? This value-orientation pair also relates to a sense of responsibility. Trompenaars adds the following management problem: "Is it more important to focus [as a manager] on individuals so that they can contribute to the collective as and if they wish, or is it more important to consider the collective first since that is shared by many individuals?"[24] Thus, this dimension measures three facets of value orientation.

Examples of individualist countries valuing individual freedom include Canada, the United States, Norway, Spain, and Hong Kong. Countries where individual freedom is valued less include France, Greece, Kuwait, East Germany, and South Korea.

Examples of countries where people prefer to work independently include Sweden, the United States, Czechoslovakia, and Switzerland. Examples of countries where people prefer to be members of a team are France, West Germany, Italy, Japan, and Singapore.

Examples of countries that make the individual accountable for problems include: Russia, Poland, Denmark, and Switzerland. Examples of countries in which individuals tend to share blame with others include Singapore, Japan, UK, and the Philippines. The United States tends to fall at the middle of the scale.

Neutral or Emotional   This value-orientation pair measures the range of emotions that people express when dealing with others in a business context.

Examples of countries where it is acceptable to express emotion when a conflict arises in a business situation include Italy, France, and the United States. Examples of countries where expressing emotion is discouraged during a conflict in a business setting include Japan, UK, and Norway.

Specific versus Diffuse   A specific value orientation is one where public and private life and public and private personal spaces are compartmentalized. It measures the range of involvement that people have with others in their lives. In specific-oriented cultures (in the United States, Australia, the UK, the Netherlands, Sweden, and West Germany), there is a clear division of business relationships and private relationships with others. A good business relationship is often kept separate from a good friendship.

In diffuse cultures, there is very little differentiation between a public and private life, and business relationships are expected to be of a personal nature. Hence the diffusion of public and private boundaries, spaces, and relationships. Countries that value diffuse relationships include: China, Singapore, Japan, Mexico, and France.

It is interesting to note that Trompenaars recorded regional differences as well. For example, in the United States, people on the West Coast have a greater tendency to express sympathy or outrage at specific issues than do people on the East Coast of the United States, who tend to respond judgmentally (approve or disapprove) to specific issues.

Achievement versus Ascription   This value orientation measures how status is accorded. In achievement-oriented cultures, status is accorded based on individual achievements. Examples of countries where this is the case include Norway, the United States, Canada, and the UK. In ascription-oriented cultures, status is accorded based on birth, kinship, gender, age, your connections, and your educational record; examples of countries include Russia, Japan, Spain, France, China, and Belgium.

Attitudes to Time   This international variable is similar to that of Hall's definition of M-time and P-time. It concerns a culture's attitude toward the past, the present, the future, and the relationship of the three to each other.

In some cultures, time is perceived as a linear sequence of discrete events leading to some point in the future or some future goal. Examples of countries that demonstrated a sequential relationship of the past, present, and future include the United States, West Germany, and South Korea.

Other cultures think of time as "moving in a circle, the past and present together with future possibilities."[25] Examples of countries where the past, present, and future are integrated include: France, Belgium, and Venezuela. In some instances, as in Russia, Italy, and the Netherlands, the cultural data gathered indicated that there is little or no relationship among the past, the present, and the future.

Attitudes to the Environment   This value orientation measures people's attitudes toward their ability to control the environment (nature).

Countries in which people believe it is worth trying to control nature include Brazil, Portugal, and China. Countries who have the opposite inclination include Japan, Singapore, and Switzerland.

Identifying International Variables for Your Model of Culture

There is an old expression in English that is appropriate to consider when identifying the international variables that you want to use in your model of culture: "Do not put the cart before the horse." In other words, avoid selecting international variables before you determine the most appropriate assessment method to use to collect cultural data.

Assessment Methods for Identifying International Variables
All of the authors of the cultural models reviewed here relied on a particular assessment method like academic research (Victor), observation and focus groups (Hall), or questionnaires and interviews (Hofstede and Trompenaars) to gather cultural data that they then analyzed to determine international variables. They did this by looking for patterns in the information they

gathered, comparing and contrasting all findings, observations, and responses they received to the initial assessment method. Consistent patterns were generalized and tested and eventually became international variables (categories that organize cultural data).

Of all the traditional assessment methods, questionnaires and observation are the most preferable for identifying international variables. Of these two assessment methods, questionnaires are the best choice because "it is possible to distribute a questionnaire to the entire user population. Questionnaires are probably the only usability method that makes such extensive coverage feasible, with the ensuing possibility for discovering differences between various user categories as well as the specific needs of various small groups of users."[26] Clearly you want this broad a scope when identifying international variables.

Regarding observation, you would need a lot of time to observe enough of a representative sample of your user community in order to make some objective decisions about which international variables would be most meaningful to your company.

Note that you may need to develop additional assessment methods to validate the international variables that your cultural data suggests.

Define the Purpose of Your Model of Culture   The purpose of each of the models of cultures reviewed in this chapter is defined in Table 3.1. This purpose guided the design of the assessment method that each author applied. For example, Trompenaars very clearly wanted to collect cultural data that indicated how people in different cultures solved problems. Since his primary audience was management, this purpose helped him develop cultural profiles of management style in different countries.

Like these authors, you should articulate a purpose for your model of culture *before* you develop the assessment method.

Some Comments about Using Questionnaires to Identify International Variables   Here is a sample survey question from Hofstede's research: " 'Try to think of those factors which would be important to you in an ideal job; disregard the extent to which they are contained in your present job. How important is it to you to . . .' followed by 14 items, each to be scored on a scale from 1 (of utmost importance to me) to 5 (of very little or no importance)."[27] From this question and its responses, Hofstede derived two international variables (dimensions in his research): individualism versus collectivism and masculinity versus femininity.

By comparison, Trompenaars, who also identified individualism and collectivism as international variables, used this question:

> A defect is discovered in one of the installations. It was caused by negligence of one of the members of a team. Responsibility for this mistake can be carried in various ways:
>
> A. The person causing the defect by negligence is the one responsible.
>
> B. Because he or she happens to work in a team the responsibility should be carried by the group.
>
> Which one of these two ways of taking responsibility do you think is usually the case in your society, A or B?[28]

All of the questions in both Hofstede's and Trompenaars's questionnaires are situational and quite clearly try to assess the "middle layer" of culture, to use a term from the Onion model. However, as Hofstede repeats again and again in his literature, questionnaires that are used to compare two or more groups of people with cross-cultural comparison as their goal must meet three criteria:

1. Samples must be *functionally equivalent* and as *homogeneous* as possible so that you limit the differences you seek to identify to cultural differences.
2. Questions must be developed and tested by usability and human factors specialists from around the world to *eliminate cultural bias* in the questions. (Hofstede made this mistake in his research.[29])
3. Data gathered as a result of the questionnaires must *avoid stereotyping* a group of people.

Some additional points to consider:

- Should questionnaires be translated into the native language of the user prior to distribution for the widest possible circulation? In general, yes. However, there are two possible problems. First, consider that good translators do not translate word-for-word but translate meaning. Translators can influence the tone and style and possibly the meaning of a question just by doing their jobs well. Second, translation makes the samples less homogeneous. Language, while a facet of culture, is in many respects an artifact of culture. It operates more at the objective layer than at the subjective layer. A good questionnaire might need to assess only one layer of culture to keep the assessment really focused and to generate reliable data. Take advantage of a multicultural and multilinguistic test team to evaluate the translations and also the physical layout, fonts, and so on of the questionnaire. Consider that if you translate and if you allow users to comment in free-form fashion to various questions, you will receive their responses in their native languages. You will then need to translate their responses into whatever your base language is, English for example, in order for the whole test team to have access to the data.
- Should questionnaires be returned in postage-paid envelopes to a location in the country of the user, in the country of the usability and human factors team, or to a country in the vicinity of the user? In general, most companies that use postage-paid response cards find that they get a higher return rate if the information is sent to an address in the same country as the user. The second recommended address is one that is in the vicinity of the user. Having all responses sent to one country only is known to decrease the amount of returned surveys. In all cases, do not require the user to pay for the postage of returning a completed questionnaire.

An excellent vehicle for gathering questionnaire data is the Internet and specifically the World Wide Web (WWW). The Graphics, Visualization, Usability (GVU) Center at Georgia Institute of Technology has been quite successful in gathering accurate survey results via the WWW, for example.[30] Of course, using the Internet and the WWW assume that your user community is connected to the Internet and that they have access to the WWW. For this reason, consider offering a paper- and postage-paid-based questionnaire, an email-based questionnaire, and a WWW-based questionnaire to encourage an even higher response rate to your questionnaire.

- Should you validate the cultural data using other assessment methods? Yes, particularly if you intend to use the cultural model and its international variables as assessment methods that evaluate the global appeal of all products that your company produces. Consider creating a storyboard of cultural comparisons that are organized using your international variables and that compare cultural data across national borders or across international markets. A tabular presentation is a good information design for this. Present the storyboard to multicultural and multilinguistic focus groups that discuss these findings in greater depth.

APPLYING CULTURAL DATA

Grouped, the international variables you identify form cultural models, which are assessment methods in and of themselves. With a cultural model you are able to gather cultural data again and again for the purposes of comparing and contrasting how groups of people think, feel, and act in different situations as defined by your statement of purpose. You can then validate this data by using the same or other assessment tools. Once you feel confident that the cultural data you have gathered is representative (without stereotyping), organize it into categories (international variables) to begin developing cultural profiles of groups of users.

With a cultural profile of your users, you can begin evaluating how to design, test, and evaluate products for the global market. In some cases, for example, you may find that there are so many similarities in the cultural profiles that cultural customization of the product and its feature set is unnecessary. In other cases, you may find that the cultural differences are severe to the point of contradiction, making some form of cultural customization necessary to create an effective, usable product.

Always balance your cultural findings against the business

needs of your company. In many cases, the business needs have already been articulated in marketing research reports. For example, your cultural findings may indicate that cultural customization would greatly enhance the product for a particular group of users. But if this group of users forms only 3 percent or less of the market share for this product, and if this group of users is not targeted as an emerging market for your company, cultural customization is not worth the effort and expense.

Use your cultural profiles to evaluate the effectiveness of the product's international user interface.

- Can the product be globalized so that it is usable in many cultural contexts without modification of any kind?
- Does cultural bias exist in the product design?
- Which cultural metaphors are most effective?
- Is cultural customization required?
- Does a facet of the product's design offend a group of users within a shared cultural context?

SUMMARY: STEPS TO DEVELOPING A CULTURAL MODEL

Remember that creating effective products for the world market must balance economy (business needs) with cultural understanding (user needs). Do not customize for the sake of customizing. Customize only when it makes good business sense to do so.

1. Determine the layer or layers of culture that you want to study.
2. Define the purpose of your model of culture.
3. Select an assessment method for gathering cultural data.
4. Develop the assessment method with the purpose of your model of culture in mind.
5. Apply the assessment method to gather cultural data.
6. Analyze the cultural data to identify international variables.
7. Validate the international variables by reapplying the assessment method or by developing another assessment method.

8. Organize cultural data to develop cultural profiles of your user community.
9. Validate the cultural profiles by developing another assessment method. Keep the data up-to-date by reapplying the assessment methods periodically.
10. Apply the cultural profiles or apply the cultural model to assess a product's design and a product's usability in a worldwide context.
11. Educate product developers on the findings of the cultural model and how to apply it in their work.
12. Document and distribute the cultural model, the cultural data, and the cultural profiles to the whole product team.

REFERENCES

1. The simple definition of culture provided here addresses the concepts that I feel are important to a discussion of how to develop a cultural model. There is no agreement on a specific definition of *culture*. In 1954, for example, A. L. Kroeber and C. Kluckhohn reported over 300 definitions of culture (*Culture: A Critical Review of Concepts and Definitions*, New York: Random House). Clearly there are more definitions than that today. For these reasons, I chose a definition that is simple and seems to be in agreement with much research on culture.
2. Note that many cultural anthropologists and international business consultants use the phrase "dimensions of culture" and not the phrase "international variables." I find the phrase "international variables" to be more direct and accurate.
3. Stewart and Bennett, 2.
4. Because of the popularity of the Iceberg Model in cross-cultural training, it is difficult to trace its origin. Here are two of the sources in which it is described, although this list is not complete by any means: Sylvia Odenwald, *Global Training*, Business One Irwin, Illinois, 1993, p. 47; from a handout by Heather Robinson and Jeanne Parrent, "Cross-Cultural Communication," presented at the *Seminar on International Technical Communication*, which was sponsored by the Society for Technical Communication and held in Seattle, Washington, March 2, 1992.
5. The Pyramid model is introduced in Geert Hofstede, *Cultures and Organizations: Software of the Mind*, McGraw Hill, New York, 1991, 5–6.

6. Hofstede, 5.
7. Fons Trompenaars, *Riding the Waves of Culture: Understanding Cultural Diversity in Business*, Nicholas Brealey, London, 1993, 22–24.
8. Ibid., 22.
9. Hall, 4.
10. Edward T. Hall, *The Dance of Life*, 229.
11. Ibid., 61.
12. David A. Victor, *International Business Communication*, Harper Collins, New York, 1992, 143.
13. Edward T. Hall, *Understanding Cultural Differences: Germans, French, and Americans*, 15.
14. Ibid., 35.
15. Ibid., 22.
16. David A. Victor, *International Business Communication*, Harper Collins, New York, 1992, 11–12.
17. Hofstede, 251.
18. Ibid.
19. Ibid., 5.
20. Ibid., 125.
21. Ibid.
22. Note that Business One Irwin, a publisher based in Homewood, Illinois, is the U.S. publisher for Trompenaars's book.
23. Trompenaars, 6.
24. Ibid., 9.
25. Ibid., 10.
26. Jakob Nielsen, *Usability Engineering*, Academic Press, New York, 1993, 211.
27. Hofstede, 51.
28. Trompenaars, 52–53.
29. Hofstede made this mistake in his research. The original questions reflected Western values and hence some re-sponses to his original survey did not fit into his original four international variables. The fifth international variable was added to address cultural differences in long-term versus short-term orientation, which Hofstede attributes to the teachings of Confucius. See pp. 159–174.
30. For more information, point a forms-capable Web browser to this URL: http://www.cc.gatech.edu/gvu/user_surveys/.

ABOUT THE AUTHOR

Nancy L. Hoft is a consultant on creating world-ready products and is the President of International Technical Communication Services in Temple, NH, USA, which caters to the computer, telecommunications, and networking industries. Some of her clients include the World Health Organization in Geneva, Switzerland, Sun Microsystems Computer Corporation, Lotus Development Corporation, Siemens Medical Systems, and Digital Equipment Corporation. She is a popular lecturer at conferences and teaches worldwide workshops on world-ready product design and on designing world-ready Web sites. Nancy is a senior member of the Society for Technical Communication (STC) and is the past chair of the International Technical Communication Professional Interest Committee. She is a Novell Certified Netware Engineer and a charter member of the Netscape Development Partners program. Nancy is the author of *International Technical Communication: How to Export Information about High Technology*, and a coauthor of *The Web Page Design Cookbook*, both published by John Wiley & Sons in 1995. She is also a contributing author to *International Dimensions of Technical Communication*, published by the Society for Technical Communication in 1996. You can reach Nancy on the Internet at nhoft@itech.mv.com or by mail at RR2 Box 493 Moran Road, Temple, NH 03084-9761 USA.

CHAPTER 4

Culture and Design

INTRODUCTION

Let me tell you about a film I saw while at university. The film is entitled *The Gods Must Be Crazy* (Uys, 1981) and it has a simple but meaningful storyline, so much so that it came to be considered a cult film. The story begins with a Westerner flying in a light aircraft across the Kalahari Desert in Southern Africa. Oblivious to the consequences, the pilot drops a Coca-Cola bottle out of his window. A short while after, a native of the Desert, a Kalahari Bushman finds the bottle, the likes of which he has never seen before, and takes it back to his people. The Kalahari Bushman believes that this glass bottle must be a gift from his Gods. The Bushmen are nomadic people who have no contact with Western Civilization. Because of the habitat where these people live, a dry desert, they have no materials or tools that are hard. So the bottle, due to its hardness, has a terrific number of uses for facilitating daily tasks. The bottle becomes a tool to prepare food, a child's toy, a musical instrument, and has a variety of other uses. Most of all, the bottle is an object or possession which has great value to these people. Soon the existence of the bottle begins to dramatically change the behavior of the Bushpeople.

The adults become jealous and self-centered and the children begin to exhibit behavior never seen by the Bushpeople before. One day, while two children are fighting over the bottle, one child hits the other on the head with the bottle and knocks him unconscious. The Elder of the Bushpeople, the same man who found the bottle, cannot believe the changes that have come over his people as a result of the introduction of this gift from the Gods. The Elder decides that his Gods must be crazy as this gift is not a good thing for his people. He then sets off on a journey to return the bottle to the Gods. The story continues from here with a great number of misunderstandings and mishaps as the Elder encounters modern Western civilization. He finally makes his way to Victoria Falls on the border between Zimbabwe and Zambia. This incredible waterfall is where the Bushman believes that his Gods reside. He throws the bottle into the falls. The Bushman, believing that he has rid his people of this horrible object, begins his journey back to his people in the desert, hoping that everything will be back to normal when he returns.

Although a very amusing film, it illustrates the negative impact that something can have when introduced into one culture from another, even something as apparently benign as a glass bottle (in this case, unbeknownst to the people who have introduced it). How do we affect other cultures by our designs? Do we enrich their lives or do we change them by upsetting some delicate balance? Maybe the products that we are responsible for designing don't have such a dramatic impact as the bottle did on the people in the Kalahari Desert, but are we truly aware of the possible consequences of our designs when they reach cultures for which they were not specifically intended.

The world is faced with a new economic order, fueled by the rapid obsolescence of technology and consumer products, vast political changes which have opened worldwide markets, and the always fluctuating state of world economies (Blaich 1985). This state of being in the worldwide marketplace has allowed, encouraged, or forced a new competitiveness in companies. Many companies can no longer depend on the home market, as unheard of competitors begin to move into previously uncompetitive markets, and local competitors spring up in what were previously foreign markets with little competition. In addition, some companies may no longer be enjoying government support in their home market in terms of finance or legislature which restricts foreign competition.

Internationalization is becoming more and more popular, but not because we felt it wasn't right to inflict our language and culture on foreign customers. We have looked to designing international products as a way to remain in a very competitive and sometimes tightly regulated worldwide marketplace. It wasn't a moral decision; it was a business decision.

Thus, the resulting trend is to conquer new markets worldwide by increasing productivity, cutting prices, and improving the localization of products. Vendors now understand that entering a new market, or continuing to compete in an old one, will take more than supplying a product that is just technically superior, aesthetically pleasing, or relatively inexpensive compared to those of competitors. Each culture has its own needs and desires when it comes to products, things that a local or national vendor may have no trouble in understanding or supplying.

The recent concentration of effort on producing products that are internationally usable has not been without results. One has only to look at the enormous increase in the number of publications and products currently available concerning internationalization, localization, and translation to realize that these usability issues have been placed in the forefront for many companies wanting to move into or remain in foreign markets. There now are a number of publications and software tools available to assist with the more concrete localization issues. For example, the advancement of translation tools, development of application programming interfaces (APIs) specifically for localization, the creation of user interface and documentation design guidelines, and the spread of Unicode are all factors that greatly simplify the activities that were once a major design and programming effort.

As individuals responsible for designing products and their user interfaces, we must begin to explore beyond the questions of "does it do the job?" and "is it usable?" This is a simplistic approach when designing a product for a variety of cultures. We need to look more closely at the questions that investigate deeper into the cultural metaphors, preferences, attitudes, and impact of our products when they are introduced into cultures for which they were not specifically designed.

Understanding and performing internationalization, localization, and translation of products allows companies to enter into new markets. All else being equal, it is the quality of the localization that will keep you in the market. Because of the growing trend in localizing products, no longer is the foreign customer delighted with a local language version of your product. Your customer now expects it. If companies in international markets are to stay competitive, they must compete on a higher level of internationalization requirements. Competition is fierce and in order to stay in the market you must be able to provide products that exhibit a level of cultural understanding that can sometimes only be attained by persons belonging to the particular culture or having a Ph.D. in anthropology.

The authors of *Made in America* (Dertouzos et al. 1989), a report produced by the MIT Commission on Industrial Productivity, state that in order to be competitive in a world that is becoming more and more international and competitive, American companies must move into markets beyond their borders. The authors list as one of their four goals for businesses who want to orient themselves to international markets, to understand foreign languages, cultures, and practices. Companies will have to obtain this type of knowledge in addition to knowledge of foreign legal systems and regulations. As we become proficient in producing products that are internationally usable, localizable, and translatable, the competitive design issues will center around cultural metaphors and profiles.

The big question is how do we come to grips with designing for other cultures? There are three ways to achieve this: The first is by education, the second is by changing our design practices, and the third is to be born and raised with it. Before the first and second methods are discussed further, it is necessary to understand culture, what it is and how it develops, in order to be able to understand and recognize the characteristics that are demonstrated as a result of it. As for the third method, since we cannot change our cultural background with each design project, the best way to attain this type of first-hand information is through the first two methods. Incorporate people from the target market by creating a multinational design team, use people from the target market as educators for the design team, and use people from the target market as participants in design studies.

CULTURE

In order to understand a particular culture and its needs in relation to your product, you must first understand what culture is and all of the factors that contribute to its being. *Webster's New Collegiate Dictionary* (1976) defines culture as "a multitude of elements and their integration." This includes "customary beliefs, social forms and material traits of a racial, religious, or social group." Sukaviriya (1990) add to this definition, "Numerous facets of a particular society together form its culture. Geographical location, interactions with neighboring countries, internal political warfare, mineral resources, agriculture, and diverse other factors all play a role in shaping each unique culture and the people who conform to it."

In addition, culture can also be affected by nationality, language, history, and level of technical development. Culture can cut across all of these attributes by including other common demographics that designers consider as common practice when designing systems, such as gender, age, education, and skills. These demographic groups represent cultures that exist within and across larger cultures normally defined by racial, religious, or social groups, for example, the medical industry, the aviation industry, or professional athletes. A culture can even be created by special interests, such as *Star Trek* enthusiasts or those with a special skill or handicap.

As an example of how easily one can misunderstand a culture to which they do not belong, last year a brief article appeared in the London *Sunday Times* (Syval 1994) concerning the BBC (British Broadcasting Company). The BBC wanted to ban some gestures within signing language (used in FV broadcast for deaf people) that were deemed to be offensive. To indicate a Chinese person, the hands are lifted to the forehead to pull the eyes into a slant. (Signing Chinese don't seem to find this offensive; their sign for a Westerner involves motioning circles around the eyes.) On investigation, it appeared that the signing deaf use many such signs that could be considered offensive by hearing individuals, but are used because they are concise. The BBC felt it was appropriate for them to interfere by trying to redesign a language that is part of a culture to which they do not belong and obviously do not understand.

Cultures are also constantly changing. Sometimes the change is dramatic, but in most cases the change takes places over time, such that it may not be perceptible by those living within the culture or by foreigners looking in from outside. Change may come from a natural progression or be initiated by events which occur either within or outside the culture. Language is a good indication of cultural change and history. For example, there is a tribe in Kenya that has a tradition of scarring their women's faces. Although seeming barbaric to a Westerner, it originated with the best of intentions. In the past, the more attractive women of this tribe were frequently taken as slaves by another neighboring tribe. The scarring was performed in order to make women less desirable. As a result of this practice, this tribe still use the word *ugly* as a term for freedom.

As designers, we must realize that there is a great deal more to know and understand about a culture than the language and the stereotypical idiosyncrasies we have learned from watching movies that depict individuals as caricatures. Zelden (1988) makes the point that most people of most nationalities are unexceptional in their ordinariness; it is the exceptions, like the loud American, the short Italian, or the fat German that give a culture its reputation. We also cannot make assumptions about a culture based on what is the norm within our own culture. The real cultural differences are not so obvious or simple to recognize. For example, Europe is a relatively small continent, but the cultural complexity is immense.

Richard Hill, in his book *We Europeans,* provides an excellent description of Europe, which illustrates the incredible contrasts that exist within this one continent. "Within a relatively limited area of the globe, [Europe] encompasses the widest range of cultural influences and the greatest variety of natural features of any continent, North America included. Europe does not have rain forests or tropical jungles. But it is, geologically, the most complex of all the continents of the world. It has glaciers, tundra, fjords, archipelagos, islands, mountains, fells, semitropical seas, even real desert (the area around Almeria in southeastern Spain). From the lakes of Sweden to the hilltowns of southern Italy, from the human warmth of the western islands to the sparkling folklore and music of the Slavs, this Europe, often unsuspected and unseen, is unique. It offers a richness of cultures and languages unparalleled anywhere else in the world" (Hill 1992).

The Europeans have mainly economic interests in common and seem to make every effort to sustain their cultural individuality (De Mooij 1994), and the EEC has made many nations in the Union become even more nationalistic. It is also important to recognize that there are some similarities across European cultures of which designers and their companies should be aware. The following is a good example of what can happen when a vendor knows one market, but makes assumptions about neighboring markets.

In the naming of a car *Pajero*, the car manufacturer found that *Pajero* means "masturbates" in Spanish. Obviously, they decided to change the name of the car in Spanish-speaking markets (Fernandes 1995). The unfortunate circumstance is that the car manufacturer did not change the name for France and possibly the rest of Europe. What they failed to understand is that the European culture is such that many people in Europe speak more than one language well and Europeans (many of them Spanish speaking) travel around Europe quite extensively for holiday and business. So it is not just in Spain that people speak Spanish; and the Spanish frequently go beyond the borders of their country. The name of the car should have been changed for *all* markets in Europe, but luckily for the car manufacturer, there seems to be a good number of people who presumably don't speak Spanish and like to drive the "Pajero."

EDUCATION

So how do we as designers increase our level of understanding? Education is one way. If you look at education in America, compared to Europe, there is a startling contrast just in the concentration of language studies. In America, fewer than 4 percent of public high school graduates have two years of foreign language study (Sprung 1990). Although more and more language programs are starting to appear in grade schools, it is not nearly enough of a change. Compare Europe, where, although language skills vary across the continent, it is not uncommon for people to speak at least a second language well. In Sweden, by the time children are twelve years of age they are beginning to learn a second foreign language, having begun studying their first foreign language at approximately eight years of age.

There are also educational ramifications on the preparation of designers. We can easily teach international standards, guidelines, and conventions pertaining to international design, but the challenge will be to introduce students to the idea of different cultures and the impact they have on design and vice versa (Burdick et al. 1985). A quote from MIT's study on American productivity (Dertouzos et al. 1989) sums up the traditional American attitude of looking inward. "Many Americans pay scant attention to life beyond the nation's borders. The educational system, from kindergarten through graduate and professional schools, has reinforced this inward-looking bias and has failed to open windows onto the world. The principal economic rivals to the United States, on the other hand, have long understood that operating in a foreign society requires mastery of the language as a prerequisite, together with significant exposure to different cultures." The overall cultural foundation needs to be broadened, starting with the very young. But we cannot teach what we do not know. Much research and investigation on the subject of the interaction of culture and technology is needed.

DESIGN PRACTICES

The second way to address our lack of knowledge concerning culture is to update our approach to collecting design information. Look at our current practices for evaluating international products. If a language variant does undergo usability testing, the studies are normally performed with a fairly stable product. To date, most of the evaluations performed on variants are after the fact. The design of the product has been completed and only the international usability of the more cosmetic details of the user interface are tested. It is too late and too costly at this stage (i.e., field-test version) to make any significant changes to the underlying metaphor. The reason language or culture variant testing is normally performed like this is because translations of the user interface are done after the user text has become stable. For most products, this does not occur until the product is nearing the end of its development phase. By this time it is too late to think about making any major changes to the product design and only superficial problems can be rectified. Another problem is that designers assume that when a product is tested extensively in its base language the language variants will be just as usable. This theory sometimes holds true, but not always. For example, icons are not normally changed for other markets and translations are frequently not perfect. These two factors alone can greatly decrease the usability of a language variant.

How does culture influence the design and use of products? The usability of the design goes beyond accommodating the requirements of localization and translation. Although this is a complicated task, producing a product that is localizable and translatable may only be scratching the surface. Design preferences evolve from cultural attitudes and expectations toward the task to be performed and the technology used to perform the task. These culturally linked attitudes or biases can be very difficult to recognize and articulate for the designer and user alike. As a result, to date, they have been very rarely addressed in the design of computer software. Even if problems with the underlying metaphor are found through testing, it is normally too costly and disruptive to the product schedule to implement any major changes to the product design. If the product is then released with a culturally unsuitable metaphor, it may not be possible to change it subsequently without a major usability impact to someone.

A good example of the result of the ignorance of a cultural metaphor is provided by Ito and Nakakoji (Chapter 6). The Western typewriter metaphor was used for the design of Japanese word processors. Ito and Nakakoji state that before the introduction of the word processor, writing and formatting styles in Japan used to be very different from those in Western countries. Document production in Japan was based on paper with 20 × 20 grids, one character per square, flowing from top to bottom and right to left. Today, the Western model is still used in Japanese word processors because users now see this as the norm. The authors of Chapter 6, who are Japanese, do not see this as a success story for the Japanese culture.

Fernandes (1995) states that designers themselves may not be aware of their own biases, a factor that makes testing the cultural validity of design metaphors even more important, as the Japanese word processor example demonstrates. Creating a design without relying on preconceived ideas concerning the overall design can be very difficult. Designers must observe and understand the activities, problem-solving style, needs particular to task, location, or language and artifacts created in the context of the world in which other cultures live and work. In order to do this successfully, the designer must focus on the needs of users in order to perform the designated task within their own environment and culture. It is also important to note that the designer may be observing the result of the previous introduction of products based on other cultural models. As discussed by Ito and Nakakoji, because the Western metaphor for word processing has already been established in Japan, to change it now could be the wrong thing to do.

So how does a design team approach this problem? Sometimes the only way to truly design a universal product is to work with a multinational design team. This allows the inclusion of a variety of cultural opinions in the early design stages. For products developed by multinational companies this may not pose much of a problem because they have the resources already in place. Unfortunately, not all companies or design teams are that fortunate. Without some sort of established connection (e.g., a subsidiary or business partner) in the target markets, companies and their design teams will need to locate and form relationships with agencies in the target market that can either provide the cultural information they require or assist in its collection.

The good news is that the methods for collecting this information are not new. The methods are those that are already widely incorporated into the process of collecting design information for systems (e.g., storyboards, contextual inquiry, walkthroughs, task analysis). Only the focus and the manner in which the information is collected have changed. The focus of the information collection is on cultural attitudes, practices, norms, and artifacts that affect the product's overall model. In order to use these same methods successfully in other cultures, the experimenter's approach may have to be altered, and additional tasks must be performed. A good example of this is in Chapter 12, where contextual inquiry techniques were used in the United States and in Europe as part of a study to collect information on in-home use of computers. As Dray and Mrazek state, due to cultural differences, their U.S. approach had to be slightly altered for Europe. For example, participants were solicited differently and translators were used for each session. It is also important to note that Dray and Mrazek were not testing a particular product, but looking at overall design considerations for producing home products. They did not focus on the usability issues of a particular product; they wanted to know how people's use of computers at home differed among cultures.

As those who have done testing in other countries will attest, issues as simple as time and location of testing and remuneration for participants may have to be addressed and altered for each new culture. Other more complicated issues, such as the experimenter's style and gender and legal requirements for soliciting participants and study procedures, are also important. Before you start, get professional advice from agencies or individuals who know the culture, language, and legal system. Use international or local (to the target market) agencies for marketing, recruitment, translation, and consultancy services. Before beginning, have all consent or release forms translated and then reviewed by a legal firm familiar with the local laws and unions. As one can imagine, the logistics of performing studies, even when the experimenters have contacts and are able to speak the language, can be horrendous. For every task and procedure the experimenters would perform in their home country, they must determine if it is correct or appropriate for another culture. Don't expect not to miss something.

One solution to decrease necessary traveling and increase the number of cultures included in your participant list is to set up testing at a major trade show or conference specifically targeted at your users. There are many such activities in Europe, and with proper planning they can become an excellent testing ground. Again, there are the same logistic problems as before, but you will also need to coordinate with the trade show or conference staff for almost all of your logistics. Be aware, when testing in one country, that participants from other countries will expect their consent forms to meet the requirements in their home countries. Testing at trade shows does make it easier to solicit participants, and you will find that displaying posters, and including requests for participants in attendee information packs, and making announcements are very successful methods. If testing in Europe, be explicit about the mother tongues you would like for participation in your study, as there are likely to be many people who speak more than one language.

CONCLUSIONS

The economic reasons for international products have been drummed into us again and again, but what about the moral issue of ensuring designs for other cultures? For those designers who are not of the opinion that neglecting cultural differences can have some very grave consequences, I will end this chapter with a very good example of what can happen when there is a lack of insight into cultural difference.

In 1970 the Iraqi government and Cargill Corporation of Minneapolis, Minnesota made a deal for the delivery of almost 100,000 metric tons of wheat and barley to Iraq. The grain was delivered in the fall of 1971. This shipment was intended as seed grain and had been treated with alkylmercury fungicide and dyed red to indicate it was not fit for human consumption. As an extra precaution, each sack of grain was marked with a warning in English and a skull-and-crossbones symbol. Farmers in the Iraqi provinces do not read English and the death symbol meant nothing to them. Although some farmers were informed verbally of the grain's toxicity, they made the assumption that if the red dye washed off, so did the fungicide. But the fungicide was not chemically bound to the dye and remained on the grain. Neither the alkylmercury or the dye gave off an offensive odor or taste (Casey 1993).

Unfortunately, the shipment arrived late to the provinces and only some of it arrived in time for the winter growing season. A large amount of the original shipment remained unused. Due to food shortages, the grain was washed, milled into flour, made into bread, and then eaten by the farmers and their families.

Within three months of the grain's arrival in Iraq, people with symptoms of methylmercury (a type of alkylmercury) poisioning began to show up in rural clinics. Ingestion of the treated grain caused serious neurological disorders and death. By the middle of 1972, 6,530 hospital admissions due to methylmercury poisoning were recorded in Iraq. Deaths that were attributed to the poisoning numbered 459. Based on additional information, the actual number of people to have suffered from poisoning could have been closer to 60,000. It was also estimated that for every death recorded, there were actually ten (Casey 1993).

Although lack of cultural insight may not always end in death, it is important to note the moral as well as the financial issues concerning internationalization of our designs. True internationalization will produce both diversity and uniformity, and compatible yet culturally distinct products. The differentiation among products designed in various cultures may decrease, but hopefully, the uniqueness of each cultural tradition will continue to bear a strong impact on the products (Burdick et al. 1985). Technological advances in software and hardware should allow us to design more flexibility into the user interfaces of our products, including changes of the overall metaphor. This will allow a single product to meet a wide variety of cultural preferences and needs. However, even with the broader perspective acquired by education or experience, our designs will still reflect our own cultural traditions, which will continue to foster creativity and diversity in our designs.

REFERENCES

Blaich, Robert. 1985. Design management in a global corporation. *Innovation, Design in the International Context*, **4**, 2 (Spring 1985): 3–5, ISDA, McLean, Virgina.

Burdick, B., C. Pelly, R. Tallon, M. Vignelli, and G. Zaccai. 1985. The international design practice. *Innovation, Design in the International Context* **4**, 2 Spring 1985: 6–10, ISDA, McLean, Virgina.

Casey, Steven. 1993. *Set Phasers on Stun and Other True Tales of Design, Technolgoy, and Human Error*. Santa Barbara: Aegean Publishing Company.

De Mooij, Marieke. 1994. *Advertising Worldwide*. London: Prentice Hall

Dertouzos, M. L., R. K. Lester, and R. M. Solow. 1989. *Made in America: Regaining the Productive Edge*. Cambridge, MA: MIT Press.

Fernandes, T. 1995. *Global Interface Design*. Chestnut Hill, MA: AP Professional.

Hill, Richard. 1992. *We Europeans*. Brussels: Europublications.

Sprung, Robert, C. 1990. Two faces of America: Polyglot and tongue-tied. In Nielsen, J. (ed.), *Designing User Interfaces for International Use*. Amsterdam: Elsevier Science Publishers B.V., 71–102.

Sukaviriya, P., and L. Moran. 1990. User interface for Asia. In Nielsen, J. (ed.), *Designing User Interfaces for International Use*. Amsterdam: Elsevier Science Publishers B.V., 45–69.

Syval, Rajeev. 1994. Deaf fight to keep their offensive signs. London: *Sunday Times*, 28 August.

The Gods Must Be Crazy 1981. Director: Jaimie Uys (South Africa).

Webster's New Collegiate Dictionary. 1976. Springfield, MA: Merriam-Webster.

Zelden, Theodore. 1988. *The French*. London: Collins-Harvill.

ABOUT THE AUTHOR

Elisa del Galdo is a native American who has been living and working in Europe since 1986. Ms. del Galdo currently resides in France were she is an independent human factors consultant specializing in the design and evaluation of software, hardware, and documentation for internationalization.

Prior to setting up as an independent, Ms. del Galdo was employed in the UK by Digital Equipment Corporation were she was responsible for the design and evaluation of software and hardware user interfaces, documentation, and icons and symbols for ten European countries. She also participated in UK National and International Standards.

In the area of internationalization, Ms. del Galdo has performed research on the design of products for localization, translation, and multilingual markets and has been responsible for or contributed to several publications, standards, and guidelines, either in the public or corporate domain, concerning the design and development of international products.

Ms. del Galdo can be reached at: del Galdo Consulting Ltd., 1 chemin du bois d'Opio, les Tomieres, 06650 OPIO France. Telephone and Fax: +33 93.77.72.59. Internet: delgaldo@riviera.fr.

CHAPTER 5

Cultural Learning Differences in Software User Training

In discussions of software internationalization, localizing a product's feature set, user interface, and documentation are often treated as the final steps in tailoring a product to the needs of users outside of its home market. For low-end products, this may indeed be the case, but for more powerful software, altering the product itself is only the beginning. Training takes features out of the development lab and into the mind of the user. It enables the user to take full advantage of a product's features and achieve the greatest return on investment.

Effective software user training requires sensitivity to users' native language and culture. Like the product itself, software training materials and methods must be modified to fit the language and culture of the target audience. This article uses Interleaf Inc.'s Japanese subsidiary as a case study in the tailoring of software training to the needs of international users.

CASE STUDY: INTERLEAF JAPAN

Interleaf is a U.S.-based maker of software for document authoring, management, and distribution. The company has subsidiaries in Japan, Australia, and throughout Europe, and its software supports over a dozen languages. Interleaf Japan was opened in September 1992 to market and provide training and technical support for the Japanized version of Interleaf 5, the company's document authoring and management software.

Interleaf 5 has been localized for the Japanese market to support features such as Japanese text editing and vertical text layout. Its user interface and end user training materials have been translated as well. This has made it possible for a native speaker of Japanese to handle end user training.

Interleaf 5 also features an object-oriented Lisp programming environment to enable customization by system engineers. This openness is one of the product's distinguishing characteristics, but the company can only derive competitive advantage from this openness to the extent that distributors and customers in Japan understand the technical process of customization. This has made effective training critical to the success of Interleaf's entry into the Japanese market.

The on-line documentation, reference manuals, and training materials for this developer's toolkit (DTK) were not translated into Japanese for the product's initial release in the Japanese market. None of the company's Japanese engineers expressed a desire to work full-time in a capacity which requires the rapid mastery and translation of new written English documentation at each release and its ongoing use for electronic mail, development, and attendance at new courses at headquarters. As a result, it has been necessary to use American engineers fluent in Japanese (including the author) to deliver technical training.

EVOLUTION OF TRAINING MATERIALS

The development of Interleaf Japan's training materials for the DTK proceeded in the following way. Lacking time to translate the training materials at the outset, the author initially lectured in Japanese using the available English training materials. In this environment, at least 10 percent of the students found the written materials a severe barrier to understanding and would fall behind the rest of the class.

Over time, the following steps were taken to meet the needs of Japanese students:

- More extensive and detailed English-language course notes were provided. These covered in written form all points which previously had been transmitted by lecture only.
- Preentered code and command samples were made available, freeing Japanese students from the need to laboriously input English commands and allowing them to simply select and run the pre-entered text. This step alone increased the speed of training by 10 percent
- The author translated the training materials into Japanese and had his draft translations proofed by native speakers. This step further increased the speed of training and, even more dramatically, its effectiveness. Students grasped concepts more quickly and displayed more confidence and enthusiasm. Far fewer students fell behind the rest of the class. This step also enabled a native Japanese engineer to teach the class.
- Additional Japanese language training materials were developed to address the particular needs of Japanese customers.

The localization of training materials for Structured Generalized Markup Language (SGML) training proceeded in a similar fashion.

Cultural Issue: Japan as a Teacher's Paradise

Japan is arguably the best country in the world to be a teacher. Teachers are addressed with the term *sensei*, a term of respect also applied to doctors, lawyers, and (perhaps incongruously) politicians. The student-teacher relationship entails considerable commitment, deference, and responsibility on the student's part to satisfy the teacher's expectations.

A teacher of adults in Japan benefits greatly from the high educational attainment of the students. Thomas Rohlen, a leading foreign expert on Japan's educational system, notes that 90 percent of Japanese "finish the twelfth grade,"[1] and that "in many respects the average high school graduate in Japan is equal or superior to the average American college graduate in the sciences, math, geography, history, music, art, and foreign language skills."[2] Of particular help in technology training is the fact that "On international tests of achievement in science and math, Japanese students outperform all others."[3] Hence, Japan represents a best-case scenario for international software user training.

Most of the students the author has trained are employees of Interleaf's 15 Japanese distributors. These students are an elite in Japanese society. Most are employees of leading Japanese software, hardware, and trading companies; most have a college degree.

In the author's experience, these students are almost without exception intelligent, attentive, and highly motivated. They take training seriously and work intently on in-class exercises. In three years of teaching, the author has caught only one student "goofing off" in class. Some students will voluntarily stay an hour or longer after class ends at 5:30 P.M. to continue or review lessons or to do optional additional modules.

Cultural Issue: Acceptance of Foreign Instructors

Companies introducing new technology abroad often use experts from the country of origin to deliver technical training; initially, there may be no alternative. This means that student-teacher interaction may be cross-cultural, with accompanying risks and opportunities. In the case of Interleaf Japan, American instructors delivered the initial technical training on all products and continue to deliver most technical training today.

Fortunately, Japan has a long tradition of importing foreign ideas and technology and foreign experts to deliver training. Japan imported elements of its culture as basic as its religion and writing system, and after the Meiji Restoration of 1868, it made intensive efforts to import foreign technology, partly by hiring foreign experts.[4] Thus, the import of foreign technology and the use of foreign technical instructors have well-established places in Japanese history and culture.

Today, this is particularly true in the field of software technology. There is a consensus in both government and industry in Japan that the country lags behind the United States in the field of software technology. The government has responded by easing visa restrictions for foreign software engineers in a deliberate attempt to encourage their use by private industry, and in consequence, foreign software engineers are relatively common at Japanese software companies and the Japanese subsidiaries of foreign software companies.

Thus, Japan represents a best-case scenario for foreign software companies which wish to transfer technology by using foreign software engineers. The cultural resistance to this approach is relatively low. This may not be the case in all countries and cultures, so companies should assess local conditions before using this approach elsewhere.

Cultural Issue: Student-Teacher Interaction

The author has tailored his teaching style to meet Japanese cultural expectations.

In the West, the Socratic method of engaging students with questions is well regarded as a highly interactive teaching style. Instructors will also pause and ask the entire group whether there are any questions.

In Japan, the educational system emphasizes rote memorization.[5] "Instruction almost entirely by lecture is a thoroughly entrenched pattern,"[6] and students are reluctant to respond to questions in front of others.[7] As a result, the Socratic method of using questions to get students to deduce new information on their own from basic axioms proved culturally inappropriate. Students found it unpleasant, and eliciting responses proved tedious for the instructor as well. Lectures followed by practice problems designed to test comprehension of material and the ability to apply it to specific cases proved much more efficient.

In addition, asking a group of students whether there are any questions proved relatively ineffective. Individual Japanese often hesitate to pose questions in front of a group of strangers; experience at Interleaf Japan has shown this to be true regardless of the instructor's gender and nationality. As a result, the instructor must instead rely on expression, body language, and eye contact to determine which individuals have questions and should be encouraged to ask them.

Clearly, effective international software user training requires cultural sensitivity as much as fluency in the native language.

Cultural Issue: Class Size

In America, Interleaf limits class size to a student:teacher ratio of 9:1 for the express purpose of ensuring a high-quality training experience. In Japan, however, Interleaf has successfully experimented with much larger class sizes. Due to the urgent demand from distributors for the training of large numbers of engineers, class sizes of fifteen to sixteen were not unusual during the company's first year in operation, and on one occasion eighteen students attended a single class. Large class size was not in and of itself perceived as a problem by the students; while numerous students requested a larger training room with more "elbow room" and better air conditioning, none of them requested a reduction in the number of students per class.

This acceptance of relatively larger class size probably has its roots in the students' experience of the Japanese educational system. High school class sizes are much larger than in America; public schools average forty-four students per class, and private schools average fifty-four.[8] Japan's consistently superior performance in international tests of educational achievement shows that at least in Japan, large class size does not prevent students from learning effectively.

As a result, Interleaf Japan has been able to train large numbers of system engineers rapidly and cost effectively. Some domestic Japanese companies have adopted the same approach; Hitachi has used large classes to train engineers at one of its "software factories."[9]

Cultural Issue: Pace and Intensity of Training

International users may request changes to the pace of training as well. In America, Interleaf offers one five-day class on Common Lisp and a second five-day class on Interleaf's Lisp extensions. In response to distributor requests for more rapid training, Interleaf Japan offered from the outset a single, condensed five-day class covering both topics.

In response to demand for additional training on modular design and application structure, the five-day class was further condensed into four days so that the final day could be devoted to these other topics.

Training was condensed by the following methods:

- Training on Common Lisp and object-oriented programming was condensed from five to two days by covering only the most critical commands.
- Training on Interleaf's Lisp extensions was condensed from five days to two days by redesigning the user interface customization modules as self-paced take-home lessons for the students to study on their own.
- Class hours were extended from 10 A.M. to 4 P.M. in the United States to 9:30 A.M. to 5:30 P.M. in Japan. Lunch hours were also reduced when necessary from one hour in the U.S. to forty-five minutes in Japan. This made each Japanese "day" of training 40 percent longer than the U.S. equivalent.
- Written documentation was expanded to cover nearly all points discussed during lectures, and a highly structured and sequenced modular class format was adopted.

Japanese students proved to be capable of covering the same scope of material at more than twice the pace originally adopted in North America. Interleaf has since considered using this accelerated format outside Japan as well.

The pace of a two-day SGML (Structured Generalized Markup Language) syntax and authoring class was not changed. A four-day SGML application development class was condensed into three days by similar methods.

Cultural Issue: Technical Literacy across Cultures

Teaching Japanese system engineers Lisp syntax, object-oriented programming, interprocess communication, and modular design in one week proved to be particularly challenging because the skill sets of the incoming engineers were from the author's perspective a generation out of date. In early training classes, the author surveyed students about their programming background and found that the majority were experienced in COBOL programming on IBM mainframes but that only a small fraction had experience in C programming on UNIX workstations. In contrast, in American computer science classes for undergraduates, COBOL is rarely mentioned, and students will usually learn to program on personal computers or workstations rather than mainframes.

Most of the system engineers had no academic training in software engineering and had only begun to study programming after they entered their companies. Japan produces far fewer graduates with computer science degrees each year on both an absolute and relative basis than does America, but the demand for software engineers in Japan is high, so Japanese companies attempt to increase the supply of software engineers via internal training for new hires who have no prior experience.

One easy way to explain a programming language's commands is to define them in terms of those of another known language. This was never an option since the author did not know COBOL and the students were unfamiliar with C and other languages of more recent popularity.

In darker moments, the author considered studying COBOL in order to bridge the psychological gap, but in the end the solution was to explain Lisp syntax and commands in as simple terms as possible without assuming prior knowledge of or making reference to any particular other programming language.

Linguistic Issue: English Fluency and the Role of the Educational System

Users of software developed in another country (including users within the company itself) are often forced to use documentation in a language other than their native tongue. There are many reasons this situation occurs:

- The software company may believe that the target users are able to read foreign language documentation.
- When a new product is first released, international users may desire immediate access before the documentation is translated.
- If the release of a new major version of a product is imminent, the company may wait until the new version has been completed to translate its documentation into foreign languages.
- For products sold in low volumes, translation of documentation may not be cost effective.

- Even when product, training, and reference documentation is translated, other kinds of documentation such as internal customer support databases are usually not translated.
- The user may exchange electronic mail or facsimiles with technical or marketing experts at the company's headquarters.

Usually this untranslated documentation will be in English, so in such situations users' degree of fluency in English becomes an important factor influencing their success in using the software. For the reasons mentioned above, some of Interleaf's users in Japan have at times used English-language documentation, so the company's experiences form a valuable test case of the ability of Japanese users to successfully use English-language documentation.

It is worth taking a moment to discuss the level of English fluency in Japan because there are many misconceptions about this subject. Foreign observers frequently criticize the Japanese educational system because students spend a minimum of six years studying English yet few Japanese are able to speak or understand the spoken language. To put this fact in perspective it is useful to ask how many Americans are able to speak or understand Japanese or any other foreign language. While the Japanese educational system does not turn out a class of fluent English speakers every year, it does require its students to spend more time studying foreign languages than does the American system.

The Japanese educational system emphasizes written English rather than spoken English; this at least in part accounts for the disparity between years of study and achieved oral fluency.[10] Even if a particular Japanese cannot speak English or understand it when spoken to, he or she may be able to understand written English; according to Rohlen, Japanese "knowledge of written English is certainly better than the average foreign language ability of our [American] college graduates."[11]

The result of this training system is that many Japanese can when forced make some sense out of English documentation. This is particularly true of university graduates and those with a technical or engineering background. The author is always impressed by the high average level of fluency in written

English among the software engineers in his training classes. While they would not be able to understand a lecture in English, as many as nine in ten can follow step-by-step English software operation instructions in training manuals when Japanese translations are not yet available. (Of course, none of them enjoy this, and in such situations they implore the instructor to provide translated documentation.)

This is not to suggest that companies need not translate their technical documentation. The author believes as a matter of principle that a company's customers should not be forced to use documentation in a foreign language and that companies should be committed to full product localization including the translation of all on-line and printed documentation. Any company which fails to fully localize its products and documentation will pay a price in resistance among potential customers, lost sales, and lost productivity among customers working with foreign-language documentation.

That said, the performance of Interleaf's distributors when the company has not yet fully translated the documentation (such as the reference and on-line documentation for the Interleaf 5 Developer's Toolkit) has been impressive. Japanese engineers have succeeded in developing sophisticated applications with thousands of lines of code, and the ratio of toolkit sales to base product sales has been higher than anywhere else in the world. Clearly, Japanese engineers can, when forced, make some use of English-language software reference materials. The Japanese educational system deserves both credit and blame for the particular strengths and weaknesses of its graduates.

Linguistic Issue: Familiarity with English Spelling across Cultures

All major programming languages today use keywords derived from English (GOTO, LENGTH, WHILE, etc.), and this can impose a significant burden on nonnative speakers unfamiliar with the highly irregular spelling of English words. Mistyping or misspelling a single character of such a keyword will invariably trigger an error message, and determining the cause of such an error is often time consuming for nonnative speakers of

English. Spelling errors which leap out from the page to the eyes of a native speaker are camouflaged among the other characters to the eyes of a nonnative speaker.

Both native and nonnative speakers of English find the language's irregular spelling difficult, but the author has observed that Japanese students in particular suffer acutely from this problem. Several reasons explain the special difficulty Japanese students face with the spelling of English words and keywords:

- The native scripts and words of Japanese are totally unrelated to those of any Western language. The language developed for a millennium in isolation from European languages, so until recently, very few Japanese words were cognates to those of Western languages.
- This situation has reversed in the postwar era and the Japanese now borrow English words (particularly technical terms) with what some would term reckless abandon. The Japanese language has an entire syllabary called *katakana* which is used largely for the rendering of foreign words into Japanese equivalents. Using this syllabary, *computer* is phonetically rendered in katakana characters for the syllables *konpyūta*, *copy* becomes *kopī*, and so on. (See Figure 5.1.) This rendering alters a word's spelling and pronunciation to conform to the limited number of syllables and sounds available in the Japanese katakana syllabary.

A native speaker of Japanese will typically first learn such a word in its Japanized katakana form and only later study the original English spelling and pronunciation. From

computer

konpyūta

コンピュータ

FIGURE 5.1   Transliteration of English terms into Japanese.

the standpoint of learning correct English, this means that native speakers of Japanese first learn to misspell and mispronounce words, then later memorize the original, correct spelling and pronunciation.

- Japanese students also face a special difficulty because English has separate sounds and letters for *L* and *R*, but Japanese has a single sound which is halfway between the two. This means that Japanese find it very difficult to distinguish between *L* and *R* sounds when listening to spoken English and equally difficult to remember which letter to use when spelling a given English word.

The practical result of these problems is that when Japanese students write computer programs using text editors, they waste far more time making and correcting spelling errors than do native speakers of English. This is especially true when students are studying a new programming language and its set of keywords for the first time. Japanese students are far more likely than native speakers of English to make a spelling error, and it takes them much longer than native speakers to locate a spelling error within a body of text. The result is a considerable productivity loss in software training. Students waste time stumbling over the spelling of English-derived keywords instead of focusing on the concepts that training is intended to convey.

Traditional spellcheckers are of little help because most of the keywords and other tokens used in a computer program do not appear in the dictionary. To date, the author has found only two ways to help students with this problem:

- For classes in which numerous commands must be entered in sequence (such as when following along with the examples in an instructor's lecture) supplying preentered commands for the students to select and run saved tremendous time and frustration for both students and the instructor. In a five-day Lisp programming course, this step alone reduced the time required to cover material by four hours, a productivity gain of 10 percent.
- That solution is not applicable to programming exercises in which the goal of the exercise is the creation of a functioning code sample. During such exercises, the author walks

around the room, checks students' screens, and points out spelling errors wherever he sees them. Purists might argue that students should find and correct their own mistakes, but in a class with limited time, the author prefers that students focus on discovering and correcting semantic errors rather than spelling errors in their programs.

Newer programming environments (such as Apple's HyperCard and Microsoft's Visual Basic) often include intelligent text editors which automatically parse and indent lines of code and check for syntax and spelling errors when the user hits Return. Such features may prove especially helpful to nonnative speakers of English.

When students use English variable and function names within their programs' code, the same spelling problem occurs. Typically, such names are a sequence of English words connected by hyphens or underbars. Curiously, the author has noted that even when a text editor and programming language allow the use of Japanese characters for variable and function names (as is the case for Interleaf Lisp) the majority of Japanese engineers at training use only alphabetic characters within their code. Possible explanations for this phenomenon include:

- *Habit.* Accustomed to code editors and programming languages which do not support two-byte token names, engineers may not take advantage of two-byte enabled environments.
- *Portability.* Since not all text editors support two-byte characters, engineers may prefer to author code in strictly one-byte characters in order to retain the option of using any available editor. Similarly, since Japanese characters must be saved in a platform-dependent encoding—typically Shift-JIS or EUC—engineers may shun the use of Japanese characters in code in order to avoid problems when editing and displaying code on multiple platforms.
- *Input Efficiency.* Because of the need to use a front-end processor and type extra keystrokes for the input of Kanji characters, the entry of Japanese token names is slower than the entry of Western character token names. The dis-

like of Japanese users for this inefficient text entry method should not be underestimated; the author has even observed Japanese sending each other short electronic mail messages in English or romaji (Japanese words spelled out phonetically using the English alphabet) simply because they didn't want to waste time using the front-end processor!

Linguistic Issue: The Importance of a Translated User Interface

It goes without saying that software users prefer a user interface in their native language, but the author experienced a particularly vivid demonstration of this fact when Interleaf first released its Standard Generalized Markup Language (SGML) option in Japan. SGML is the international standard file format for saving and exchanging structured text documents. Interleaf offers an SGML option for Interleaf 5 which allows users to edit documents in this format.

Interleaf initially offered this option only for the English version of Interleaf 5, so training classes had to be conducted using Interleaf's English version with its English user interface. Moreover, the first training class in Japan began one week after headquarters completed the 300 pages of English language training materials, so the author had no choice but to use the English language training materials in class. Naturally, the class was challenging for both the instructor and the Japanese students.

When Interleaf released a version of the SGML option for use with Interleaf 5 for Japanese, the class became dramatically easier to teach. The user interface for the small number of SGML option commands was still in English, but it was running on top of Interleaf 5 for Japanese with its Japanese user interface. As a result, nearly all of the commands on screen were presented in the students' native language. The students were able to locate and use commands much more efficiently, so the class moved much more quickly and students made far fewer mistakes. This was true even though the students were still using English-language training materials.

Some time thereafter, the author was given time to translate the SGML training materials into Japanese. Unsurprisingly, the students were ecstatic, and the class moved still more quickly. In a three-day SGML Toolkit class, students finished the second of three practice problems up to three and one-half hours earlier than did previous classes which used the Japanese-language training materials, achieving a productivity gain of 15 percent. This increased speed also gave the students more time to work on a final open-ended practice problem, resulting in an important qualitative improvement in their depth of understanding.

Linguistic Issue: The Usage of Cognates

Nonnative speakers of Japanese often find technical Japanese easier to understand than ordinary Japanese speech or writing because so many of the words have been borrowed from English. This cuts the learning curve for foreigners seeking functional fluency in technical Japanese, but such borrowed words must be used with care in lectures or training materials as their usage or meaning often changes across languages.

The term *copy* is a case in point. In English this can refer to photocopying a document, copy-and-paste in a text editor, or looking at a printed sample and entering the identical text into the computer. The katakana equivalent *kopī* in Japanese, by contrast, only conveys the first two meanings. The author discovered this when he instructed students in Japanese to copy the text from a sample document into their SGML text editor, only to be greeted by blank looks and a student's question, "How can we select text on the hard copy?"

As this example makes clear, even technical terms borrowed from English must be used with care in other languages and cultures.

CULTURAL DIFFERENCES DOWN UNDER

One need not work in a non-Western or non-English-speaking culture in order to discover significant cultural issues in software user training. An American colleague of the author's has spent two years in the hardship post of Sydney, Australia and notes that language differences there have a significant impact on the students' satisfaction with training:

> [Consider] spelling. Centre, colour, organisation, catalogue, etc. I run my class materials through the Australian spell checker. Just making these small changes helps the students feel that the course material has been done "just for them." Sometimes we do use the basic American stuff, and just disparage the seppos (that's Australian rhyming slang: seppo = septic tank = yank) for being too self-centred to care about the rest of the world.[12]

He also notes that Australians' famously laid-back approach to life has influenced his training style in the opposite direction:

> The classes I teach here tend to be a little more structured than the ones I teach in the States, because if they're not, nothing gets done. And New Zealanders are even more so (but they're great fun to party with).[13]

CONCLUSIONS

For many software products and services, localizing the user interface and functionality is only the first step toward enabling international users to get the most value out of their investment in technology. Training is what takes features out of the user interface and into the user's mind. The delivery of high-quality software user training requires sensitivity to the user's native language and culture.

REFERENCES

1. Rohlen, Thomas P. 1988. Education in Japanese society. In Okimoto, Daniel I. and Thomas P. Rohlen (eds.), *Inside the Japanese System: Readings on Contemporary Society and Political Economy*, Stanford, CA: Stanford University Press, 25.
2. Ibid., 25-26.
3. Ibid., 1988, 25.
4. Duus, Peter. 1976. *The Rise of Modern Japan*. Boston: Houghton Mifflin, 84–85.

5. Rohlen, Thomas P. 1983. *Japan's High Schools.* Berkeley: University of California Press, 316.

6. Ibid., 244–245.

7. Ibid., 244.

8. Ibid., 19.

9. Cusumano, Michael A. 1991. *Japan's Software Factories* New York: Oxford University Press, 193.

10. Rohlen, 101.

11. Ibid., 322.

12. Wright, Spence, electronic mail to author, 18 April 1995.

13. Ibid.

ABOUT THE AUTHOR

Eric Krock has a B.A. in Japanese and a B.S. in Computer Science from Stanford University. He opened Interleaf's Tokyo subsidiary in September 1992 and continues to work there as a trainer and technical marketing consultant. His responsibilities include authoring and translating technical documentation, training Japanese customers on the use and customization of Interleaf software, and technical marketing. He can be reached by electronic mail at ekrock@jp.ileaf.com.

CHAPTER 6

Impact of Culture on User Interface Design

INTRODUCTION

This article discusses user interface design and culture, especially Japanese culture compared with North American. Our goal is not to articulate specific requirements for internationalizing and localizing user interfaces. We have studied cultural effects on the use of computer systems in order to understand the important characteristics and aspects of user interface design. Some aspects of a user interface come into consideration only when the interface is examined from cross-cultural perspectives.

Word processing software is a good example for illustrating the cultural impact in software design. Most word processing software is designed from the typewriter metaphor. Concepts and notions used in word processors, such as tab-stops and margins have been well known and naturally understood by those who have experience using typewriters. This, however, was not the case in Japan. As Japanese language uses Japanese and Chinese character sets, which contain approximately six thousand characters, the use of typesetters was very limited. Even formal documents, such as business correspondence, used to be hand-written before the word processor era. Typewriters were used only by a limited number of professionals and English-major students.

When word processing software programs for Japanese were

introduced in Japan (some were imported from the United States and some were developed authentically), most of the programs were based on the typewriter metaphor in the same way as the Western word processors. As such, Japanese users had to face unfamiliar concepts such as "tab-stops."

What would have been an alternative if word processors for Japanese did not use the typewriter metaphor? Writing and formatting style in Japan used to be very different from that of Western countries. We used to use rule-lined writing pads. A letter-sized writing pad typically had 20×20 grids, and one character was written in for each grid, from top to bottom and right to left. We measure the length of a document by the number of characters, not words. If authentic word processing software for Japanese had been developed without being influenced by the software developed in the United States, the ruled writing-pad metaphor might have been used.

So why do Japanese still use the Western typewriter metaphor for Japanese word processors? Interestingly, Japanese users of word processors got accustomed to the Western-style word processing interface so much so that they would find it rather awkward if word processing software was based on another metaphor. We have seen many such cases where "acclimatization" overwrites differences in the cultural background. For example, there were attempts to develop Japanese-like programming languages, which resulted in no success because other Western programming languages were already commonly used.

We do not think the case of word processor programs was a success story. Rather, it is a bad example of what can happen when designers do not understand the cultural impact of software design, and we should learn from this experience.

When developing a new system, considering cultural impact would not harm but benefit the usability and usefulness of the system. For example, suppose you as an interface designer face a design trade-off: fancy-looking graphics with comforting sound versus shorter response time. In Japan, users may appreciate a prompt response. However, some cultures prefer friendliness to fast service and it might be more important for them to show responses in fancy computer graphics with 300 ms longer response time than to show responses in simple text.

Although tempting, it is misleading to simply generalize such differences as "cultural differences." Cultural differences often stem from much deeper and more complex background social context, not just "preference of speed versus friendliness." On the other hand, there are differences among different groups of people. What is important for user interface design is to have a mechanism to understand such differences and accommodate them when identified. Such mechanisms, then, will level out differences whether they are cultural or individual.

Note that user-adaptation mechanisms (Schneider-Hufschmidt, Kuehme, and Malinowski 1993), which allow individual users to customize user interfaces as they like, are a good starting point. Existing adaptable and adaptive mechanisms are designed to accommodate individual preference. However, differences that stem from cultural background go beyond such surface-level adjustment. The mechanisms we suggest in this chapter provide "good" human-computer interaction designs to users across multiple cultures, not just usable tools for users of a specific culture.

In what follows, we first discuss the impact of culture on human-computer interaction design by using two models to illustrate our point. The case study section on culture-specifics in Japan describes cultural impacts on user interface designs by closely examining system usage in Japan as contrasted to that of North America. We then discuss our approach to dealing with cultural impact in user interface design. We suggest viewing multicultural user interface (and system) design as cross-cultural collaborative work between system designers and users who belong to different cultures. To support such collaboration, we propose using community knowledge-bases, which are to evolve through the experience of developing and using user interfaces across multiple cultures. We briefly introduce our prototyping efforts and conclude the chapter.

IMPACT OF CULTURE ON HUMAN-COMPUTER INTERACTION

In this section, we illustrate aspects of user-interface design that background culture is likely to affect. Instead of trying to enumerate such aspects, this section suggests a classification scheme for them. We use schematic models to illustrate cultural impact by dividing user-computer interactions into two modes: *listening* mode, in which people are presented with a computer's reaction, and *speaking* mode, in which people give instructions to a computer system.

Listening Mode: Information Presented from Computers to Users

Three Phases in the Listening Mode Figure 6.1 illustrates three phases of users' reactions along the timeline after a computer system presents information on the display. By "presentation of information," we include any type of system reaction, such as presentation of a message, change of icon shape, or generation of sound. At the initial moment, people perceive the system's state changing. Then, people associate the perceived phenomena with what they have already understood. In the last stage, they logically reason about what they have understood, and proceed to the speaking mode to plan the follow-up reactions.

1. Perception Phase People either voluntarily or involuntarily become aware that objects on the display change their states. Representations concerning this initial recognition phase are

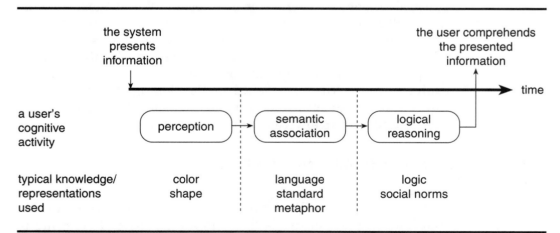

FIGURE 6.1   The *listening* mode.

"intuitive" information, such as color or shape. For example, a user recognizes that a list of characters is presented in "red" on the screen in this phase.

2. Association Phase In the association phase, people associate semantic meanings to what they perceived in the preceding perception phase. For example, the user understands that a list of characters is a message written in English, and associates the "warning" meaning to the presented message because of the red color used.

3. Reasoning Phase After understanding the semantic association of the information or behavior presented by a computer, users reason about the presented information. For example, the user tries to understand why the warning message is presented at this moment and how it is related to what the user has done previously.

Cultural Impact in the Listening Mode Using the model presented in Figure 6.1, we describe the cultural impact on the user interface, using Japan as a contrast to the United States. Figure 6.2 illustrates that the semantic association phase has more cultural impact than the perception phase, and the logical reasoning has even more.

1. Perception Phase The perception phase has the least cultural impact. Design concerning this phase should be done by considering cognitive aspects of users as human beings. Representations related to this phase, such as physiology of color and the size of a shape, do not depend on languages or cultural background but on sensory monitors of humans.

2. Semantic Association Phase Representations related to the semantic association phase should be more culture-sensitive. Culture-specific aspects of representations related to the association phase can mostly be dealt with by surface-level adjustment, such as languages, icons, color, and formats of numbers, dates, and time. In fact, most studies about cross-cultural issues in user interface design is limited to this surface-level user interface adjustment (Kellog and Thomas 1993).

Much of the literature suggests that iconic representations are problematic among different cultures (Fernandes 1995;

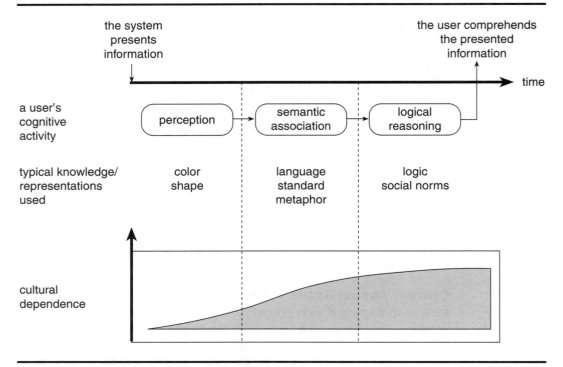

FIGURE 6.2   Cultural impact in the listening mode.

Jones et al. 1991; Russo and Boor 1993). For example, Figure 6.3 illustrates icons developed for Japanese software compared with those for software developed in the United States. As is obvious, some graphics are culture dependent, for example, the shape of a house, a wrapping cloth to hold documents, and mailboxes.

Different cultures have different psychological associations for color. For example, purple indicates dignity and nobleness in Japan but is an icon for death and evil in ancient Greece (Fukuda 1994). Russo and Boor (1993) argue that different cultures require different mappings between logical flow and physical flow of objects on the screen (e.g., Arabic may prefer the flow from right to left).

FIGURE 6.3   Comparison of NEXTSTEP icons (the upper row) and Japanese icons (the lower row).

Presentations of text for different languages differ dramatically. The Japanese language uses approximately several thousand Chinese characters, which is much more than the number of characters used in many Latin languages. Consequently, displaying Japanese needs many more bites to display the characters, and requires much larger space on the display. It also requires the balance of textual representations with figures. It is sometimes required to write from top to bottom instead of from left to right on the display. Each character has the same height and width, and no spaces are provided between words. As such, Jones et al. (1991) provides a detailed guideline for developing an international user interface. For example, "English text usually expands when translated into another language," therefore, "do not encapsulate text in boxes."

Formats for dates differ among different countries. Japan uses the regnal designation for representing the year in addition to the Christian Era, which is written in the year-month-day order. Many European countries use the day-month-year order, in contrast to the United States, which uses the month-day-year order.

To overcome cross-cultural breakdowns in user-interface design, standardization and the use of metaphors can play a role in designing representations related to the semantic association phase. A typical success model of multicultural interface design is a street sign. There is a conventional standard, for example, a white horizontal line with red background means that parking is not allowed. Even if you have never been to a country or had driver's education there, you can almost always guess what a street sign means. Using metaphor in interface design avoids heavy dependence on language. The multimedia technology allows us to more easily implement metaphors in user interface design. On the other hand, it is important to remember that even the use of metaphors cannot be perfect. Such an example is the trashcan icon; things thrown into a trashcan are recoverable in some countries, but they are gone for good in other countries, which may give users the wrong expectation for the associated functionality of the icon.

3. Reasoning Phase   The reasoning phase is affected most by culture. Although formal reasoning, such as mathematical reasoning or logical reasoning, is universal, much of cognitive reasoning depends on social norms and background culture.

There is a Japanese saying that means "one needs to understand ten by listening to one." In Japanese culture, it is a shame if one does not understand the whole even when it is only partially explained. In contrast, in American culture, it is expected that everything is clearly defined and articulated. The existence of job descriptions is a good example. In Japan, it is atypical to have explicit job descriptions in any organization. Workers are expected to infer and understand what they are required to do.

Speaking Mode: Instructions from Users to Computers

The speaking mode is when users want to indicate their intention to the system. In our model, the mode consists of four phases.

Four Phases in the Speaking Mode   Figure 6.4 illustrates the four phases by which users react and convey their intentions to a computer system.

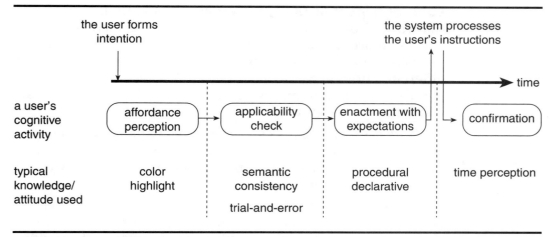

FIGURE 6.4   The *speaking* mode.

1. Affordance Perception   The affordance perception phase is when users identify what they can do with presentations displayed by the system. The phase actually consists of the phases in the listening mode because users understand what the presentations on the screen indicate. For example, the user looks around on the screen and identifies highlighted icons that seem clickable.

2. Applicability Check   The applicability check is when users validate their choice of actions; that is, whether the chosen action plan will actually let users do what they intended. For example, users read the label on the icon which they viewed in the previous affordance perception phase and examine whether the label indicates their intended action.

3. Enactment with Expectations   This is the phase when users enact their selected action plan. For example, this is the phase when users physically click on the mouse button after bringing the mouse cursor onto the icon display.

4. Confirmation   After the enactment, users need to confirm that the enacted action has carried out what they expected of the system.

Cultural Impact in the Speaking Mode   Figure 6.5 illustrates that the cultural impact in the speaking mode increases as the phases proceed. Most cross-cultural user interface design research focuses on how to present information appropriately in different cultures. Not much attention has been paid, for example, to the expectations users have when they give a certain instruction to the system.

1. Affordance Perception   Since users need to listen to and understand presentations by a computer system, the cultural impact in the affordance perception phase can be illustrated with the model of the listening mode described above.

2. Applicability Check   Culture affects people's attitudes in this phase. Users' attitudes for checking the applicability of what they planned to do in the preceding affordance perception phase differ across cultures. For example, a trial-and-error method is perceived as tedious and time-consuming in Japan, whereas some

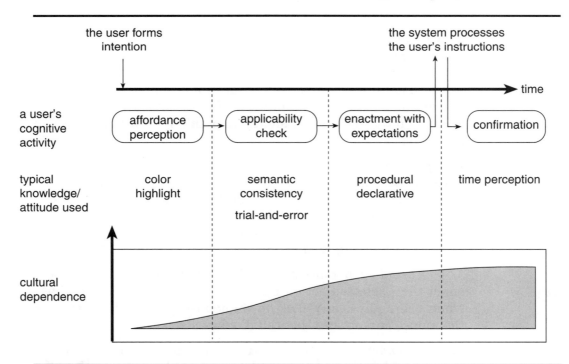

FIGURE 6.5   Cultural impact in the speaker mode.

cultures associate the method with freedom and exploration, which have positive connotations. In general, Japanese users do their best to avoid breakdowns. It is often quoted that Japanese users read instruction manuals very carefully before they start using a system, as opposed to typical North American users who immediately start using a system to "see what will happen."

People use semantic consistency in checking applicability of their decision. Culture affects how consistently semantics are assigned to representations on a user-interface display in terms of the degree of appreciation for particularity. Some cultures value uniformity, and like to have a uniform or global mechanism for multiple tasks. For example, Japanese prefer uniformly arranged buttons in the same color. To the contrary, some cultures value particularism, and like to have a specific style of interface object assigned to each task.

3. Enactment with Expectations   "The diversity of languages influences the thoughts and actions of people who speak them" (Whorf 1956). Although we do not have any empirical evidence at hand, when people perform actions to objects in Japanese, they tend to first identify objects, then designate which action to perform to the objects. This may stem from the fact that in Japanese grammar, a subject is followed by objects followed by a verb; for example, "watashiha ('I') sono-fairu-wo ('the file') kesu ('delete')" means "I delete the file." In English grammar, a subject is followed by a verb, then objects. In a typical graphical editor, users are required to first select an object on the window, then select a menu item to specify an action. In this sense, Japanese users may find this sequence of actions more natural than North American users.

Another factor on which culture has impact in the enactment phase is how the enactment process is indicated or described to users. In Western cultures people prefer descriptions written in a declarative manner, while in the Oriental and Russian cultures people like to have a description written in a procedural manner (Kellogg and Thomas 1993). In some cultures people prefer processing jobs in parallel, while in other cultures tasks should be performed sequentially. It has been observed that German users prefer writing precise queries for information retrieval, while people in the Latin countries (Italy and Spain) prefer browsing through the information space. Finally, different languages require different paragraph structures, for example, a topic sentence can be found at the beginning of each paragraph in English, while it is often found in the end of each paragraph in Japanese. Also, one needs to be careful in performing translation because some languages may have different connotations for literally translated terms. These considerations should be taken into account when writing help messages and on-line manuals for the system.

4. Confirmation As indicated in the model, we assume that the culture has the most impact in the confirmation phase. The biggest difference is the perception of time, on which depends how much they value the speed of service. In some cultures people are in general patient and do not mind sacrificing fast service for other factors, such as friendliness. In Japan, fast service is the most important factor.

On the other hand, Japanese users demonstrate more patience in achieving a long-term goal in system usage than users in other countries. They are more willing to spend time getting ready to start by reading instruction manuals carefully, setting up the system, and getting used to the system. Japanese users can wait longer to see a payoff take place for their setups. This is related to the observation that Japanese users try to avoid errors and breakdowns as much as possible. They do expend more effort in the prevention of breakdowns than in repair.

Lastly, communication overlap illustrates an interesting aspect of time perception in different cultures. Studies have shown that time intervals between two people talking in a conversation differ in various languages. In many of the Western languages, they alternate; in the Asian languages, they alternate and pause for a while; and in the Latin languages, the two conversations overlap (i.e., one interferes with the other). This aspect may need to be reflected in the way users turn from the listening mode to the speaking mode.

A CASE STUDY: CULTURE-SPECIFICS IN JAPAN

This section illustrates differences of use situations of computer systems between the United States and Japan. The differences illustrated are somehow subjective, and it is not our intention to provide ethnographical evidences. Rather, these anecdotal differences are to emphasize what types of differences are identified between the two cultures, which need to be understood when designing a system to be used in different cultures.

We focus our discussion on three characteristics: collectivism, synthesis, and human relationships.

Individualism versus Collectivism

Japanese culture values the collective, compared to other cultures which value individualism. The collective nature emerges in several cases in system usage and system evaluation.

First is the use of groupware, especially group decision-supporting systems. In Japan, it is not likely that individuals explicitly show their strong opinions and policies against their company. Their contributions to the company are appreciated as teamwork, not as individual contribution, even if a single individual has come up with a really interesting idea. It is not good to be recognized individually; but the team should be recognized. A team leader remembers which team member has contributed most, which will lead to promotion for the contributor at a later time.

"Harmony" in the meeting is regarded as very important (Ishii 1990), and a meeting agenda should be discussed enough before the meeting starts (except some meetings such as discussing technical details). Junior workers are not supposed to object to any of the opinions of their senior workers if "big" bosses are present in the meeting. This may affect anonymity issues discussed by Valacich et al. (1992), who reported that anonymity in using groupware enhances the group performance. This may be more so in Japan where an individual does not want to be recognized among the others. Fernandes (1995) points out that this issue is also important to consider when evaluating system usage as "Japanese users would not speak up especially when their bosses were present."

Second, Japanese users would like to have idiosyncrasy as a group at an organizational level, not at on individual basis. For example, in the course of deploying Lotus Notes, needs for companywide system customization are much stronger than individual-based system adaptation. Japan used to use "off-con" (abbreviated from *office computers*) for word processing and accounting jobs. These are specialized microcomputers, with software that is totally customized to individual users or companies. The market share of personal computers in Japan used to be comparatively low as compared to that of the United States (34% in Japan and 55% in the USA in 1993) because of the existence of off-cons. Japanese companies were not interested in purchasing shrinkwrapped software packages and installing them on personal computers because "they would lose their identity as a company." Now that functionalities of packaged software surpass those of off-con software, companies have started using personal computers. Still, they need their "specialized software" for their own company.

Internal Control versus External Control

In the western culture, individuals want to have control over their surrounding environment (e.g., characterized by western medicine, which tries to conquer the illness), while in the oriental culture, individuals try to accommodate the external environment (e.g., oriental medicine, which tries to compromise and harmonize with nature). These characteristics are reflected in the typical attitude Japanese users take in the use of computer systems.

We have observed differences in the initial acceptance of a newly deployed system between Japan and the United States. In Japan, people tend to have less resistance against and to be more willing to use new technologies. This is because in general, Japanese workers are very obedient to their senior workers or managers. When a manager decides to bring change into a workplace, such as introducing a new computer system, the subordinate workers will accept the change. In these situations, achieving critical mass (i.e., a technology becomes useful only if a certain percentage of group members use it) and the prisoner's dilemma (i.e., if everyone acts in pursuing their own best interest, the result gets worse not only for the group but also for the individuals) (Grudin 1991) seems to be less problematic.

A difference also lies in where users ascribe the difficulty in using the system. If Japanese users cannot use the system, it is likely that they conclude that it is their fault. If they do not understand how a command works, they are likely to blame themselves that they have not read the instruction manual carefully. Consequently, they are relatively negative toward adapting the system to themselves. Implicit assumptions here are that their system is designed based on the best intention by the system designers—so the system must be designed in the best way—and that modifying the user interface according to their personal preference is a bad thing to do. Thus, Japanese users try to overcome the difficulties in using the system by getting accustomed to the system. On the other hand, in the United States, the notion that it is designers who are to blame if the system is not usable has prevailed (Norman 1993). Users try to adapt the system so that the system becomes easier to use before they try to get used to the seemingly clumsy interface.

Jiro Kawakita, who invented a psychological method (KJ method) to help people synthesize enumerated ideas through the brainstorming method and produce a summary of the ideas, points out differences in analyzing and synthesizing ideas between Japan and the United States (Kawakita 1984). Americans are better at the process of identifying units of ideas (during brainstorming sessions) than Japanese, while Japanese are good at the process of "intuitively" identifying a summary when faced with a collection of ideas, each of which "seem relevant to one another." In making a summary, or headline, one should minimize the conceptualization without making too much abstraction. Japanese are good at keeping vague parts around a concept so that they can be used to establish relationships among concepts that are "heterogeneous but look similar." Americans, on the other hand, are good at articulating the boundary of a concept by eliminating the vague parts, which then lose some similarities.

Kawakita describes why the KJ method, which is a method for producing a new meaning by combining and integrating individual objects, was invented in Japan and not in Western society, where the brainstorming method has prevailed. He argues that although Americans may not have as good intuitions in identifying a summary as Japanese, they are pretty patient in gradually constructing a global solution from what had been achieved. This is the reason why the trial-and-error method has been widely accepted in Western society. When this ability is combined with organizational cooperation, they can achieve large-scale creative projects. On the other hand, Japanese are not good at constructing a global concept from small chunks of ideas, but are good at accepting the reality with flexible attitudes. They appreciate a method not for analysis, but for synthesis.

People versus Technology versus Economy

Culture affects how people value and prioritize human relationships, technologies, and economy. Successful human-computer interface design cannot be achieved without considering these issues. For example, technical support is considered more important than price in Japan, while the price is a driving force in choosing a system in the United States.

Until recently in Japan, it has been quite uncommon that people change their jobs. The average length that a person remains in the same company used to be somewhere around twenty to thirty years. In this situation, the problem of the mismatch between those who have to do the work and those who get the benefit is less problematic. For example, a successful software reuse case in a Japanese industry is partly due to the fact that the same group of people who built the software did not mind extra work (e.g., documenting design rationale) for future maintenance and reuse because they are the ones who would maintain and reuse the same software later.

The notion of an open market and capitalistic competitiveness is somehow blurred in Japan in terms of human relationships. When a seminar on the topic of open systems was given to a Japanese audience, a question was raised why we need open systems in the first place. The answer was obvious—so that the market becomes competitive and consumers can get hardware and software of the same quality with less cost. Then, several Japanese engineers and managers pointed out that they already had established friendly relationships with their providers, and that they did not want to change their providers even if other competitive companies offered the same products with a lower price. People-people relationships count more in doing business in Japan. Japanese business is based on an assumption that such "invisible" trust-relationships will improve the quality of service, which cannot be attained at any price.

ISSUES AND APPROACHES

Design and deployment of technologies should differ in different cultures especially if the technologies involve cognitive tools and a number of people. Cole and Griffin (1980) described technologies as "cultural amplifiers." While technologies transform the nature of culture and thought to amplify human productivity, technologies are developed based on motivations derived from different relations with different elements in different cultures. Introducing software to a new culture brings many unpredictable factors to light. The functionality of a system is often unconsciously affected by underlying traditions of the culture where the system is designed, as illustrated with the word processor software story in the introduction to this chapter.

We have become aware that simply translating help messages and on-line documents is not enough for internationalizing and localizing user interface. We have seen that different cultures use different languages, formats of dates and numbers, and graphical representations. We have started developing guidelines for such surface-level adjustment. These efforts so far, however, remain on the level of technical and national localization (Fernandes 1995). We need cultural localization, which means dealing with values, tastes, and the history of the user's culture (Fernandes 1995), by going beyond surface-level adjustment.

There is no universal interface that can be applied to any culture. There is no way to enumerate the necessary guidelines and procedures to fully accommodate any culture. The important steps are to first understand the target culture, and reflect the findings into the human-computer interaction design. As breakdowns and problematic situations are found through the usage of the system, the system needs to be refined to better serve users in the target culture.

Our approach is to design cross-cultural human-computer interaction by supporting cross-cultural collaboration among people from different cultures: those who design a system from one or more cultures, and those who use the same system coming from another culture. Two modes of cross-cultural collaboration take place in internationalizing and localizing the user interface: during design and during use.

In order to understand the culture where the software is to be marketed and used, user interface designers first have to understand the characteristics of the culture. One way of understanding is to talk to potential users of the culture, and use questionnaires and surveys to identify their requirements. Another way is to investigate already successfully used artifacts in the culture, probably made by local developers.

During use, we view computer systems as communication media (Winograd and Flores 1986). Interacting with a computer system implies asynchronous communication with people who designed and programmed the system. Thus, using an internationally designed system means collaborating with designers who belong to different cultures.

In the human-human collaboration, the collaborative work is done by developing a shared context by which to communicate (Krauss and Fussell 1991). Shared understanding emerges through the evolving context, and intention can be shared by grounding the communication in the shared context (Fischer, Nakakoji, and Ostwald 1995). Most of computer-supported collaborative work (CSCW) research assumes that stakeholders belong to the same culture (Greif 1988). A unique challenge in supporting cross-cultural collaboration is to develop such shared understanding and context among collaborators from different cultures, who fundamentally see the world in a different way. One approach to support cross-cultural collaboration during the design time is to integrate design artifacts and communicate ideas and other explicitly represented information within a hypermedia environment to serve as context to be shared (Ostwald and Nakakoji 1994). Explicitly represented and stored information can be used as "community knowledge" that can provide the design rationale for internationalizing and localizing user interface designs, and provide design knowledge as case-based design aid (Kolodner 1993) for future development.

We have developed prototype systems to support such community knowledge-bases. Figure 6.6 illustrates an interface of one of our prototype systems, which supports software designers

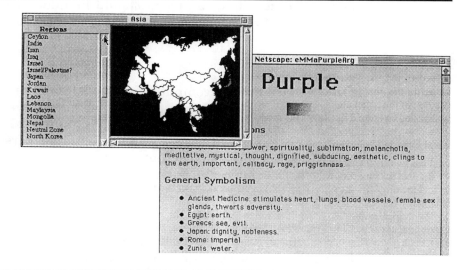

FIGURE 6.6   Culture-specific information retrieval system.

in accessing information in a community knowledge-base about the use of color in different countries. As discussed above, color has different psychological and social associations in different cultures. The system allows a designer to access a World Wide Web page that provides color information of the designated country by using the map.

To support cross-cultural collaboration during usage requires a system designer to embed mechanisms to construct shared understanding between the users and the system a priori. For example, users need a way to identify a profile of their culture. Users must be able to identify their culture to the system by using techniques such as a questionnaire and a template so that the system can adapt to the culture. The system, at the same time, must be able to create a user model to capture users' interaction style by monitoring users' behavior, such as what commands are frequently used. In addition, providing feedback to users is especially important for cross-cultural interaction design in order to make sure that users interpret the system's provided information as designers originally expected. If breakdowns are detected, the users should be allowed to adapt the interface to their way of understanding in their culture.

CONCLUSION

Designing a human-computer interface traditionally incorporates two views: a task perspective and a cognitive perspective. The task perspective requires the analysis of tasks that users want to perform with the system. Cognitive perspective provides information about human nature, such as keystroke-level analysis. Developing an interface for multiple cultures or for a culture that you are not familiar with requires the addition of a cultural dimension, including language, social factors, rules, norms, and values.

In this chapter, we used Japan as an example to illustrate how and why software developed for Western countries has not worked well in some cases. Although we have limited our discussions on racial and geographical culture, there are other "cultures," such as gender, generation, cooperation, or professionalism (Bodker and Pedersen 1991). Moreover, as virtual communities who share common interest evolve over computer networks, new types of cultures will emerge. In fact, some characteristics we pointed out earlier no longer hold in some cases; for example, Press reported a study in which older people were slower in using a system because they read everything on the screen before making a choice while children were less focused, randomly clicking objects on the display (Press 1995).

However, we see no fundamental differences among different types of cultures: They are characteristics of groups of people. Our approach to viewing cross-cultural human-computer interaction design as cross-cultural collaborative work will be able to deal with the impact of any type of culture, whether it is geographical or virtual.

REFERENCES

Bodker, K., and J. Pedersen. 1991. Workplace cultures: Looking at artifacts, symbols and practices. In Greenbaum, J., and M. Kyng (eds.), *Design at Work: Cooperative Design of Computer Systems.* Hillsdale, NJ: Lawrence Erlbaum Associates, 121–136.

Cole, M., and P. Griffin. 1980. Cultural amplifiers reconsidered. In Olson, D. R. (ed.), *The Social Foundations of Language and Thought*, W. W. Norton, 343–364.

Fernandes, T. 1995. *Global Interface Design*. London: Academic Press.

Fischer, G., K. Nakakoji, and J. Ostwald. 1995. Supporting the evolution of design artifacts with representations of context and intent. *Proceedings of the Design of Interactive Systems, ACM*, Ann Arbor, MI, August 1995, 7–15.

Fukuda, K. 1994. *The Name of Colors (Iro no Namae)*. Tokyo: Shufunotomo, Inc. (In Japanese).

Greif, I. (ed.) 1988. *Computer-Supported Cooperative Work: A Book of Readings*. San Mateo, CA: Morgan Kaufmann.

Grudin, J. 1991. Interactive systems: Bridging the gaps between developers and users. *Computer* **24**, 4 (April 1991): 59–69.

Ishii, H. 1990. Cross-cultural communication and computer-supported cooperative work. *Whole Earth Review* (Winter 1990): 48–52.

Jones, S., C. Kennelly, C. Mueller, M. Sweezy, B. Thomas, and L. Velez. 1991. *Developing International User Information*. Bedford, MA: Digital Press.

Kawakita, J. 1984. *Hassouhou (Abduction: How to Develop Creativity)*. Tokyo: Chuuou Kouron, Inc. (In Japanese).

Kellogg, W. A., and J. C. Thomas. 1993. Cross-cultural perspective on human-computer interaction: A report on the CHI'92 workshop. *SIGCHI Bulletin* **25**, 2: 40–45.

Kolodner, J. L. 1993. *Case-Based Reasoning*. San Mateo, CA: Morgan Kauffann.

Krauss, R. M., and S. R. Fussell. 1991. Constructing shared communicative environments. In Resnick, L. B., J. M. Levine, and S. D. Teasley (eds.), *Perspectives on Socially Shared Cognition*. Washington, D.C.: American Psychological Association, 172–200.

Nakakoji, K. 1994. Crossing the cultural boundary. *BYTE* **19**, (June 1994): 107–109.

Norman, D. A. 1993. *Things That Make Us Smart*. Reading, MA: Addison-Wesley Publishing Company.

Ostwald, J., and K. Nakakoji. 1994. *EVA: A Medium for Conceptual Coordination in Collaborative Design Across Cultural Boundaries*. Boulder, CO: Department of Computer Science, University of Colorado.

Press, L. 1995. McLuhan meets the net. *Communications of the ACM* **38**, 7 (July 1995).

Russo, P., and S. Boor. 1993. How fluent is your interface? Designing for international users. *Human Factors in Computing Systems, INTERCHI'93 Conference Proceedings, ACM*, 342–347.

Schneider-Hufschmidt, M., T. Kuehme, and U. Malinowski (eds.). 1993. *Adaptive User Interfaces—Principles and Practice.* Amsterdam: Elsevier Science Publishers.

Valacich, J. S., L. M. Jessup, A. R. Dennis, and J. F. Nunamaker, Jr. 1992. A conceptual framework of anonymity in group support systems. *Proceedings of the 25th Annual Hawaii Conference on System Sciences, Vol. III: Group Decision Support Systems Track,* IEEE Computer Society, January 1992, 113–125.

Whorf, B. L. 1956. *Language, Thought, and Reality: Selected Writings of Benjamin Lee Whorf.* Cambridge, MA: MIT Press.

Winograd, T., and F. Flores. 1986. *Understanding Computers and Cognition: A New Foundation for Design.* Norwood, NJ: Ablex.

ABOUT THE AUTHORS

Masao Ito, a Japanese software developer and a researcher, recently established a new company, NIL Software Corp., to develop computer-aided software engineering (CASE) tools, which support a software designer's thinking processes. This is challenging because the designer's thinking process takes place internally, and is not visible to a computer system. Ito is interested in finding an innovative solution for user interface design to deal with the issue using the Zen-Buddhism approach.

Kumiyo Nakakoji received her B.A. degree in computer science from Osaka University, Japan, in 1986, and her Ph.D. from the Department of Computer Science and the Institute of Cognitive Science at University of Colorado, Boulder, in 1993, through a scholarship provided by Software Research Associates, Inc., of Japan. Her recent research interests include a knowledge-based approach for multimedia authoring environments and cross-cultural considerations in human-computer interaction design and in software engineering. She was a co-organizer of the Cross-Cultural Issues in Human-Computer Interaction workshop at InterCHI'93. Currently, she is an Adjunct Assistant Professor at University of Colorado and a visiting Assistant Professor at Nara Advanced Institute of Science and Technology while working for Software Research Associates, Inc. of Japan.

CHAPTER 7

Arabization of Graphical User Interfaces

LOCALIZATION AND INTERNATIONALIZATION PROBLEMS FOR THE ARABIC LANGUAGE

The Arabic script presents major and specific processing problems that are not encountered in Latin-based languages, or even in Far Eastern languages. The software localization process cannot be handled directly by regular *MNLS (multinational language supplement)* architecture support which is available on most UNIX systems for European languages. Specific internationalization support must be added either to the application itself or, and this is the objective of LangBox international's products, to the operating system interface. The main Arabic language support problems are the following: character codeset and standard encoding, character shaping and text direction algorithms, character fonts, global screen direction and mirror effect, numerals and Hindi digit shapes, Arabic vowels and collating sequences, neutral characters, dual keyboard management, and optical character recognition.

Character Codeset and Standard Encoding

The recommended codeset used for representing Arabic script under the UNIX environment is ISO 8859-6 (the same as ECMA

XLANGBOX-ARA storage codeset in DATA PROCESSING (ISO 8859-6)

	0	1	2	3	4	5	6	7	8	9	A	B	C	D	E	F
0				0 ·	@	P	‘	p						ذ	-	
1			!	1 ١	A	Q	a	q					٠	ر	ف	
2			"	2 ٢	B	R	b	r					آ	ز	ق	
3			#	3 ٣	C	S	c	s					أ	س	ك	
4			$	4 ٤	D	T	d	t				$	ؤ	ش	ل	
5			%	5 ٥	E	U	e	u					!	ص	م	
6			&	6 ٦	F	V	f	v					ئ	ض	ن	
7			'	7 ٧	G	W	g	w					ا	ط	ه	
8			(	8 ٨	H	X	h	x					ب	ظ	و	
9			)	9 ٩	I	Y	i	y					ة	ع	ى	
A			*	:	J	Z	j	z					ت		ي	
B			+	;	K	[	k	{				؛	ث			
C			,	<	L	\	l					،		ج			
D			-	=	M	]	m	}					ح			
E			.	>	N	^	n	~					خ			
F			/	?	O	_	o					؟	د			

(C) LangBox International

FIGURE 7.1   The ISO 8859-6 codeset.

114 and ASMO 708, see Figure 7.1). Several other codesets exist on the PC environment or in constructor specific implementations (i.e., IBM, WANG), and codeset converters to or from these codesets to ISO are then needed. The alphabet of the Arabic language is well defined. Each letter receives one ISO character

value. However, this ISO 8859-6 codeset is incompatible with other languages covered by the ISO 8859 family (i.e., European, Cyrillic, Greek) since it is an 8-bit codeset. Data stored in the Arabic codeset cannot be displayed on a regular ISO 8859-1 or *Latin 1*-based system. This problem can be solved with extended multibyte standards such as Unicode. Also, and this is the case for European localization as well, ISO 8859 is an 8-bit codeset, meaning that the application must be *8-bit clean*. The 8-bit support of applications was a problem with old software initially designed for ASCII support and the U.S. market. Most UNIX applications now support 8-bit code sets.

Character Shaping and Text Direction Algorithms

The graphic form (glyph) shown in the ISO 8859-6 character chart is not the identity of that character (like in Latin 1 for example). The same Arabic character may correspond to up to four different glyph types. The glyph type of a character depends on the position of the character within a word. The possible glyph types are the *initial shape* (a character that begins a word), the *medial shape* (a character that is surrounded by other Arabic characters), the *final shape* (a character that is located at the end of a word), and the *independent shape* (a character that is surrounded by white space).

Some characters can be linked to another character on either side (each character has four possible glyphs), some characters can be linked only on their right side (and have only two possible glyphs), and some characters cannot be linked on either side (and have only one possible glyph). Also, in some character sequences, the formation of ligatures is obligatory. These ligatures associate one specific character form to the joining of two Arabic characters. They are necessary for well-rendered Arabic text. In addition to this, Arabic text is written from right to left, and mixed Arabic/Latin strings include text in both directions which is presented on the same line. In fact, text is stored in sequential order in the backing store. Logical or backing store order corresponds to the order in which text is typed. The conversion from backing store format to the readable one represents one of the major problems in the processing of Arabic script. In order to be the most useful, powerful, and especially transparent regarding applications, this conversion must be handled by low-level text-rendering routines.

Character Fonts

The Arabic character font also has another particular need. Arabic is always written in "cursive" or handwritten form, where characters are linked together as if they were written by hand. The linking rules are well defined, but the font needs to be adapted to this style, and the display device must be able to join all characters designed in order to avoid blank columns between characters. The nicest solution is to use proportional width fonts, which are very important for rendering Arabic script. Some devices, such as alphanumeric terminals, cannot handle this kind of font, and use fixed-width fonts instead; the result is less enjoyable but remains readable.

Global Screen Direction and Mirror Effect

Due to the right-to-left writing direction of the Arabic language, the common way to read a document is to start from the top right-hand corner. This is also the case for an application screen or a printed document. This characteristic of the Arabic language is also a problem for standard applications. These applications are designed for Latin-based character sets which have built their screens starting from the top left-hand corner position. Also, several little details, such as the menu cascading in a *GUI* (*Graphical User Interface*) application, need to be right-to-left oriented. These characteristics are very difficult to localize if they are not included in the original design of the software.

Numerals and Hindi Digit Shapes

Numerals are mainly handled in the same way as in Latin languages. Numbers are read from left to right with the highest-order digit on the left side. However, there are two possibilities for numeral shapes. In North African countries, the digit's glyphs are the "Arabic digits" (i.e., the same as for Latin use). In Middle Eastern countries, the digits used are the "Hindi shapes." The display of one of these two possible digit representations must be user configurable.

Arabic Vowels and Collating Sequences

The Arabic vowels (named "Tashkil") have a specific status in Arabic text. In fact, in common use, these characters are simply not used and Arabic text is written only with consonants. Any possible synonym confusion is cleared according to the context. However, in some cases (e.g., official or legal documents), vowels may be added to the text. These vowels look like Latin accents that are displayed above or below a consonant letter. The problem here is that from a collating sequence or a pattern search point of view, a word with vowels and the same word without vowels must have the same intrinsic value. Also, text input with vowels must be displayed or printed with or without vowels.

Neutral Characters

Normally, Arabic characters are always written from right to left, and Latin characters are always written from left to right. For some technical reasons and in order to be able to display text correctly in right-to-left mode some application screens or forms are initially built in a left-to-right direction. Some characters must be able to take the global writing direction despite their own direction value. It is necessary then to define a set of neutral characters which are able to use the global writing direction when being written.

Dual Keyboard Management

In most cases, European language keyboards have one specific keyboard layout, including all needed Latin letters. Since the Arabic alphabet is different from the Latin character set and because a user must always be able to input Latin and Arabic characters from the keyboard (ISO 8859-6 includes both ASCII and Arabic characters), a dual keyboard management system is needed. The keyboard management system must allow the user to switch from one language to the other using a single keystroke. This is also the case for languages that use Cyrillic, Greek, or Thai character sets.

In order to be coherent, the solution must include either an engraved keyboard with both ASCII and Arabic letters on each key, or to be more flexible, a set of keyboard stickers to be installed by the user on the existing keyboard. Sometimes the second solution is not acceptable to users and it is necessary to supply an engraved keyboard.

Optical Character Recognition

Because Arabic is a connecting-letter language, it is quite difficult to use the same method and algorithms for optical character recognition as for Latin languages. The main problem is the ability to extract a single letter from a word.

ARABIC STANDARDS AND CULTURE

Handwriting

One of the most difficult points of the Arabic writing culture is the ability to reproduce the cursive handwriting aspect of the text on a computer screen or within an application. Initially, with character-based interfaces such as typewriters, dump terminals, and dot matrix printers, results were acceptable, but were not appreciated by all users. This kind of interface always uses fixed-width fonts and, even when *context analysis* and *automatic shape determination* are implemented, the final rendering (on a screen or on a printed document) is not high quality.

Since the appearance on the market of graphical interfaces (such as Microsoft Windows on PCs and X Window on UNIX platforms) and the ability to use proportional-width fonts and *WYSIWYG* (*What You See Is What You Get*) systems, the rendering of Arabic text on a screen or on a PostScript printer more closely reflects user expectations.

Codeset Uses

Some Arabic standards, like the keyboard layout, are conflicting and are not always clear. The Arab Organization for Standardization and Metrology (ASMO), has determined a specific layout, but user habits have developed standards from the use of specific manufacturer products. For example, regarding the ligature *Lam-Alef*, this ligature (visual shape coming from the juxtaposition of two ISO letters "Lam" (L) and "Alef" (A)) appears on an IBM keyboard standard. To be compliant, Microsoft has also implemented this same solution. Since this character does not exist "as is" in the ISO codeset, the ASMO layout does not include this key, and most users find this unacceptable. In fact, this problem is due to market competition rules that give a de facto standard to the first solutions. The localization of an application must also take into account these kinds of problems.

Local Differences

Arabic writing is the same for all Arab countries. However, the speaking of Arabic may be different and therefore different country dependencies must be implemented. This is the case for month names, which are different in North Africa, around the Nile Valley area, and in the Middle Eastern countries.

No Abbreviations

Abbreviations and acronyms (like IBM for International Business Machines, N.Y. for New York, or P.M. for time indication) do not exist in Arabic. In Arabic, we always need to specify a complete word. This characteristic needs to be taken into account when translating messages and labels of user interfaces into Arabic. The length of messages will grow. In some cases, the real visual length of labels and messages should be greatly reduced using a proportional-width font. One of the characteristics of Arabic cursive writing is that the beginning and the middle shapes are narrower than final or isolated shapes. The result of a normal string is very condensed.

Justification of Text

The general behavior of some applications is not directly applicable to Arabic language usage. This is typically the case for word processing and their justification features. The standard algorithm to justify text in Latin is to add spaces between words on the line in order to achieve both left and right alignment. The method used for text justifying in Arabic is to stretch the last letter of a word in the line. This stretching is called *keshide*, and to be fully compliant with the Arabic culture, a word processor must implement it.

LOCAL EXPECTATIONS AND DOS-BASED SOLUTIONS

PC User Habits

As explained above, the DOS market created most of the Arabic implementation standards. Microsoft Arabic DOS and Arabic Microsoft Windows have reinforced this aspect. A user moving from this kind of environment to a UNIX environment will expect to find the same Arabic features and uses. However, after initial discontentment, users will normally adapt themselves to a new system.

Some of these PC solutions could not be implemented on the UNIX environment. For example, in Arabic DOS character applications, users press **Right Shift + Left shift** to toggle their keyboard layout between Arabic and Latin mode. If you press the same key sequence on an alphanumeric terminal (such as VT100 or Wyse), the UNIX operating system and therefore the application will simply receive nothing from the serial line connection. Hence, it will be unable to use this sequence to switch between two internal logical keyboard mappings.

Calligraphic Styles

Also, during the past thousand years, a number of Arabic calligraphic styles have grown in popularity and are in standard use today. The most famous Arabic calligraphic styles are Naskhi, Baghdadi, Farsi, Kuffi, and Requah.

IMPLEMENTATION CASE STUDY AND SPECIFIC PROBLEMS FOR APPLICATIONS

There are two main types of user interfaces on the UNIX workstation: the character-based user interface, mainly used on server or remote alphanumeric terminal connections and the graphical-based user interface used on a workstation console or on X Terminals. The graphical user interface is X Window-based in most cases, but could also be a constructed proprietary environment dedicated to a specific workstation. This is the case for Intergraph EnvironV or SUN Xview or GKS system libraries. The determination of the user interface depends on the application implementation. The solution used to *Arabize* an application is different according to this user interface type.

For the above reasons, LangBox International specialized in design and development of bilingual and multilingual operating systems, including Arabic, Farsi, Hebrew, Greek, Cyrillic, Turkish, and Thai. LangBox has implemented bilingual capabilities on a large number of platforms operating under both the character-based applications and X Window/OSF Motif-based applications. These specific enhancements have been implemented within the operating system and its libraries in order to offer transparency for the end user applications under the following product solutions:

- "LANGBOX for Arabic" package (called LANGBOX-ARA) for character-based applications
- "XLANGBOX for Arabic" package (called XLANGBOX-ARA) for pure X Window applications

Both LANGBOX-ARA and XLANGBOX-ARA packages allow the following features:

- Providing a global solution to Arabic and Latin simultaneously
- Maximum transparency of applications
- Total transparency to storage and display of data in national languages
- Ease of internationalization of applications
- Conformity with national and international standards

These two products are not able to cover all needs, but a major part of the UNIX application is working either in the old terminal interface mode or using the OSF/Motif interface which comes on all workstations today. However, other user interfaces may be covered by a set of subparts of this product. In this classification, we can find some proprietary GUI library equivalents to Motif (like Intergraph I/FORMS or Silicon Graphics Tinyui) on which we find label, text, button, and cascade menu widgets. We also find subparts of some applications that make a direct display through proprietary routines (like PostScript mapping area in geographic information system (GIS) applications or OpenGL graphic data representation window in presentation applications). Specific cases like these have already been Arabized using basic LANGBOX routines.

LANGBOX-ARA: The Character-based Arabization Support

Standard UNIX operating system support of character-based internationalization (locale) supplies only support for European languages which is generally based on the ISO 8859-1 character codeset. This multinational language supplement (MNLS) allows keyboard mapping, handling of collating sequences and character types, and date and time format. But it cannot handle Arabic characters and, in general, it cannot handle languages with a right-to-left writing direction.

The LANGBOX-ARA system is built around UNIX System V. When loaded onto the UNIX system, LANGBOX-ARA provides the user with a full bilingual environment within the operating system interface, the system development, and the character-based applications. To conform to the UNIX operating system, LANGBOX-ARA is also designed to run in a multiuser and multitasking environment and to coreside with the standard UNIX facilities. Having LANGBOX-ARA added to a UNIX system does not prohibit its users from operating in a pure UNIX environment.

The internal solution exists to enhance the terminal device driver with specific Arabic process routines that are able to manage both input and output character flow. These routines make dual keyboard mapping management possible at the input level and full screen management possible at the output level, including context analysis, automatic shape determination, font selection, and mirroring effect. The Arabic font is initially loaded on the terminal's local RAM or on the device.

While operating under the LANGBOX-ARA bilingual environment, users can select and set their default language, English or Arabic. Users can log into the system in the language of

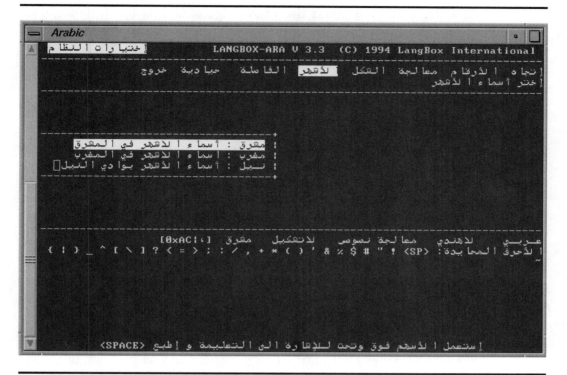

FIGURE 7.2 Arabized character-based application.

their choice and communicate with the host using the standard UNIX commands and tools. The commands could be entered either in Latin or in Arabic and are executed by the LANGBOX-ARA shell command interpreter. The system responses are displayed in the language chosen by the user (see Figure 7.2).

Although set with a default language prior to login, a LANGBOX-ARA user can start multiple work sessions (shell child processes), each with a different base language. He will be able to alternate languages within the same work session, at the command line, directory and file level, or when running a standard UNIX application (e.g., text processing, spreadsheets, database management, etc.).

In addition to the bilingual UNIX user interface, LANG-BOX-ARA provides a comprehensive bilingual software development environment for programmers. The programmer will be able, with or without the knowledge of the Arabic language, to develop with ease bilingual applications or to adapt, with minimal effort, current English software packages to run in a bilingual mode under the LANGBOX-ARA environment.

LANGBOX-ARA provides an enhanced environment for the internationalization of applications as compared with classical techniques. Also, the merge of LANGBOX-ARA support and the MNLS files for ISO 8859-6 codeset (which are part of the product) enable applications already designed for European localization to be adapted to the Arab market very quickly. Usually, application programmers need to incorporate international character string manipulation, context analysis (automatic shape determination), display processing, and font set within the application. Under LANGBOX-ARA, 8-bit clean character-based applications will run with no modification.

XLANGBOX-ARA: The Graphical-based Arabization Support

With the development of the graphical interface (like X Window) on workstations, other kinds of applications have been designed. These applications are clients that communicate with a graphic server through network connection facilities. Here, the main application routines work directly with bitmaps and the concept of character flow has disappeared. A transparent Arabization is more difficult to implement. We need at least to link the application with an Arabic graphical library, or use an Arabic shared library at the runtime level (if the operating system allows it). Also, some application concepts must be implemented to allow correct behavior. For example, we always need to refresh the complete line after each input character. Moreover, fonts could be selected through a resource file or a command line option. Even if all these features are present, parts of the application cannot behave correctly in Arabic (like cut and paste for example), and a specific implementation must be done for the Arabic support by adding specific source code lines.

The XLANGBOX-ARA library package is built around the MIT X Window and OSF/Motif libraries. When added and linked to an application that uses these interfaces, XLANG-

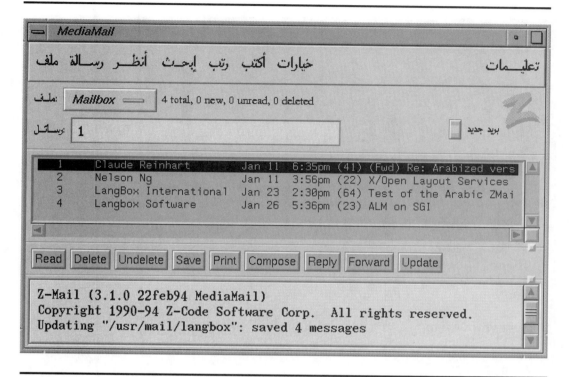

FIGURE 7.3   Arabization of a standard Motif application: Z-Mail.

BOX-ARA provides the user with a full bilingual environment in runtime application operations (see Figure 7.3).

The XLANGBOX-ARA package is specially designed for software developers willing to address the Arab countries' market. They can prepare a standard Latin application with minor changes. As a set of demonstrations and X Window samples, OSF/ Motif and UIL programs are Arabized and included in the package (see Figure 7.4).

Arabization level parameters can be selected and set at the runtime level. These parameters can be either user independent or in the application. They include context analysis (automatic shape determination), dual keyboard state, mapping, numeral shapes, and vowels.

XLANGBOX-ARA is composed of the following parts:

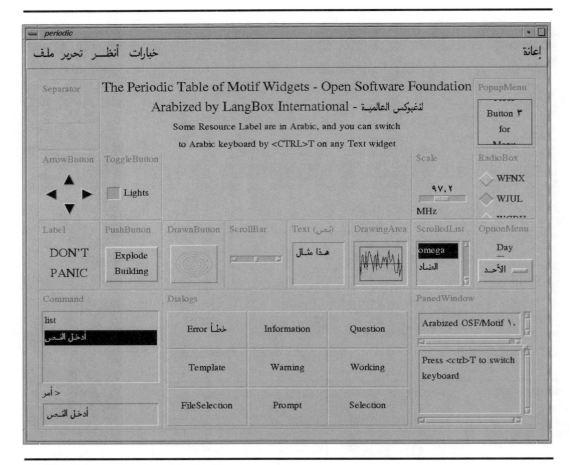

FIGURE 7.4   Arabized Motif widgets.

- The Arabic context library
- The X Window Arabic extension
- The OSF/Motif Arabic extension
- Arabic fonts for the server
- The printing support
- The demo set

These parts can be used together or separately depending on the need and the internal organization of the application to be Arabized.

The Arabic Context Library This library contains the specific Arabic string manipulation routines. These routines allow the following:

1. "Contextation" of ISO 8859-6 strings coming from a storage area; this makes it readable according to the Arabic context (generally for a display purpose).
2. Character position calculation: These routines allow the location of the new position value for a character after or before a contextation.
3. Attribute range selection: These routines allow the calculation of a new attribute.
4. Range of a string after or before a contextation.
5. Contextation parameter management: These routines allow the retrieval or setting of specific Arabic parameters used during the context analysis of strings.
6. These parameters are mainly the following:
   - Left-to-right/right-to-left main direction
   - Hindi/Arabic numeral shape
   - Vowels enabled/disabled (tashkil)
   - Automatic shape determination on-off
   - Data processing/word processing
   - Neutral character management
   - Arabic floating point symbol
   - Arabic dual keyboard management.

This library is an independent one. It can be used for any application that wants to handle Arabic strings directly.

The X Window Arabic Extension This library already contains Arabized X11 routines for string manipulation, string rendering, and keyboard management. In order to be used, this library must be added to the link phase of the application. This may be done by relinking the applications that follow the static linking format, or by setting path value in an environment variable when using the dynamic linking concept.

The OSF/Motif Arabic Extension This library is an extension to the famous Open Software Foundation "Motif Library." This complement allows the transparent handling of primitive Motif widgets (e.g., text widgets, label widgets, list widgets). As for X Window, this library must be added to the link phase of the application. One of the main reasons that the Arabic handling support must also be included in this library and not only in the X Window library is the global writing direction handling within widgets such as Text or List, on which a mirroring effect must be implemented in order to provide a full right-to-left presentation. For example, the first character in a text widget must be on the top right side of the widget box. The X Window level cannot cover this kind of need. Also, in the same way, the very useful cut-and-paste and drag-and-drop features which are available under the Motif environment need to be adapted to the Arabic language. In fact, to be transparent, the cut-and-paste internal X Server buffer must get an internal consecutive data area in one block. This is not straightforward on mixed Latin/Arabic strings, where the internal order is completely different from the visual order. (See Figure 7.5.)

This attribute splitting is not automatically done by the regular Motif library, and a specific enhancement is needed. In the same way, any cursor pointing using the mouse within an Arabic text also needs to be converted to an internal pointing position to enable transparency for editing actions. The correspondence between the internal buffer structure that follows the ISO codeset and the visual buffer that depends on the Arabic context must be checked and always highly valid.

The selection from position (4) to position (15) in the internal ISO string:

1	2	3	4	5	6	7	8	9	10	11	12	13	14	15	16	17	18
I	n	ف	ي	t	h	e		b	o	o	k	ا	ل	ك	ت	ا	ب

gives:

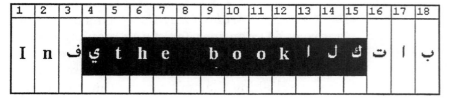

FIGURE 7.5   Highlighting in bi-birectional text.

Arabic Fonts for the Server XLANGBOX-ARA supplies a set of Arabic fonts for the X server running on the target machine. These fonts are in both "snf" and "bdf" format for heterogeneous network connections. Several sizes are available and can be selected either from the application itself or from a resource file. XLANGBOX-ARA contains fixed spacing and proportional spacing fonts that give better-looking results for Arabic.

Printing Support This subpackage consists of a set of printer fonts that are downloaded directly onto the supported printer, using specific XLANGBOX-ARA commands. It also includes a new specific line printer spooler that must be used instead of the standard lp or lpr types, for printing Arabic files as well as an ISO 8859-6 to PostScript filter tool and Arabic PostScript fonts.

The Demo Set This set is given for X11/Motif developers. It facilitates the understanding of how Arabization can be included in an existing application (see Figure 7.6). This demo set includes samples for:

- Sample character-based program
- Pure X Window (X11) interfaced program

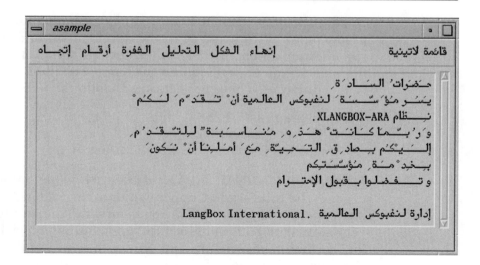

FIGURE 7.6   Sample of an Arabized Motif text widget.

- OSF/Motif sample application
- OSF/Motif and UIL build applications

Several Arabic software developers' recommendations are also included.

LANGBOX-ARA and XLANGBOX-ARA Availability

LANGBOX-ARA and/or XLANGBOX-ARA are available on the following operating systems:

- SUN SunOS and Solaris on SPARC series
- Silicon Graphics IRIX
- SCO UNIX System V
- IBM AIX RISC System/6000
- CDC's EP/IX
- BULL BOS
- INTERGRAPH CLIX
- Data General's DG/UX
- Siemens' SINIX
- VAX VMS (Arabic context library only)

Other User Interfaces

During the development and marketing of the above two main products, we were involved in the development and the supplying of Arabization to some other specific user interfaces. The main problems always remain the same, but their implementation is different. These projects are as follows:

- Intergraph I/FORMS Graphical Library
- UNISYS System9 GIS
- Graphical Drawing and Presentation Tool

Intergraph I/FORMS Graphical Library This interface was used on the Intergraph Clipper workstation, using CLIX operating system and EnvironV graphic server. This environment is very similar to X11 and Motif features, but is proprietary. Also, font format is proprietary and implies a new font development. The main advantage of this interface is that 80 percent of the Intergraph Clipper applications are built on it and use dynamic linking. Even the screen forms are external and may be edited or modified very quickly using a form builder to change, for example, font attributes and labels.

UNISYS System9 GIS This geographic information system (GIS) runs on the SUN platform and is based on X11 library for menu and message displaying. Pure graphic data viewing is done in an independent window and uses proprietary routines, even for label and text attribute display (see Figure 7.7). The

FIGURE 7.7   Arabized GIS application.

menu and text input were designed initially for Latin messages and even more for English-only messages. This "historic" characteristic created some problems for Arabic support. The first problem was 8-bit character support. Some 8-bit characters were used internally and eaten by the application. An 8-bit cleaning of the application was necessary.

The second problem dealt with input line refresh. This is a more frequent problem found in low-level display routines. To be faster, the application refreshes only the last typed character at the end of the string and the low-level routines from Xlib receive only this character. For Arabic, a new context analysis must be done on the full entry line and sometimes the full line needs to be redisplayed by the application. For example, if the user enters Arabic letters 1, 2 and 3 on the keyboard, each letter could take an independent (i) shape, a beginning (b) shape, a medial (m) shape, or a final (f) shape depending on the word context.

Entered key letter	Stored string (ISO)	Displayed string (CTX)
1	1	1(i)
2	12	2(f)1(b)
3	123	3(f)2(m)1(b)

The minimum effort (without any display optimization) is required to force the redisplay of all the lines (the ISO one) after each inputted character. When the application makes its own refresh of an inputted string with XDrawString() calls, this refresh must redisplay the complete string after each incoming character. If this is not done, it must be modified in the GIS application source code. In this section, if input is handled directly by X11 routines (i.e., not using a high-level widget under Motif), other editing features have to be also adapted to Arabic (backspace management, cursor move, and insert mode). In fact, the backspace action will be OK, but the cursor motion will continue to move on the ISO string internally (the stored one) and the cursor will be displayed on the contextation string, but the two positions are not in phase.

To cover this feature in the GIS application, we had to call an external function implemented in a specific "shared library" (e.g., libGISarabic.so), which calculates the physical cursor position from an internal position. For the standard English GIS version, this function could be just a stub code, as follows:

```
int GIS_arabic_position(i)
{
    return(i);
}
```

It could be dynamically replaced by a true Arabic function for the Arabic GIS version. To be exhaustive, both visual-to-internal (for mouse pointing) and internal-to-visual (for cursor display) kinds of routines must be implemented.

Also, the mapping area attribute display routines which need to be enhanced with Arabic context analysis routines and specific scaleable fonts (hershey format) have been developed to cover this part on the interface. The plotter printing was designed to dump a mapping area window and did not need specific treatment since Arabic support was already done in the mapping area itself. But sometimes it must follow the same considerations. For example, the original code was:

```
char name[100];
name = getTextAttr(...); /* get the string value from
                          * the database
                          */
MapDrawStr(name, x, y, size, ...); /* draw on the map */
```

The Arabic version of the same code is:

```
char name[100];
char ara_name[100];
name = getTextAttr(...); /* get the string value from
                          * the database
                          */
GIS_arabic_cntx(name, ara_name);/* Make Context
                                 * analysis
                                 */
MapDrawStr(aname, x, y, size, ...);/* draw on the map */
```

This new GIS_arabic_cntx() routine was implemented in an external shared library (libGISarabic.so). For the standard English GIS version, this function could be just a dummy code, as follows:

```
void GIS_arabic_cntx(in, out)
char *in *out;
{
    strcpy(out, in);
}
```

Graphical Drawing and Presentation Tool   We also worked on a presentation tool which is able to create and manipulate several kinds of graphic objects, such as lines, boxes, pictures, text and 3D objects. This tool is based on two kinds of GUI library: the dialog/menu toolkit library (for menus and control action area), and the OpenGL library (for data area).

> *The dialog/menu toolkit library.* This GUI library is similar to Motif and is based on X11/Xt layout. Several widget types are involved in string display:
> - Label widgets that may be covered by an X11 Arabization level
> - Text widgets that need an enhancement (like Motif XmText) in order to allow the input/output, edition, and selection in Arabic
>
> *The OpenGL library.* There are no direct text management routines in this library and all text attributes included in the data area need to be handled in the application source directly, before calling OpenGL routines. Also, Arabic PostScript Type 1 fonts are needed since the display engine uses this format. Specific Arabic management needs to be included in three different locations in order to cover all possibilities.

> **1.** *The Single Text and Multiline Text Object.* After consulting on this part of source code, it appears that the internal text object structure is composed by a chained list of a chunk of text. Each chunk contains a subpart of text having the same character attribute within a single line. The maximum length of a chunk is 20 characters. If this length is reached,

the system allocates a new chunk, appointed by the first, to store the rest of the text. This internal solution causes a problem for the Arabic language, since the output line rendering needs a context analysis of at least a whole and full line. The Arabization of this kind of object will need an internal rebuild of the full single line, an Arabic context analysis process on this line, and a rendering of the new visual codes through regular routines. Also cursor positioning actions and cut-and-paste selections must use the same kind of procedure. This internal particularity of the application complicates its Arabization. Also, such a new code modification needs to be very optimized to avoid the loss of performance.

2. *The 3D Text Object*. The 3D text objects are handled by a specific 3D dynamic library. This library includes C++ object classes that include their own rendering routines. According to this class structure, the text data is stored line by line in an internal array. Its display is also done line by line and needs to call Arabic context analysis routines before the internal application routines convert each character of the string into drawing segment set. In the same way, the 3D cursor management routines need to make calls to specific routines in order to be coherent with the visual display.

FUTURE IMPLEMENTATIONS

In order to standardize and avoid many of the localization problems not only for languages such as Arabic, Hebrew, Farsi and Urdu, but also for Thai or Far Eastern languages, constructors and working groups like X/Open Consortium need to define new standards for operating systems. For example, since X11R5 has included the Input Method specifications to partially solve the problems of Far Eastern languages input, X11R6 now includes the Output Method and Output Context specifications especially designed for languages such as Arabic. A well-written application, taking all of these services into consideration, should be localized faster than any other language in the world. LangBox International is already working on the development of such dynamic layout services, which will be automatically used by X11R6 routines if they are installed in a system. Concerning the old applications, the problem will remain because source code modification is needed in most cases.

ABOUT THE AUTHORS

Franck Portaneri graduated from the University of Nice, Sophia Antipolis, France, and received his M.S. degree in computing. He worked on the conception of one of the first bilingual Latin/Arabic UNIX operating system. He has been working in the multilingual field since 1986 and leads several internationalization and localization projects. He is the author of several publications dealing with UNIX localization.

Fethi Amara graduated from the University of Nice, Sophia Antipolis, France, and received his M.S. degree in computing. During his Ph.D. studies, he worked at INRIA (National Institute of Research in Informatics and Automatics) on multilingual desktop publishing within the MALIN Project (MultiAlphabetism and Lingualism in Informatics). He joined the LangBox team in 1990. He is the author of several publications dealing with multilingual user interfaces.

CHAPTER 8

A Chinese Text Display Supported by an Algorithm for Chinese Segmentation

INTRODUCTION

The absence of a word delimiter in Chinese causes problems in displaying and editing texts from this writing system in the sense that some X-Window/Motif styles, like word selection, are not easy to preserve. Also, systems that are designed for nonnative speakers would be improved if displays showed word boundaries. A solution is presented in this chapter which utilizes the research achievement in Chinese segmentation from the Computer Research Laboratory, New Mexico State University to support Chinese text display and editing on Xmat text widget, developed in CRL NMSU. A segmentation algorithm has been customized at several levels in fulfillment of various requirements of the text operations. Tests and results that illustrate the expected behaviors of the segmenter on the text display are presented, followed by a discussion of possible future work.

The Problem

In natural language processing and in graphical text display, *tokenization and segmentation* is a necessary first step in providing the basic features for this process. Generally, tokenization determines how a word is composed from characters, while segmentation determines how a sentence is composed from words. For the writing systems of most European and some Asian languages, tokenization, though still not trivial in some cases, is relatively easy, because word boundaries are always indicated by certain explicit delimiters, such as whitespace, hyphens, or slashes. By looking for delimiters, a text display system can implement editing features like *double click to select a word* without heavy computation cost. Segmentation is almost trivial because there are few ambiguities in tokenization. Thus, for these writing systems, tokenization and segmentation may not be the decisive issues for language processing and display systems.

However, for some other languages, such as Chinese and Japanese, tokenizing and segmenting by a computer are quite difficult (see Jin 1994; Jin/Nie 1993; Jin 1992). For Chinese text, there are the following difficulties:

1. There is no explicit delimiter between words. Figure 8.1 shows samples of Chinese text and a Japanese text without delimiters between words.
2. Some substrings in a sentence may actually be a word in a Chinese lexicon, but not in the context of the sentence. For example, if the correct segmentation of the sentence ABCDEFG (one English character denotes one Chinese character) is A BC DE FG and CD is a dictionary entry, then CD should *not* be tokenized as a word in the sentence.
3. Sometimes a sentence can be segmented in more than one way and each resulting sentence represents a different, or even contradicting, meaning.

The first two are problems arising from tokenization while the third is a segmentation problem. None of them could be solved without natural language processing (NLP).

As for text display systems, the questions are:

How to augment, while still being compliant with, the original operating and display conventions, for example, implementing the "word select" operation, of the base system without heavy computation

How to represent, or help the user resolve, ambiguities that occur in tokenization and segmentation

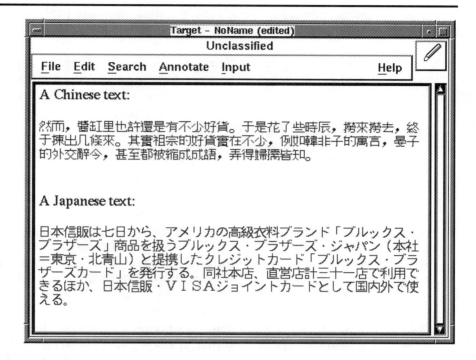

FIGURE 8.1   Chinese and Japanese text sample. Sentences appear as strings without word
delimiters.

How to allow the user to edit segmentations in addition to
the literal text

How to store and retrieve the segmentation information, if it
is required

How to maintain performance for interactive editing

Since *tokenization* and *segmentation* are two closely connected
issues, the terms *segmentation*, or *segment*, will generally refer
to both tokenization and segmentation in the rest of this chapter, unless specified.

Previous Work

This work is based upon previous research and development in
two different areas: Chinese segmentation, an NLP (natural

language processing) effort; and multilingual text display, a GUI (graphical user interface) effort.

Chinese Segmentation   Chinese segmentation, as one of the major subjects in the area of computer-based Chinese processing, has been studied intensively in the past decade. The major approaches include the heuristic method, the statistical method, and the hybrid method.

The knowledge-based heuristic approaches (Jin 1994; Jin/Nie 1993; Jin 1992; Chen/Liu 1992; Liang/Zhen 1991; He/Sun 1991; Wang/Li/Huang 1991) have the advantage of simplicity and efficiency. Because the heuristics used in the system correspond closely to the knowledge about languages (e.g., words and word structures), no meaningless words will be produced. So a high-quality result seems to be assured. However, the heuristic segmentation algorithm relies heavily on word knowledge, typically on-line dictionaries. The quality of the dictionary will have a great impact on the overall performance of the system. Also new words are constantly being produced from time to time in real life. The limitation of system knowledge often results in weakness in the operation. Especially, those purely dictionary-lookup approaches have no guarantee of producing syntactically and semantically correct segmentation. As a result, the problem of recognizing unknown words still remains as a major obstacle to performance improvement.

The statistical approach (Sproat et al. 1994; Sproat/Shih 1991; Chiang et al. 1992; Chang et al. 1991; Sun et al. 1992) uses such statistical information as character co-occurrence frequencies in a large corpus. Statistical models used in these approaches typically consider the occurrences of isolated characters. This approach has the advantage of being independent from the application and no dictionary is required per se. However, several problems have been encountered in this approach. First, large amounts of space are needed to store the model's parameters. Second, the probabilities estimated from the statistics calculated for one set of training data need to be revised when new texts are introduced or when an existing system is used in a different situation. The revision operation may be very costly.

Moreover, most statistical approaches bear the limitation that only the frequencies of single characters and their frequencies of occurrence in combination with other single characters are used. Chinese words, however, may contain several characters. It would be difficult to accurately handle words containing more than two successive characters. If the first order Markov model is extended to a higher order, new problems are encountered: (1) The prevalence of many single "functional" characters, such as prepositions, interrogative and negative markers, and conjunctions, can cause an explosion in statistical data in terms of frequency of occurrence, and (2) collecting enough data to extend the model beyond a first-order level in a uniform fashion is difficult. Several methods have been proposed to handle these problems (Sproat/Shih 1991; Chiang et al. 1992; Chang et al. 1991). However, they all involve considerable increases in the model's complexity and computational costs.

Recently, in an attempt to overcome problems in both approaches, a hybrid approach incorporating heuristics with statistics has been studied (Nie et al. 1994). This approach attempts to recognize the basic words similar to the heuristic method and solve the unknown word recognition problems by statistical methods. By this approach the range of word recognition is extended and the quality of segmentation is improved a great deal. However, ambiguous segmentation is still a problem which hasn't been completely solved (Jin 1994). The underlying algorithm for Chinese segmentation adopted in this work was originally developed by Jin at the Computing Research Laboratory (CRL) of New Mexico State University (NMSU) and is still an ongoing research effort.

Xmat: Multilingual Text Displayer and Editor   Another fundamental facility underlying this research is the Xmat text widget, an *X*-Window *M*ulti-Attribute motif *T*ext widget, provided by M. Leisher from the Computing Research Laboratory (Leisher/ Ogden 1993). Before the development of the Xmat text widget, there were a number of text widgets providing graphical interface for text editing. But none of them offer complete support for multiattribute (including multilingual) text processing (Yang 1994). The only partial solution was the internationalization support provided in the MIT distribution of X11R5, which has its limitation. X11R5 does not support those codesets (i.e., the internal format of the codes of language characters) that require more than one machine byte to represent a character, like Chinese and Japanese.

Xmat gives sufficient support for multilingual text display and editing. Currently, the Xmat text widget supports ten different kinds of attributes (while annotation, as a new kind of attribute, will possibly be supported in the near future) with the *codeset* attribute as one of them. The codesets that have been implemented include:

ascii	ASCII
atext_arabic	Arabic
ja_JP	Japanese
ko_KR	Korean
koi_cyrillic	Russian
it_IL	Hebrew
it_LN	Latin1
it_LV	Latvian
viscii	Vietnamese
zh_CN	Chinese GB
zh_TW	Chinese Big5

Figure 8.1 is an actual screen dump of a text window from an application utilizing Xmat text widget. Among many others, *text marker* and *text span* (to be implemented) are two features from the Xmat text widget that are particularly useful in representing, saving, and retrieving the segmentation information. For more information about the multilingual text widget refer to Leisher/Ogden (1993).

Overview

The overall purpose of this work is to utilize the research results of Chinese segmentation mainly from CRL NMSU, by customizing and integrating them into the Xmat text environment. The segmentation results could then be represented in an X-Window/ Motif-compliant way to solve the segmentation problems caused by introducing Chinese text into a graphical text display.

The original development of the segmentation algorithm used the PROLOG language, an ideal language for NLP research. The algorithm has been rewritten into C when applied to this project for reasons of performance. Moreover, the original algorithm only works at file level. It takes, as its input, a plain Chinese text file and generates the segmented text into a new file. In rewriting, it has been refined into three different levels: (1) word level, (2) sentence level, and (3) file level, in order to fulfill different requirements from the text displayer and editor.

The Motif convention for word selection is augmented so that the words can be selected by double-clicks even though there are no explicit delimiters between the words. A new method called *select circle* is introduced to represent the ambiguities in word selection, a case that never occurs in English texts. Any sentence from the text on display can be segmented dynamically by a simple mouse click **<btn3np>**. The result (i.e., the segmented sentence) is displayed in a separate auxiliary text window. In less than 10 percent of cases there is more than one way to segment a sentence. All possibilities are displayed. This is referred to as the *multiple readings* of the sentence.

Segmentation editing is introduced as an aspect of text editing. The user is allowed to edit both the literal string and the segmentation of a text. These two kinds of editing are separated and interact with each other by a drag-and-drop mechanism. The user is now allowed to edit both (text string and segmentation) at the same place. The reason for separating two aspects of editing is to emphasize the distinction between them.

Text can be displayed in either the implicit segmented mode (ISM) or the explicit segmented mode (ESM). In ISM, text is displayed in its original form and there are no explicit delimiters between words. The user can ask where the left and right boundaries of a word are by double-clicking to select it. In ESM, special symbols are explicitly inserted between words. Currently a small vertical bar is used as the special delimiter, but the user may choose other symbols (e.g., whitespace). Text can be alternated in the display between these two modes. Persistent storage of segmentation information along with the text is supported by an SGML-like markup language. It is also possible to store this information using an *annotation manager*, a recently developed package as an extension to Xmat.

DESIGN CONSIDERATIONS

General

As indicated earlier, the main purpose of this work is to utilize the results of research in Chinese segmentation in order to solve the problems that occur when displaying Chinese text with the text widget. Let's first have a close look at the problems with Chinese text display.

The original cause of almost all of the problems discussed in this chapter is that there are no explicit word delimiters in Chinese text like whitespace is used in English text. This causes little difficulty for human reading, but does disrupt the Motif style for text display and edit. An obvious example is BSelect Click 2 in a text widget which is used to select a word (Open Software Foundation 1991). Its implementation is almost trivial if the text contains Latin text only. All it has to do is to look for the closest delimiter at both sides of the mouse click point and make a range selection for all characters between the two delimiters. If this strategy remained for Chinese text, however, BSelect Click 2 would have no way to find where the boundaries of the word are.

One solution is to use an explicit delimiter in the text. This would result in the text shown in the example in Figure 8.2. The advantages could be that (1) there is no need to reimplement BSelect Click 2, and (2) this kind of text appearance is helpful for the nonnative user to understand the text. But there exist cases when the original appearance of the text should be kept intact. Native users usually prefer not to use this kind of text appearance. Moreover, a more severe problem is that almost all Chinese on-line texts are not in this form and it is difficult and prohibitively time consuming to convert them into this form by human editing.

This suggests two solutions:

1. Reimplement BSelect Click 2 so that it will work on any Chinese or Chinese-English combined texts in their original format (with no delimiter in the text).
2. Provide a program (*text segmenter*) to automatically convert a text with no word delimiter (*unsegmented text*) into the text with explicit word delimiters (*segmented text*).

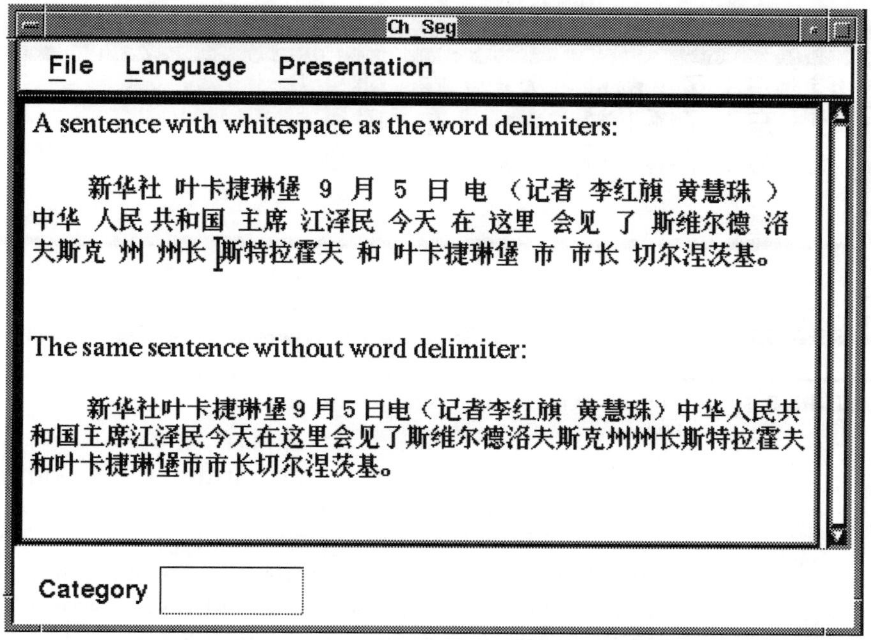

```
┌──────────────────────────── Ch_Seg ────────────────────────────┐
│  File   Language   Presentation                                 │
├─────────────────────────────────────────────────────────────────┤
```

A sentence with whitespace as the word delimiters:

　　新华社 叶卡捷琳堡 9 月 5 日 电 （记者 李红旗 黄慧珠 ）
中华 人民 共和国 主席 江泽民 今天 在 这里 会见 了 斯维尔德 洛
夫斯克 州 州长 斯特拉霍夫 和 叶卡捷琳堡 市 市长 切尔涅茨基。

The same sentence without word delimiter:

　　新华社叶卡捷琳堡 9 月 5 日电（记者李红旗 黄慧珠）中华人民共
和国主席江泽民今天在这里会见了斯维尔德洛夫斯克州州长斯特拉霍夫
和叶卡捷琳堡市市长切尔涅茨基。

Category [_____]

FIGURE 8.2　　A sample Chinese sentence with and without word delimiters.

In both the reimplementation of BSelect Click 2 and the construction of the text segmenter, ambiguity is a major problem. Since both rely heavily on dictionary lookup to find the possible boundaries of a word (we will discuss the implementation in detail in the next section), sometimes there are one or more substrings in a sentence that appear as words in the dictionary. It usually requires semantic knowledge from the context to judge which substring is a meaningful word and which is not.

Figure 8.3 shows the three different segmentation results (we call them readings) for the same sentence. In English, the sentence means "I forgot where Liberate Street is." Among them only the first is meaningful; the other two do not make any sense. But it is not easy to distinguish the correct one without semantic analysis.

FIGURE 8.3   Three different readings for a sentence.

Figure 8.4 displays a more interesting example. This sentence has two different readings and both are meaningful. Moreover, the literal meanings of the two results contradict each other. The first reading means "The president's forced-resignation calms down people's anger," while the second reading has a totally contradicting meaning as "The president's forced-resignation (makes) people angry."

For this kind of problem, neither dictionary lookup nor semantic analysis can tell which is the correct one. That can only be determined according to the context.

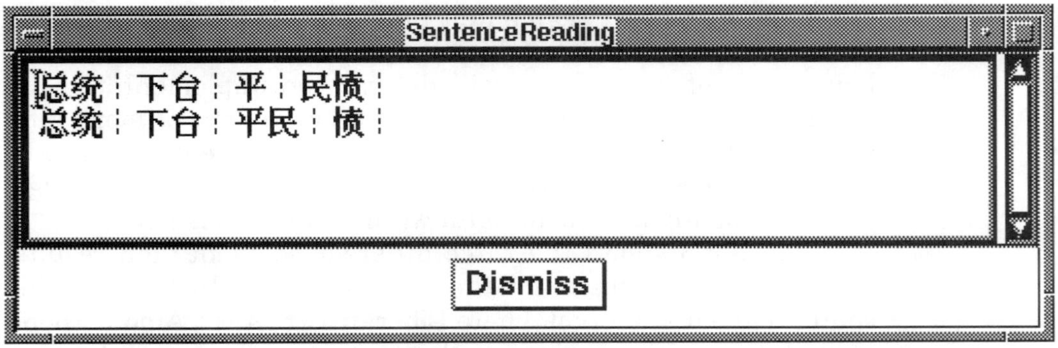

FIGURE 8.4   Two different readings both make sense yet contradict each other.

Now the question is, how much should the text widget be involved in the segmentation procedure? The answer is that it depends upon the level of the text operation. In the following section, we will categorize the operations into three levels as word, sentence, and file, and discuss the corresponding segmentation requirements.

The Operation Levels

The segmentation-related operations are categorized into three levels as word, sentence, and file.

Word Level   At the word level, we focus on how to find all possible words which cover a certain text point, usually the point where BSelect Click 2 happens, and represent their boundaries.

1. For text in implicit segmented mode: As indicated before, for a given point in a sentence there may exist more than one substring which contains all dictionary words covering that point. For example, given a sentence consisting of seven characters (here we use English characters to denote Chinese characters), ABCDEFG, and the current cursor position at D, substring CD and substring DEF are all dictionary entries (both include D). We are not able to tell which is the correct one by semantics at this point by the dictionary lookup alone. Although more sophisticated algorithms are available to solve the ambiguity, they are usually time consuming. It may not be a good idea to spend ten seconds or so in responding to a simple BSelect Click 2. So instead of invoking a semantic analysis procedure, we simply present all possibilities to the user through what we call *select circle*, which is described below.

   The first BSelect Click 2 on character D will make a selection on DEF, the longest word. Next time, without the cursor moving, it will make a selection on CD, the second longest word, and then D itself since each single Chinese character could possibly be a word. Now if we BSelect Click 2 on D one more time, DEF will be selected again.

2. For text in explicit mode: BSelect Click 2 behaves as its convention, selecting the portion of string between two boundaries.

Sentence Level   At the sentence level, we focus on how a sentence can be segmented. Issues under consideration include the recognition and representation of ambiguity, and the support to the user editor for segmentation as well.

Approximately more than 90 percent of all sentences in a selection of text are not ambiguous. For the others, we need to present all of the possibilities to the user, along with a preferred suggestion.

Sentence ambiguities come from the overlapping of those substrings appearing as dictionary entries in the sentence. Consider the previous example: In the sentence ABCDEFG there are four substrings found as words in the dictionary: AB, CD, DEF, and EFG. Each single Chinese character could possibly be a word. So there could be eight different readings (r) for this sentence:

> r1: AB CD EFG
> r2: A B CD EFG
> r3: AB C D EFG
> r4: AB CD E F G
> r5: AB C DEF G
> r6: A B C DEF G
> r7: AB C D E F G
> r8: A B C D E F G

Obviously, this is not a good result. Actually, the number of multiples could be largely reduced based on a fairly safe assumption:

Suppose r: S1 $X_1X_2 \ldots X_n$ S2 and r': S1 $X_1X_2 \ldots X_n$ S2 are different readings generated from a same sentence, where S1 and S2 are the substring as the first and last part of the sentence and X_i ($i = 1, 2, \ldots n$) are substrings in between, which make r' different from r. In reading r, $X_1X_2 \ldots X_n$ is recognized as one single word, but in reading r', it is segmented into n words as $X_1 X_2 \ldots X_n$. In this case, r' could be eliminated, or, say, r' could be absorbed by r.

Apply this assumption to the example: r2, r3, and r4 are absorbed by r1, r8 is absorbed by r7, and r6 and r7 are absorbed by r5. Then only two readings are left:

r1: AB CD EFG
r5: AB C DEF G

which is a better result. In implementation, we use a leftmost-first strategy to pick r1 as the default result for the explicit segmented sentence, and present both to the user in a separate small dialog text area. The user is allowed to edit the segment result (but not the text) in that text area and substitute the correct one by a drag-and-drop operation, if the user disagrees with the default result.

File Level At file level, the procedure for segmenting a sentence is called successively for each sentence in the file to convert the text display from implicit segmented mode to explicit segmented mode.

To convert text from explicit segmented mode back to implicit segmented mode, simply remove all delimiters between words.

The Lexicon Database

Most of the previous work to do with Chinese segmentation has placed emphasis on the completeness and preciseness of the segmentation result. Some algorithms strongly attempt to group as many characters as possible together to form big segments. This will benefit consequent language processing since, normally, it is considered that with larger dictionary coverage, more possibilities will be found and better results will be achieved. The cost of ambiguity resolving is not considered as a critical issue by these algorithms.

When applied to graphical text interfaces, however, the performance of the segmentation algorithm becomes an important issue and the size of dictionary needs to be reconsidered. With a larger-size dictionary, more words can be identified, but the possibility of segmentation ambiguity increases as well.

For example, consider a phrase UVWXYZ, and suppose UV

means "Chinese," WX means "news," and YZ means "network." A small dictionary may only have words UV, WX, and YZ. So there is no ambiguity. The phrase will be segmented as:

UV WX YZ   [Chinese] [news] [network]

But a larger dictionary may contain also UVWX and WXYZ, which will cause the extra ambiguity as:

UVWX YZ   [Chinese news] [network]

and

UV WXYZ   [Chinese] [news network]

The reason is that the large dictionary contains compound words. The existence of compound words is one of the several reasons for this kind of unexpected ambiguity. Other reasons could be the derived words and person names in the dictionary. Rarely used words and technical terminology usually cause trouble more than they help.

This segmentation system used the Chinese lexicon from CRL, which is still under construction. It is a synthesis of several Chinese-Chinese and Chinese-English dictionaries, taking into account the frequency of words from on-line Chinese text and excluding all compound words and derived words. There are currently about 57,500 entries in this lexicon.

The search management mechanism utilizes a Btree so that the searching cost is bounded to the logarithm of the dictionary size.

THE IMPLEMENTATION

This work is implemented under X-Window/Motif environment and SunOS operating system on Sun workstations, using C programming language. As we discussed earlier, the segmentation operation for the graphical text display is divided into three levels: word, sentence, and file.

At the word level, we extend the word selection convention

by a mechanism called *select circle*. At the sentence level, we utilize and customize the algorithms from previous research to segment a whole sentence and enumerate all possible readings, if there exists more than one segmentation. At the file level, we provide the user an ability to switch the text display between ISM (implicit segmented mode) and ESM (explicit segmented mode).

Select Circle

Overriding the Translations of the Xmat Widget *Actions* and *translations* are the underlying mechanisms we use to implement select circle. An action is one of the techniques implemented in the X11/Xt toolkit which links certain operations and procedures to a user interface. An action is always triggered by some X event or event combination through an Xt mechanism called the *translation table*. For more information on the action and translation table, refer to Chapter 4 of *X Toolkit Intrinsics Programming Manual* (Nye/O'Reilly 1992).

Actions for Select Circle As discussed in the section on design considerations, select circle is an extension to the Motif style for BSelect Click 2 in order to represent the multipossibilities of the word selection. To implement this extension, we define and register several new actions and override the translation table entries of the Xmat widget. The most important one among them is the action for select circle. There are three cases, based on where a double click BSelect Click 2 happens, to be handled by this action:

Case 1: BSelect Click 2 happens on an ASCII portion of the text. For this case the action simply follows the X convention.

Case 2: BSelect Click 2 happens on a Chinese string. The action looks at the text region consisting of (a) the Chinese character that BSelect Click 2 happens on and (b) the Chinese strings with the length of the longest word in the Chinese dictionary at both sides of the character in (a). Then it searches this region exhaustively to find all possible words.

The following example illustrates the search. Suppose the length of the word in the lexicon is four characters (in reality, the maximum length of the word in a lexicon could be eight or nine characters) and the user clicks on D in the text:

```
......ABCDEFG......
```

Then the search will go through all possible words as listed at the left side of the following table. The results are shown at the right side.

look up	is a word?
ABCD	no
BCDE	no
CDEF	no
DEFG	no
BCD	no
CDE	no
DEF	yes
CD	yes
DE	no

So, in this example, a select circle will be created by words CD, DEF, and D itself. Obviously, the cost for the select circle is $O(\text{maximum-word-length}^2)$ which is a constant.

Case 3: BSelect Click 2 happens on a double-byte alphabet or digit portion. For this case the action emulates the X convention.

In a Chinese and English mixed text, what happens upon a BSelect Click 2, that is, what is selected, depends on where the double click happens and the neighboring characters. For the three cases discussed above, case 1 and case 3 do not have ambiguity, that is, multiple possibilities of selection, but case 2 has, as shown in the example.

Test and Result   Figure 8.5 shows the results from a sequence of BSelect Click 2 on the last character but one in a Chinese sentence. The sixth and seventh characters together form a possible word and so do the seventh and eighth. The seventh character could be a word by itself.

When a user keeps double-clicking, the selection iterates

FIGURE 8.5   A test for select circle in Chinese text.

among these three. This is a main feature at the word level. For the ASCII portion and double-byte alphabet/digit portion in a text, selection behaves the same as the Motif convention.

Sentence Readings

Sentence reading is at the second level of the segmentation mechanism. In this level we try to find how many different ways a (Chinese) sentence could be segmented based upon the result of dictionary lookup.

The procedure for sentence reading generation is triggered by the X event of **\<btn3up\>**.

As for select circle, there are also three cases: (1) ASCII string, (2) Chinese character, and (3) double-byte alphabet/digit. Let us use an example to illustrate the procedure. Consider the example given in the section on operation levels at the sentence level. In sentence ABCDEFG, there are four substrings that could be found as "word" by dictionary lookup. They are AB, CD, DEF, and EFG. If we send this sentence as the input to the sentence segmentation procedure, it will generate the intermediate result as:

```
A 4 2
B 2
C 4 2
D 6 2
E 6 2
F 2
G 2
```

Note that one Chinese character takes memory space of two ASCII bytes. The result says that the four-byte (or two-character) substring that starts from A, namely AB, could be word, and A by itself could also be a word. Similarly, the six-byte (or three-character) substring that starts from character D, namely DEF is a possible word, and D by itself is also a word.

By sending the intermediate result for our sample

ABCDEFG to this procedure, the output will contain two different readings as:

```
AB CD EFG
AB C DEF G
```

Figures 8.6 and 8.7 show the segmentation for a selected sentence. To segment a particular sentence, move the mouse pointer to any place on that sentence and click the right mouse button. The sentence to be segmented will be surrounded by a box and the result will be presented in a small popup window. We use a small virtual vertical bar as the delimiter, but the user may also choose whitespace.

In most cases, there is only one sentence generated. For most of the rest there are two different readings. But sometimes, in rare cases, none of the readings provided are correct. Then the user may want to make some corrections by hand. We consider this an aspect of text editing and allow, but restrict, the user doing this in the small popup window. For example, in Figure 8.8, the first delimiter at the second line is removed to make the determination, and the following classifier is a single word.

FIGURE 8.6   Select a sentence to segment.

FIGURE 8.7   Multiple readings of the selected sentence.

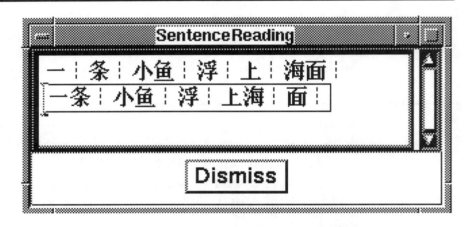

FIGURE 8.8   User editing: The delimiter between the determinative and the classifier (measure word) is removed.

Implicit and Explicit Segmented Modes

At the file level, ISM (implicit segmented mode) and ESM (explicit segmented mode) are two modes used for text display. In ISM there is no delimiter between words; the text is displayed in its original style. The user can check the boundaries of a word by a BSelect Click 2, which selects one or one of several words by select circle, or segment a sentence by clicking on the sentence using the right mouse button. Sometimes the user may also want to see the whole file in the ESM, that is, with delimiters between words.

The text displayed on the widget in ISM can be converted into ESM by successively invoking generating-a-reading procedure, a simplified version of generating multireading. Actually, the only difference between them is that the latter recursively generates all different readings for the sentence, and the former returns only the first reading it finds but indicates the existence of multireadings by a boolean flag. When the segmented sentence is displayed on the text widget, it will be underlined if this boolean flag indicates the ambiguity of the sentence.

To convert text from ESM to ISM is trivial. Simply remove all delimiters and underlines from all sentences.

The actual use of user editing for sentence segmenting lies in the file level. At this level, a whole section of text can be segmented and displayed. Figures 8.9 and 8.10 show two text

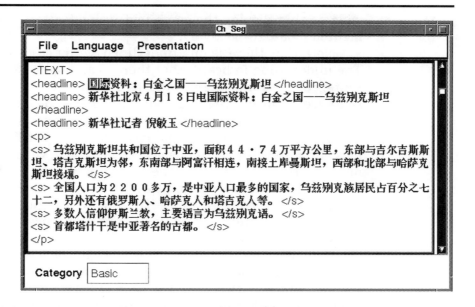

FIGURE 8.9   A text displayed in ISM.

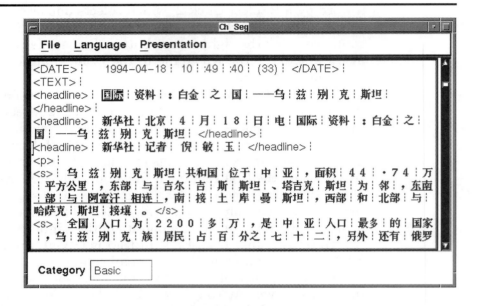

FIGURE 8.10   A text displayed in ESM.

widgets that display the same text in implicit and explicit segmented mode, respectively.

Note that there is one underlined sentence in Figure 8.10. The underlining indicates that there is ambiguity found for this sentence. So if the user conducts a sentence segment on this sentence, multiple readings will be generated. For a sentence with multiple readings, the system chooses one among several as the default. The default is based on a longest-first and leftmost-first strategy. If the user does not agree with the decision made by the system, he or she can bring up the auxiliary window which gives all possibilities. From this window, the user can pick the correct reading, if it exists, and make a replacement of the default reading in the main text area by the drag-and-drop mechanism.

If none of the candidates presented in the sentence reading window is correct, the user can do some hand editing on the reading which is closest to the correct version. The user is *not* allowed to input or delete any character in the sentence reading window.

DISCUSSIONS

This project is a very successful attempt at Chinese text segmentation. There has been no similar work reported before, although considerable research and development has been conducted in both language segmentation or multilingual display. Previously, research in language segmentation usually aimed at providing benefits and convenience for further language processing procedures such as part-of-speech tagging or semantic analysis, while the value in supporting graphical text display had not been properly realized. On the other hand, developments of multilingual text display and editing usually concentrate on issues like internal code (codeset), font/size variation, printing, and input method. But problems concerning presentation and operation conventions created by introducing writing systems other than English have not gained the deserved attention. This work demonstrated the possibility and benefits of applying the research resulting from language segmentation, especially Chinese, to the user interface of multilingual displays.

There are more issues which deserve to be addressed:

1. Algorithms for language segmentation usually need to be revised before being applied to a user interface. Many segmenters may not consider computation cost a critical issue. They ask for relatively large memory space and execution time. But for GUI operations, like mouse clicking, the response time is a big issue. So some high-cost procedures may not be adoptable. For example, why do we use select circle to represent the multiple words, rather than try to solve the ambiguity? It is true that there have been so many methods which reportedly do this. But there is no solution without heavy computation and to be kept waiting ten seconds or more just for the response from a mouse click may not be acceptable to the user.

2. Client/server computation could be a potential solution. By installing the lexicon database and a set of segmentation procedures on the segmentation server, the front-end display could be released. The client just needs to send the plain sentence to the server, which has the required com-

putability to do the segmentation or even sophisticated processing like sentence disambiguation, and wait for the outcome from the server. This way, much more of the achievement from segmentation research could be applied to support the user interface.

3. In the current system, an SGML-like notation is used to keep and represent segmentation results in persistent media. However, the annotation mechanism in the Xmat text widget is also a very good way to store, retrieve, and manipulate the segmentation information. The main advantages of using the annotation ability are:
   - A sentence or text could be presegmented, segmented on the fly, or edited by the user manually and saved back to disk without converting the data format.
   - It is very easy to attach new data/messages on them, like part-of-speech tags.
   - It is easy to convert to and from SGML format.
   - It is a rich feature for text appearance.

CONCLUSIONS

This chapter illustrates that the research results of Chinese segmentation are of great value in solving the tokenization and segmentation problems in graphical user interfaces for Chinese display. This could be a new application area beyond its traditional domain. However, to be applied in a GUI project, customizing of the algorithms is required because of the difference in considerations and emphasis. Generally, performance is the deciding factor as to whether the segmentation method can be adopted.

On the other hand, multilingual text representation has evolved considerably in the past few years; issues like font size variation, input methods, and printing have drawn a lot of attention from developers in this field and significant results have been achieved. However, issues like style and convention in introducing multilingual text display have not been studied sufficiently. Actually these issues might not be solved solely by GUI efforts.

Although this type of research is in its initial stages, encouraging prospects have been clearly demonstrated.

REFERENCES

Chang, J. S. et al. 1991. Chinese word segmentation through constraint satisfaction and statistical optimization. *Proceedings of the Fourth R.O.C. Computational Linguistics Conference*, 147–165.

Chen, K. J. and S. H. Liu. 1992. Word identification for Mandarin Chinese sentences. *Proceedings of the Fifth International Conference on Computational Linguistics*, vol. 1, 101–107.

Chiang, T. H. et al. 1992. Statistical model for segmentation and unknown word resolution. *Proceedings of the Fifth R.O.C. Computational Linguistics Conference*, 123–146.

He, K. K., H. Xu, and B. Sun. 1991. The design principle for a written Chinese automatic segmentation expert system. *Journal of Chinese Information Processing* **5**, 2: 1–14.

Jin, W. 1992. A case study: Chinese segmentation and its disambiguation. *MCCS-92-227*, Computing Research Laboratory, New Mexico State University.

Jin, W. 1994. Chinese segmentation disambiguation. *Proceedings of the International Computational Linguistics COLING'94*, Japan, 1245–1249.

Jin, W. and J. Y. Nie. 1993. Segmentation du Chinois—Une Etape Cruciale vers la Traduction Automatique du Chino is. In Bouillon P., and A. Clas (eds.) *La Traductique*. Montreal: Les presses de l'Université de Montreal, 349–363.

Leisher, M., and B. Ogden. 1993. Multi-attribute text: The low level library and text widget. *Computing Research Laboratory Technical Report*, New Mexico State University.

Liang, N. Y. and Y. B. Zhen. 1991. A Chinese word segmentation model and a Chinese word segmentation system PC-CWSS, *Proceedings of COLIPS*, vol. 1, no. 1, 51–55.

Nie, J. Y., W. Jin, and M. L. Hannan. 1994. A hybrid approach to unknown word detection and segmentation of Chinese. *Proceedings of International Conference on Chinese Computing '94*, Singapore, 326–335.

Nye, A., and T. O'Reilly. 1992. *X Toolkit Intrinsics Programming Manual*. O'Reilly & Associates.

Open Software Foundation. 1991. *OSF/Motif Style Guide*. Englewood Cliffs, NJ: Prentice Hall.

Sproat, R., and C. Shih. 1991. A statistical method for finding word boundaries in Chinese text. *Computer Processing of Chinese and Oriental Languages* **4**, 4: 336–351.

Sproat, R., C. Shih, W. Gale, and N. Chang. 1994. A stochastic finite-state word-segmentation algorithm for Chinese. *Proceedings of the*

Thirty-second Annual Meeting of the Association for Computational Linguistics, 66–73.

Sun, M. S. et al. 1992. Some issues on the statistical approach to Chinese word identification. *Proceedings of the Third International Conference on Chinese Information Processing*, 246–253.

Wang, L. J., T. Pei, W. C. Li, and L. C. Huang. 1991. A parsing method for identifying words in Mandarin Chinese sentences. *Proceedings of the Twelfth International Joint Conference on Artificial Intelligence*, vol. 2, 1018–1023.

Yang, J. 1994. An efficient data structure to maintain the text attribute of multi-lingual text widget Xmat and a GUI for handling the attributes. *MCCS-94-280*, Computing Research Laboratory, New Mexico State University.

ABOUT THE AUTHORS

Professor Wanying Jin is a research fellow at the Computing Research Laboratory (CRL), New Mexico State University. Her research interests are machine translation, Chinese segmentation, and natural language processing. She is the designer of the Chinese segmenter and one of the designers of several machine translation systems developed at CRL. She has a number of research papers published in various international conferences and journals, and a series of MCCS research papers published by CRL.

Before joining CRL, Wanying Jin was an associate professor in Shanghai University of Technology at Shanghai, China, a visiting scholar in the AI laboratory at the University at Texas at Austin, and a visiting professor at Rochester Institute of Technology. She graduated from the Mathematics and Physics Department in Tong-Ji University in 1962. She had been teaching at various universities in China for twenty years before working in the United States.

Lei Chen is a software engineer in Object Systems Integrators Co. (OSI), Atlanta, Georgia. Currently, he focuses on the design and implementation of GUI for commercial network management products. His professional skills involve GUI design, object-oriented design and programming, client/server and other network programming, relational database application, and multilingual information processing.

Before joining OSI Chen was a research assistant in Computing Research Laboratory (CRL) at New Mexico State University, software engineer at Shanghai Computer Software Laboratory in China, and system manager at ThreeStar Industrial Co. in China.

Lei Chen received his M.S. degree in Computer Science at New Mexico State University in 1994; an M.S. in Computer and Information Science at Shanghai University of Technology in 1988; and a B.S. in Computer Engineering at Shanghai University of Technology in 1985. He was honored to have his name listed in Baron's *Who's Who of Asia Pacific Rim*, 1992 edition. He also received the Phillips Petroleum Scholarship Award in 1995.

CHAPTER 9

Case Study: Managing a Multiple-Language Document System

INTRODUCTION

Those involved in the development of software for international use are familiar with topics such as date and time formats, reading order, hyphenation, and color. These issues often come into play when localizing products to a specific culture. These products are often developed for one language and culture, and then translated or localized to another language and culture. However, with the globalization of our economy and the resultant increase in the number of companies doing business across national boundaries, an additional challenge must be faced. That challenge is the concurrent use of a single system (i.e., hardware, software, and data) by users representing any number of languages and cultures.

INTERNATIONAL CHEMICAL DATASHEET SYSTEM

One such system which attempts to deal with certain aspects of this issue is the International Chemical Datasheet System (ICDS), developed in partnership by Eastman Kodak Company and International Business Machines. ICDS is a mainframe database application developed for those who must create and distribute documents known as Material Safety Data Sheets

(MSDSs). An MSDS is a multipage document containing health and safety information which must be provided to any purchaser of a chemical product. The document must be provided in the customer's own language and must meet the regulatory requirements specified by that customer's government. As Kodak's international business grew, their Health and Environment Laboratories recognized the need to control the rising translation costs for these documents, and to reduce the duplication of effort taking place at Kodak sites around the world. ICDS was developed for this purpose.

CHALLENGES OF A MULTIPLE-LANGUAGE SYSTEM

This case study will focus on the issues of managing a database application containing data in multiple languages, and the concurrent use of a system by users of different languages. ICDS makes use of language libraries to facilitate the creation of MSDSs. These libraries consist of phrases and sentences commonly used in MSDSs. Each time a new language is implemented in ICDS, the library of phrases must be translated and then imported into the database. These phrases are translated one time into the new language, thus greatly reducing translation costs per document as the phrases are reused. Adding a new language is a multistep process which must guarantee the preservation of special characters associated with a particular language. A variety of characters from varying languages may all share the same hexadecimal code, and once stored, there is nothing unique about that hexadecimal code that would indicate which language it is intended to represent. Therefore, emphasis must be placed on storing data for a given language in a way that is consistent with the method that will be used to retrieve it. Likewise, each time that the data is retrieved for the purpose of display or print, special attention must be given to interpreting the data in a manner consistent with the method used for storage.

CODE PAGES

At the heart of many issues related to a multiple-language system is the representation of individual characters. All characters which are stored in a computer system, regardless of the language, must be stored using a numerical encoding method which assigns a unique number to each character. Among the more commonly used encoding methods are ASCII and EBCDIC.

The relationship between the numerical values and the characters they represent is described using what are called *code pages*. A code page acts as a cross-reference describing the one-to-one translation of characters in a particular language's character set to the numerical value that represents that character in the computer's memory. A partial example of a code page is given in Table 9.1.

Although these encoding methods generally work well, there are some inherent limitations. First, there is a limit to the number of characters which can be represented. Seven-bit encoding schemes (allowing up to 128 values) and 8-bit encoding schemes (allowing up to 256 values) are simply not large enough to accommodate the character sets of many languages. While attempts are being made to standardize encoding schemes which accommodate the larger character sets, a very significant number of computer installations are still dependent upon these 7- and 8-bit schemes.

Another problem arises when multiple code pages exist for the same encoding scheme. Each code page represents a different *mapping* of the numerical values to characters. While this does allow the same scheme to be used for different languages, thus reducing many of the costs associated with hardware and software production, it does bring about potential problems. One such problem is the potential conflict between the code pages. The term *conflict* is used to describe the situation where the same numerical value represents two different characters, or a single character is represented by two different numerical values depending upon the code page being used.

PC Code Pages

Consider the example of code page conflict illustrated in Tables 9.1 and 9.2. Suppose that a user in the United States attempts to create a French document for her counterpart in Canada. The document is created on an IBM PC using the U.S. English code page (DOS code page 437). Please note in Table 9.1 that this code

TABLE 9.1   **U.S. English (437) Code Page**

32		61	=	90	Z	119	w	148	ö
33	!	62	>	91	[	120	x	149	ò
34	"	63	?	92	\	121	y	150	û
35	#	64	@	93	]	122	z	151	ù
36	$	65	A	94	^	123	{	152	ÿ
37	%	66	B	95	_	124	|	153	ö
38	&	67	C	96	`	125	}	154	Ü
39	'	68	D	97	a	126	~	155	¢
40	(	69	E	98	b	127		156	£
41	)	70	F	99	c	128	Ç	157	¥
42	*	71	G	100	d	129	ü	158	
43	+	72	H	101	e	130	é	159	ƒ
44	,	73	I	102	f	131	â	160	á
45	-	74	J	103	g	132	ä	161	í
46	.	75	K	104	h	133	à	162	ó
47	/	76	L	105	i	134	å	163	ú
48	0	77	M	106	j	135	ç	164	ñ
49	1	78	N	107	k	136	ê	165	Ñ
50	2	79	O	108	l	137	ë	166	ª
51	3	80	P	109	m	138	è	167	º
52	4	81	Q	110	n	139	ï	168	¿
53	5	82	R	111	o	140	î		
54	6	83	S	112	p	141	ì		
55	7	84	T	113	q	142	Ä		
56	8	85	U	114	r	143	Å		
57	9	86	V	115	s	144	É		
58	:	87	W	116	t	145	æ		
59	;	88	X	117	u	146	Æ		
60	<	89	Y	118	v	147	ô		

page does provide the special characters that would be needed. Suppose that the characters ì, í, á, and ¥ are used throughout the document. The document is saved on a disk and sent to Canada where the document is viewed on a computer using the French Canadian code page (DOS code page 863). However when viewing the document, it appears that all the ì, í, á, and ¥ characters have been converted to =, ', |, and Ù respectively.

In reality, the representation of the characters in the computer's memory (or on the disk) has not changed at all. What has changed is the code page used to interpret the characters. Taking the ì character as an example, we see from Table 9.1 that the numerical value that was stored during document creation would have been 141. However, looking at the code page in Table 9.2 which was used by the Canadian user to view the document, we can see that the value 141 translates to the = character. The underlying data is still "correct," but this example highlights the problems which can arise as a result of code page conflicts.

Host Code Pages

The problem described above becomes further complicated when desktop computers are being used to communicate with mainframe computers, as was the case with ICDS. The introduction of the mainframe computer brings with it a whole new set of code pages that must be coordinated. Even for the same country and language, a mainframe code page, or "host" code page may be very different from the code page used by the desktop computer. Communication between the two therefore requires strict attention to the code pages in use, and the method used by the communication software to perform the translations.

TRANSMITTING DATA

The interaction of desktop and mainframe code pages was felt most heavily in the ICDS project during the process of preparing language translations. ICDS was designed to contain libraries of common phrases which had been translated into many different languages. Since translation was often performed by an outside vendor, a mechanism was needed to manipulate the translated phrases which were received. Following a review and reconciliation process, these phrases were merged into the ICDS libraries which resided in a DB2 database on an IBM mainframe. Figure 9.1 illustrates the typical path that a set of translations would follow and the points at which proper code page selection was made.

TABLE 9.2   French Canadian (863) Code Page

32		61	=	90	Z	119	w	148	Ë
33	!	62	>	91	[	120	x	149	Ï
34	"	63	?	92	\	121	y	150	û
35	#	64	@	93	]	122	z	151	ù
36	$	65	A	94	^	123	{	152	
37	%	66	B	95	_	124	|	153	ö
38	&	67	C	96	`	125	}	154	Ü
39	'	68	D	97	a	126	~	155	¢
40	(	69	E	98	b	127		156	£
41	)	70	F	99	c	128	Ç	157	Ù
42	*	71	G	100	d	129	ü	158	Û
43	+	72	H	101	e	130	é	159	ƒ
44	,	73	I	102	f	131	â	160	|
45	-	74	J	103	g	132	Â	161	´
46	.	75	K	104	h	133	à	162	ó
47	/	76	L	105	i	134	¶	163	ú
48	0	77	M	106	j	135	ç	164	¨
49	1	78	N	107	k	136	ê	165	
50	2	79	O	108	l	137	ë	166	3
51	3	80	P	109	m	138	è	167	¯
52	4	81	Q	110	n	139	ï	168	Î
53	5	82	R	111	o	140	î		
54	6	83	S	112	p	141	=		
55	7	84	T	113	q	142	À		
56	8	85	U	114	r	143	§		
57	9	86	V	115	s	144	É		
58	:	87	W	116	t	145	È		
59	;	88	X	117	u	146	Ê		
60	<	89	Y	118	v	147	ô		

Translations were often received in a spreadsheet format along with numbers which helped to identify and link the phrases across language libraries. These translations were then manipulated by the Language Administrator on an IBM PC–compatible computer using spreadsheet and word process-

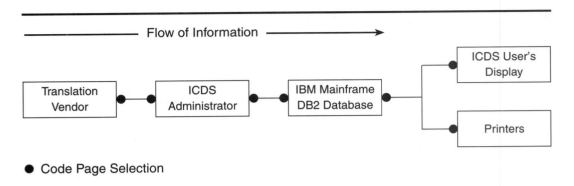

FIGURE 9.1 Data flow and code page selection points.

ing software which accommodated the special characters. The code page for the PC would need to be set consistently with the code page used to create the translations. When the translations were ready to be transmitted to the mainframe, they would be saved in a DOS Text format ("tx8").

The next step was to transmit the translations from the PC to the mainframe. This step took careful coordination. The communication software which was used had to be configured with two code pages. The first code page was the one which was used in creating the translations—the PC code page. The second code page was the code page on the mainframe that would be used to view the documents using this particular set of translations. It was the responsibility of the communication software to perform the necessary conversions when transmitting the data.

STORING DATA

Once the data had been successfully transmitted to the mainframe environment, it could be loaded into the DB2 database. This was one of the few steps where the code page(s) being used was not really relevant. The purpose of this step was simply to load textual data into the database. Since no interpretation of the data was taking place, the code page being used did not impact the results.

What was important, however, was storing information

along with the translation that would identify what language (and hence what code page) was used to create the data. The numerical values used to represent the translated characters provide no clues as to the language they are intended for, so language and code page information must be stored separately. Storing this information along with the textual data was crucial for it to later be interpreted correctly.

ACCESSING DATA ON-LINE

Once loaded into the database, the information was available for users to access from locations around the world. As in previous steps, the key element to being able to successfully retrieve the information was to use the same code page as was used to store the information. This again was performed using communication software which allowed the user to specify both the host code page and the PC code page to be used.

Terminals

Using simple display terminals, as opposed to desktop computers with communication software, did not prove to be very successful. This was due largely to the difficulty involved in setting desired code pages. In most cases the code page could only be set at the terminal control unit, which served many different terminals. This solution was not acceptable as it would adversely affect users who did not want or need the code page which was being set.

The solution was to use desktop computers along with communication software which provided easy switching of code pages. Using this combination of tools, a single user could retrieve MSDS documents in any number of languages from the same workstation without affecting other users on the system. Likewise, other users around the world could simultaneously access information from the system in their own native languages. The burden of interpreting the data was moved from the mainframe to the desktop where each user could accomplish the desired task independent of other users.

Controllers

Although the terminal control units played less of a role in this solution, there were still some surprising problems which arose. We found that certain control units were actually *filtering* the data before it reached the workstations. They were apparently configured in such a way that characters whose EBCDIC values were outside a certain range were considered *nondisplayable* and were converted to dots before being passed on to the workstation. This range was defined in such a way that many of the non-U.S. English characters (such as é, ö, ñ, etc.) were being filtered. As a result, even with the correct code pages being specified by the workstation communication software, unreadable information was being displayed for the user. Reconfiguring the control units, however, solved this problem, and allowed the communication software to have full control of character conversion.

PRINTING DATA

As one might expect, printing the documents posed many of the same challenges as displaying them. Again there was a software and a hardware element to the solution.

SCRIPT/VS was the primary software component which was used, allowing information to be formatted for the majority of mainframe printers in use. This software performed essentially the same function as the workstation communication software, using the appropriate code pages to perform character conversion and font selection. Having selected the appropriate fonts, the information could then be formatted for the destination printer.

In some cases, the printers themselves had to be reconfigured. Similar to the filtering which took place at the terminal control units, the default for some printers was to print only a subset of the full character set for the various code pages. Many of these printers were successfully reconfigured. Others were simply not capable of printing many of the special characters.

OTHER TRANSLATION ISSUES

There was one other issue in the area of translations that had to be taken into consideration. This had to do with field lengths for fields which would contain information from multiple languages. Special attention must be given to field lengths when designing a database for multiple languages due to the significant length variance which can occur from one language to another for the same phrase. A relatively short phrase in English, for example, may be quite long when translated to German. Variable-length fields are one way to accommodate unknown data lengths, but this situation may also require a certain level of self-imposed discipline on the part of the users.

CONCLUSION

The ICDS project represented substantial progress for Kodak and was considered very successful as an early venture into international systems. At the same time, it revealed many biases that exist in the systems world that pose formidable obstacles in using systems transparently for multiple-languages—biases that one would not expect in a world whose basic elements reduce to just 1s and 0s. This case study points out several areas in which hardware and software alike have been developed without consideration for their use in multiple-language environments. In many cases the resulting barriers are artificial and quite unnecessary. Still, there are many veritable challenges which the next generation of systems must address.

ABOUT THE AUTHOR

Residing in the United States, **Steve Copeland** is a partner with the consulting firm Schiesser-Copeland Consulting (SCC). SCC specializes in the design, development, and implementation of information systems. In addition to providing consulting services, Copeland has also developed software products for a variety of specialized industries including the IPS software package designed for college intramural sports programs.

Prior to his involvement with SCC, Copeland worked for Eastman Kodak Company for 10 years. During his tenure with Kodak, Copeland served as the Lead Systems Analyst in the design and implementation of the International Chemical Datasheet System (ICDS). ICDS is a database application developed in partnership with International Business Machines which is used to manage health and safety documents in a variety of languages and formats.

Copeland can be contacted at the following address:

Schiesser-Copeland Consulting, 1507 Wren Road, Bowling Green, OH 43402. Phone: (419) 352-8429, Internet: copeland @cs.bgsu.edu.

CHAPTER 10

The Design of Multilingual Documents

INTRODUCTION

Among the challenges facing those who produce products for multilingual markets (products that are available in more than one language) is how to design and deliver cost effectively the right documentation in the right format for all customers. Some markets require their documentation be delivered in more than one language due to government legislation, for example, Canada. In other cases, where linguistic markets are small, the only way to produce cost-effective documentation is by combining the linguistic preferences of a geographic area. In addition to providing more than one language within a document, the particular needs of a product and its market may dictate variations in language presentation techniques within a single document.

This chapter contains detailed information on a variety of layouts and formats for producing multilingual documentation as a solution to some of the publishing problems created by international markets and users. This chapter includes information on the design of covers, frontmatter, navigational aids, order of languages and identifiers, tables of contents, indexes, and the implementation and labeling of artwork. Design recommendations are accompanied by comments concerning the advantages and disadvantages of each technique. This chapter avoids discussing more general internationalization issues pertaining to the writing of documentation and production of graphics. There are several other publications which cover these issues in great detail (Hoft 1995; Jones et al. 1991). In addition, this chapter does not address standard documentation design guidelines, as there are many other publications that address these issues (BSI 7649 1993).

Throughout this chapter, examples of manual designs are used. In order to illustrate different languages a variety of methods have been used. The language names are represented in their own language in alphabetical order (e.g., Deutsch, English, Español, Français, and Italiano). The languages selected as examples have no relevance to language selection when providing manuals to customers. This is a business decision. Illustrations are simplified by not including too many details and representing language variants by using different shades of gray or patterns. Although color is not used in this particular publication, its use in multilingual document design can be very effective. The use of color has been demonstrated by using shades of gray. Information on the use of color in documentation and its localization implications can be found in other publications (Fernandes 1995).

WHAT IS MULTILINGUAL DOCUMENTATION?

A multilingual document is defined by the fact that the information it contains is present in more than one language and those languages can be viewed simultaneously by the user. In well-designed multilingual documentation, the languages usually appear in a consistent pattern throughout the document. There are a variety of possible arrangements and layouts of the information by language variant. There are cases where mixing style within a single manual can be effective, but this is not normally a recommended practice. It is more usual for a single formatting style to dominate a document with only variations in style in the front- or backmatter of the publication.

WHY PRODUCE MULTILINGUAL DOCUMENTATION?

There are two categories of requirements that affect the justification for producing multilingual documents. The first category, and maybe the most important, is based on country or region-specific legislation. In the second category, factors such as business justification, marketing strategies, usability, and cost reduction affect the decision to produce multilingual documents.

Many countries have legislation that requires particular types of documents to be multilingual or provided in all official languages. For example, countries such as Canada (French and English), Belgium (French, Flemish, German), Switzerland (French, German, Italian), and Finland (Finnish, Swedish) have multilingual publishing requirements. Other countries, such as France, Spain, Denmark, Germany, and Austria have legislation that requires specific information, particularly user manuals, to be provided in the local language. There are also many international organizations and companies that require publications in more than one language, for example, organizations such as the United Nations, which has six official languages, and the International Standards Organization (ISO), which has two official languages. Even some countries which are unilingual have legislation that requires translation of information on safety, installation, and user documentation.

It may be advantageous to provide customers with documentation that not only meets legislative requirements, but also meets the corporate and user needs of a global marketplace. International companies which have an official company language find that productivity is improved when documentation for computer-related products is provided in the employees' mother tongue as well as the company language. There are several advantages. Users are more receptive to new products and find problem solving or error correction easier when the documentation is provided in their mother tongue. Users in a locale can communicate or train other users in their own language, but also having the same information in the company language allows users to converse across locales in a common language.

The cost-saving factor can be deceiving. At first it may appear that the production of multilingual documentation will be more expensive. Cost savings as a result of providing multi-lingual documentation may stem from a decrease in the activities required to provide the correct language version to a customer. Some companies provide language versions with every product shipped and the customer just disposes of the language versions they do not need. Vendor costs of packaging and distribution can be decreased just because the manufacturer only has to include one set of documentation for each product. In this case, the cost of producing a single multilingual version can be less compared to providing several separate language versions. Investigate thoroughly all of the hidden costs of producing and distributing manuals in order to have an accurate indication of cost.

Another benefit that is attractive to customers is that providing both company and local language documents allows the company to hire the most capable applicant, regardless of their proficiency in the company language. Thus, there is a variety of factors which can influence an organization's decision to produce multilingual documentation. Below is a list of some of the reasons why the choice of a multilingual format can be beneficial to both the vendor and the customer.

- When icons or graphics are not rich enough to provide the necessary safety information.
- Where legislation requires information be provided in the local language.
- When the locale has more than one official language.
- Where international customers have an official company language, but the employees are of a variety of mother tongues and have varying language skills.
- When customers are located in regions that are unofficially bilingual (for example, in Miami, Florida).
- Economically and logistically, it can be cheaper and simpler to provide and distribute one document in many languages than many documents in many languages.
- Using documentation in a mother tongue can increase levels of productivity and reduce errors.
- When it is difficult to forecast numbers for production of manuals. By producing one manual for all languages, over-production can be reduced.

- The production of multilingual documentation forces simultaneous shipment of local versions. The product language variants reach the market sooner and begins to make a profit sooner.

DOCUMENT FORMATS

All multilingual document formats are constrained by the size of the original language document and the ability to configure the different formats electronically for publishing in an efficient and cost-effective manner. Some formats are more difficult to produce than others. The level of difficulty depends heavily on the availability of tools to produce the formats, the document content and function, the percentage of graphics, the number of languages, the complexity of the chosen format, and the design and size of the original document.

Some publications may call for a mixing of formats because the document contains different types of information. For example, consider a manual that contains installation instructions and the user guide for a single product. The installation instructions may contain a great deal of graphics. An effective way to present this information is to use a single illustration for all languages. This is known as a *stacked format*. The user guide may be very complex and contain step-by-step instructions. An effective way to present this information is to provide separate language sections. This is known as a *collated format*. The following sections provide descriptions of a variety of multilingual documentation formats.

Collated

Of all the formats available, the collated format is the easiest to produce and publish. This is because it is the closest to a unilingual version of a document that a multilingual document can get. It is simply a collection of several different language versions of the same document. A collated manual is created by taking two or more complete language variants and placing them one on top of the other. All the language variants are then bound into a single manual. This format is usable for almost any publication when the original document is under approximately 150 pages. The disadvantage of this type of manual is that in some cases it can become very large and its size can eventually be restricted by available binding methods. Also, depending on the frequency of use of a publication (e.g., tutorial, user guides, reference, installation), a large manual may become unwieldy.

Even though this method is one of the easiest to produce, the production of an effective collated multilingual manual requires the designer to address some additional design issues. A designer must consider how to convey on the front cover and spine of the manual that it is multilingual and also provide navigational aids within the manual to assist users in finding their particular language version. The manual will also need a title or cover page for the beginning of each new language version. These internal cover pages are unilingual and in the language of the section they precede.

Figure 10.1. shows an example of a collated manual using dark gray pages to illustrate the use of internal covers and white pages to represent the corresponding language sections. Color is not essential for the actual document pages. An alternative to color is to use heavier-weight paper for internal cover pages or a combination of both color and paper weight varia-

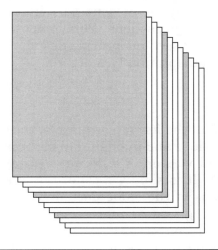

FIGURE 10.1   Collated format.

tions. This manual would also include a multilingual cover and spine, and possibly a document map placed just inside the front cover of the manual. See further sections in this chapter for more details on these elements.

Facing Pages

This method can only be used for bilingual documents. Languages are arranged such that one language appears on even-numbered pages and a second language appears on odd-numbered pages. This is the result of two different books which are paired to form a single publication, but each language version represents a complete publication in itself. No information is shared between the two language versions. The manual should be designed such that facing pages contain the same information. Figure 10.2 illustrates the facing-pages format. Figure 10.3 illustrates the use of the facing-pages format with callouts to a common illustration that extends or unfolds from the book such that it can be viewed simultaneously with the text. This design is particularly effective for documents that contain complicated and expensive-to-reproduce graphics. A particular advantage of using this method, as opposed to providing two separate collated books

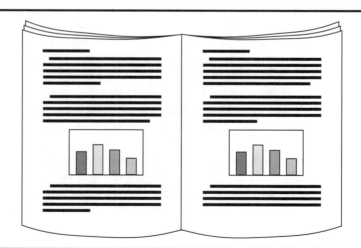

FIGURE 10.2   Facing pages format.

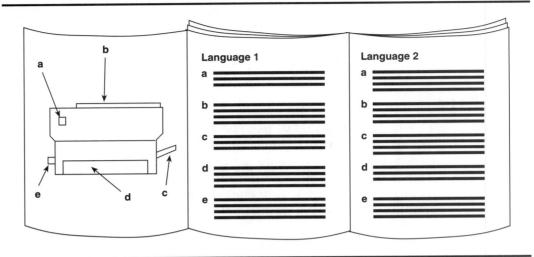

FIGURE 10.3   Facing pages with extended artwork.

within one publication, is that readers can refer to translations.

This format also allows user access to information in the local language, but where communication among colleagues of various mother tongues, is required, users can converse in the common language or organization language. This provides users with a standard translation and can alleviate problems that may occur when users try to translate from their mother tongue into the common language. Translation is a very difficult skill and even minor differences in translation can make very great differences in interpretation that can lead to a variety of problems. A single shared translation, done professionally, can lessen problems caused by on-the-spot translation.

A disadvantage of this format is that it may prove to be very difficult to produce manuals electronically as software must be able to handle the intertwining of two separate files. It also does not work well with two languages which have different writing directions or when translation results in gross differences in the length of the document. These two situations make it difficult to produce a manual with corresponding pages.

Side-by-Side

This format is used almost exclusively for bilingual documents, and only occasionally for trilingual documents. This is the format commonly used in Canada, where legislation requires public documents to appear in two languages. For this format each language is presented on every page by producing columns of text that run side-by-side down the page. The page is split vertically, with one language on the right and another on the left. When illustrations or figures are contained in the document, the design should try to allow for the use of a single figure for both languages. Figure 10.4 illustrates a page in side-by-side format where both languages are sharing a single graph. Note that the graph includes a caption for both languages.

Unfortunately, this format is not suited to documents that contain a great deal of graphics. Due to the fact that translation is very rarely a one-for-one exchange of words, it is very difficult to match exactly the positioning of one figure within two columns of text at the identical point. Text can expand between 30 and 100 percent, so even matching headers side-by-side

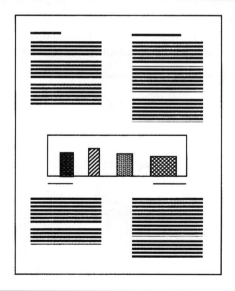

FIGURE 10.4   Side-by-side format.

across columns maybe difficult. It may be necessary to leave whitespace at the end of sections for one of the languages. An advantage of this format is that, although it looks complicated, it is fairly easy to produce electronically because each language can be dealt with separately.

Stacked

In this format translated language versions of text are stacked vertically. This format can only be used successfully where there is little text to be displayed. Preferably, the text should be a sequence of short or bulleted steps that can easily be divided into "stackable" chunks. Documents for which the stacked format is suitable often include a great deal of graphics or icons, such as installation guides or safety information. The number of languages should normally be limited to four, but in cases where there is very little text and a large percentage of the information is graphical, there can be up to ten. For example, illustrations of hardware using stacked callouts to label components are suitable for up to ten languages, providing the page size does not limit the amount of text or size of the illustrations. Figures 10.5 and 10.6 illustrate the use of the stacked format with artwork. In both figures each different shade of gray represents a different language.

The quality of illustrations and the layout of the text will determine the amount of success a user will have using docu-

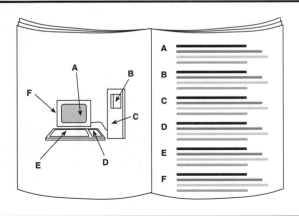

FIGURE 10.5   Stacked format using artwork callout.

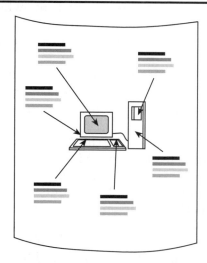

FIGURE 10.6   Stacked format for artwork labels.

mentation in this format. Numbering of the sequences of steps to be performed is always useful for guiding the user to the next step, but depending on the language mix, the document may require an additional numbering scheme for languages which do not use Arabic numerals. Languages that are not read from left to right and top to bottom may find following a sequence of steps in a counterclockwise direction unnatural. The same problem occurs for labeling a sequence of steps using letters when the mix of languages uses different character sets or vastly different collating sequences. Therefore, numbering and arrangement of a sequence of tasks to be performed based on the habits of one locale may not be appropriate for others. When preparing these types of documents it is best to use a professional graphic designer who is familiar with the idiosyncrasies of other cultures to assist in the layout of combined text and graphics.

Tumble

The tumble format is a bilingual format and can appear in two variations. Two complete language variants of a manual are placed back-to-back. When the manuals are bound together, they are oriented such that, when the manual is flipped over, the other language variant is oriented properly. Each variation has some similarities which are as follows:

- The spine of the book is bilingual.
- The manuals are two separate books.
- Each manual has its own separate cover page.

The difference in the two variations is the selection of the two languages to appear in the manual. When two languages of the same writing direction are used it is a *horizontal* tumble. When two languages of different writing directions and book reading direction are used, it is a *vertical* tumble.

In the case of horizontal tumble, a language pair is chosen which have identical writing directions. Language variants are positioned back-to-back and head-to-tail. When reading one language variant, the reader flips the book along a horizontal axis in order to position the second variant properly. See Figure 10.7 which shows the arrangement of pages from each variant as they are positioned relative to each other. In the case of vertical tumble, a language pair is chosen which have opposite writing and book reading directions, such as Japanese and English. Language variants are positioned back-to-back and head-to-

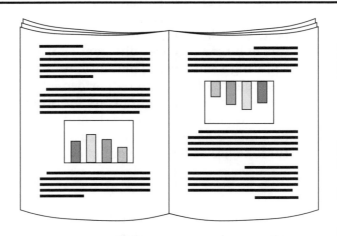

FIGURE 10.7   Horizontal tumble format.

head. In order to position the second variant properly for reading, the user flips the book along a vertical axis. See Figure 10.8, which shows the arrangement of pages from each variant as they are positioned relative to each other. Although Figures 10.7 and 10.8 show pages of text arranged similarly to the facing pages format, this does not occur in the actual book design. In the actual design the two language versions within the tumble format are separated by an internal back cover.

When viewed, the front and back book covers would both be front covers (e.g., one in English, one in French). Each front cover is positioned the same way as text within the book. For example, an English and French book would be flipped along a horizontal axis to view alternate book covers properly. The direction and placement of text on the book spine needs to be arranged such that titles are displayed correctly when the corresponding language variant within the book is placed correctly on a bookshelf. Where language variants meet, somewhere close to the middle of the book, a divider, usually a single sheet of heavier-weight paper, is placed to mark the end of each language version. The weight of these interior pages should be approximately 120grams/m2. This helps users to easily navigate to the end of the manual to view items such as an index.

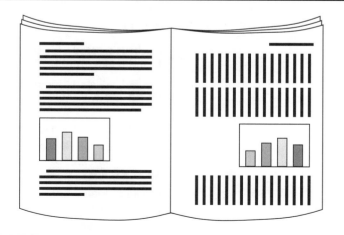

FIGURE 10.8   Vertical tumble format.

Format Selection

When producing a multilingual document, the design of the document in terms of arrangement of languages is an additional task. The organization and flow of the original language document must work well for a single or multiple languages. It is best to determine the format most appropriate for the type and amount of information to be presented and organize the material in the original language with a multilingual format already in mind. Investigate possible formats in the beginning stages of producing your document as it may be necessary to organize some material differently than for a single-language document. Nothing can hinder the creation of a multilingual document more than a poorly designed, poorly organized, or poorly written original language document. There are many references available which give details of what is necessary to produce an international and localizable original version; these guidelines should be followed closely (del Galdo 1990a; del Galdo 1990b; Hoft 1995; Jones et al. 1991; Sanderlin 1988).

Table 10.1 provides a set of guidelines for the selection of

TABLE 10.1   **Document Format Guidelines**

Pages in Original Document	Number of Languages	Acceptable Documentation Format	Types of Documentation
1	2–10	stacked, collated, side-by-side, facing pages, tumble	packing inserts, safety information
1–10	2–6	stacked, collated, side-by-side, facing pages, tumble	quick reference guides, trouble-shooting guides
10–50	2–4	stacked, collated, side-by-side, facing pages, tumble	installation guides, getting started manuals
50–100	2–4	stacked (with approximately 50% graphics)	installation guides, tutorials
50–150	2	collated, side-by-side, facing pages, tumble	user guides, tutorials
more than 150	1	separate publications	

document format based on the size of the original document and the number of languages required. It is possible to mix formats in a single document, but this must be done carefully with extra attention paid to techniques for making the change in format obvious to the user. It is also possible to split documents if many languages are required and no multilingual format would be suitable for a document containing all of the necessary languages. For example, if the market for the document includes six languages, four of which are European and two of which are Asian, it may be better to split the manual into an Asian version and a European version. Both versions should probably contain the original language version as well. If the original language is English, the result would be one version of the manual containing, for example, English, French, German, and Italian and the other version would contain, for example, Chinese, Taiwanese, and English. In this particular case, including English in the Asian version is a good idea as it would also be acceptable for Singapore and Hong Kong, where both Chinese and English are spoken.

COVER AND SPINE DESIGN

Designing the cover of a manual that is multilingual may not be as simple as it first appears. Of course the one essential factor with both the cover and the spine design is that they convey to the user the title of the manual and the languages available within it. It may not be possible to display exactly what languages are presented in the manual on the spine, but it should be possible to provide some indication, by using symbols or icons. All of this information is in addition to any other information the vendor must include on the cover or spine. Some of this additional information includes the vendor's name, the product name, publisher's name, authors, editors, or order numbers. Today, many manuals are A5 format or smaller. Including all of the necessary information on the front cover and spine of the book may not be any easy task.

Depending on the number of languages contained in the manual, just displaying the title in all languages may require most of the front cover. To begin with, the title of the manual may be long and when translated into European languages it may be up to 100 percent longer. When translated into languages which use different character sets or writing direction the arrangement will become even more complicated. There are various methods for space saving and language identification on manual covers.

A simple solution to reduce the size of the manual title is to subdivide it. Many computer-related manual titles contain two or three parts: the company name, the product name, and the manual title. If the product name and the company or vendor are not to be translated and are the same in every locale, the title can easily split into two parts. Therefore only the manual title would have to be translated. Figure 10.9 demonstrates the method of splitting titles for translation on a cover page and an example multilingual symbol. Languages are presented in alphabetical order, using the English sorting sequence. Each language is graphically given equal weight. Figure 10.10 demonstrates three example book spine designs which, using a

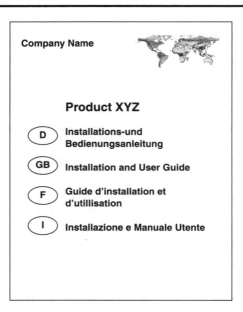

FIGURE 10.9   Multilingual cover page.

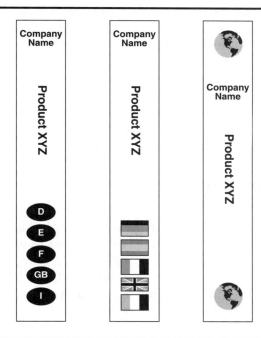

FIGURE 10.10   Multilingual book spine variations.

variety of symbols, indicate that the book contains more than one language.

The addition of graphic symbols to help users identify their language quickly is also useful. Typically flags of nations or international vehicle registration plates (e.g., D, GB, E, F, I) are used in the EEC (European Economic Community). Europeans commonly see these symbols on the back of vehicles and will also recognize the flag of their own country.

These methods of language identification do have their disadvantages. Printing in the colors required for country flags is expensive and both the flags and country abbreviations do not include all countries that speak that particular language. For example, the French flag may be used to indicate the French language within a document, but the audience for the document may be Walloon (Belgian French), Swiss French, Moroccan, and Canadian French. Therefore, the use of a symbol specific to a particular country may not be appropriate. There is also the problem that using, for example, the Spanish flag to indicate a Spanish *variant* may not be immediately recognizable to Spanish speakers from Central and South America. Either do not use flags to identify languages or change the flags to ones that are appropriate for each particular region. One last consideration when using national flags is that they do occasionally change. Always ensure that the flag designs are current and can be easily editable if necessary.

TABLE OF CONTENTS, DOCUMENT MAPS, AND FRONTMATTER

A table of contents is absolutely necessary for documents of substantial length. They are used to view "at a glance" the contents of a document, in addition to being a "map" which the user follows to find desired information. When the publication is multilingual, the table of contents must also be multilingual. This can cause problems because there may be a lot of information that needs to be presented clearly and accurately. In multilingual documents, where figures are not repeated for each language version, it is advisable to include a list of figures in addition to the table of contents. Depending on the format of the document, figures may be several pages from the corresponding text in the user's particular language version. Figure 10.11 demonstrates a variation of a normal table of contents. This figure illustrates the format of the document as a stacked body (i.e., all languages on each page) and a collated index.

A document map is a table of contents that provides information in addition to section or chapter headings and page number. Document maps include other navigational aids such as graphics or color and additional text used to provide a description of the manual organization. Therefore, document maps are interchangeable with a table of contents. The information should include the languages available, location of each language (e.g., layout and order), and any information that will help the user identify his or her own language and understand the layout and structure of the manual due to inclusion of more than one language. This could include any use of graphics or symbols used to identify languages within the document.

Getting Started ____ 1
- Einführung
- Introducción
- Manuel d'initiation
- Introduzione all'uso

Putting the Computer into Operation
- Inbetriebnahme des Computers
- Activacion del ordenador
- Mise en service de l'ordinateur
- Avviamento del computer

Technical Characteristics and Regulations ____ 15
- Technische Merkmale, Normen und Sicherheitsregeln
- Características técnicas, normas y seguridad
- Caractéristiques techniques et normes de sécurité
- Caratteristiche tecniche e normative

Installing Options and Peripherals ____ 30
- Installierung der Optionen und Peripherien
- Instalación de las opciones y de los periféricos
- Installation des options et des périphériques
- Installazione delle opzioni e delle periferiche

1

Setting up the Computer ____ 45
- Konfiguration von Arbeitsmerkmalen
- Configuración de las prestaciones operativas
- Configureation des caractéristiques de fonctionnement
- Configureazione delle caratteristiche operative

Operating Problems and Error Messages ____ 60
- Betriebsstörungen und Fehlermeldungen
- Problemas de funcionamiento y mensajes de error
- Problemes de fonctionnement et messages d'erreur
- Problemi di funzionamento e messaggi di errore

Index ____ 75
Stichwortverzeichnis ____ 80
Indice alfabético ____ 85
Index analytique ____ 90
Indice analitico ____ 100

2

FIGURE 10.11 Multilingual table of contents.

Figure 10.12 displays a document map which uses block tabs, shaded blocks, and pages to convey to the user the design of the document. In addition to the graphics there is text within the shaded blocks giving information on the document structure. This type of information is best presented as close to the first page in the manual as possible. For multilingual publications, text should be limited and graphics simple and explicit. The text should be available in all languages. If possible, this information should be kept to one page or two facing pages.

The frontmatter of a book usually includes a title page, a copyright page, a table of contents, and a preface. Because of the difficulty in presenting this information, front matter of multilingual books should be kept to a minimum. There is some difficulty in presenting this information because it may differ from country to country. Countries may have legal differences in copyright laws, thus requiring a major difference in language variants. In addition, a table of contents very quickly becomes unwieldy when presenting more than one language. One method to reduce the amount of frontmatter is to move some information (e.g., preface) to the main body of the book.

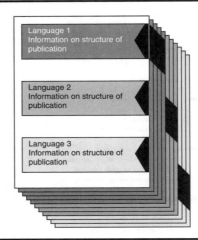

FIGURE 10.12   Document map.

NAVIGATIONAL AIDS

Within a unilingual manual the inclusion and use of navigational aids (e.g., index, table of contents) is a habit to both document designer and reader. Within a multilingual manual additional navigational aids are essential. The use of navigational aids is highly recommended in order to minimize the impact on usability by layout variations due to a multilingual design. It is important to convey to the user the information and language structure of the manual.

There are various techniques for providing navigational information to the user. Whether users are searching for a particular piece of information or working their way through a document affects what type of aids are most useful. For most manuals, these two types of navigational aids are required. As with document format, all of the different types of navigational aids have their pros and cons relating to cost, space required, time to produce, and effectiveness depending on format. Some of the techniques most commonly used include variations in paper (color, weight, and finish), colored text blocks, symbols, and tabs.

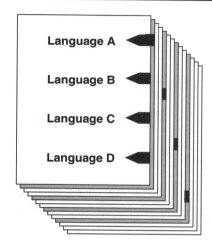

FIGURE 10.13   Paper variation as a navigational aid.

Paper Variations

Variation of the paper used within a manual is a very effective and easy way to identify important pages within a document. However, the variation of paper can also be costly. By changing the paper type for a particular page, users can easily locate a page which they may refer to every time they use the manual. When using the manual for the first time, users will be drawn to this page and immediately become familiar with its location. When using colored paper, use colors that have a good contrast against white, such as a saturated pink, blue, or green for single pages. For sections of a book that may be denoted by color, for example, a collated index placed at the back of a stacked format manual, each language index can begin with a different-colored single page or the entire index can be produced on a different color paper. Figure 10.13 illustrates the use of colored single pages (appearing as darker gray) to mark the beginning of a language version. The top page is a document map. Both the top page and the dark gray pages should be 120grams/m2. The lighter gray pages at the back of the document are the index and are of 80grams/m2 paper.

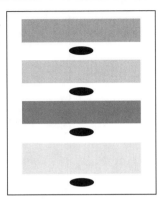

FIGURE 10.14   Shaded text blocks.

When color is used to denote an entire section of a manual, normal-weight pages (80grams/m2) are sufficient. Also use paler colors for multiple pages. When using single colored pages to identify a document map or an internal cover page, it is best to use heavier-weight paper of at least 120grams/m2. Variations in paper finish can also be used, such as a dimpled effect (similar to watercolor paper) or a polished or glossy surface. Although these can be aesthetically pleasing they are no more effective than variations in color or weight and are more expensive.

Color, Symbols, and Graphics

Colored text blocks, language symbols, or small graphics can also be used to denote where one language ends and another begins. These methods are best used within a stacked format. Figure 10.14 shows blocks in shades of gray which would have a different language variant overlaid, each color or shade denoting a different language. It is best to use pale colors for this technique to ensure that they are not distracting, but are easily identifiable. Language symbols can be used for the same purpose by placing a symbol in the margin next to where the language begins. These two techniques are effective for a stacked format, especially when all the language variants for a single "block" of information span more than one page. Users can then

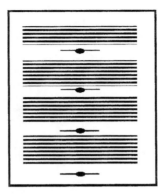

FIGURE 10.15   Use of small graphics.

easily scan pages to find the next block of information in their language. The use of a small graphic may also be useful, but is most effective when all of the language variants of a block of information fit on one page. Therefore, each language variant is in relatively the same position on every page. Figure 10.15 shows the use of a small graphic to denote changes in language in a stacked format page.

Tabs

Tabs are a very effective method to identify languages, sections, or transitions within a document. There are three types of tab that will be discussed: extended tabs (see Figure 10.16), cutaway tabs (see Figure 10.17), and color-block tabs (see Figure 10.18). The first two types of tab require physical alterations to the document and are costly to produce. Extended tabs are those tabs that extend out from a page indicating the beginning of a section. These are commonly found in older-style address books. Extended tabs are sometimes constructed from heavier-weight paper or plastic. As you would expect, these are so costly; the expense is normally prohibitive. Cutaway tabs often found on dictionaries and pocket-size address books. This entails the cutting away of the edge of the pages in a section, leaving an

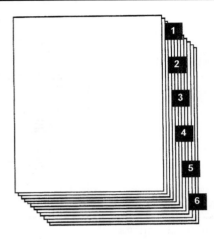

FIGURE 10.16   Extended tabs.

extended portion of the pages which increases in size as you move through the book by section. This can also be expensive, but normally costs less than the use of extended tabs. Both of these types of tab normally require some sort of marking on the tab itself, either text, color, or a symbol, to indicate what will be found at that tab.

The most cost effective way to use tabs is to mark corre-

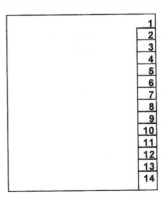

FIGURE 10.17   Cutaway tabs.

sponding pages with a color-block that rests against the outside edge of the page. See Figure 10.18. These colored blocks (black is usually used) must be referenced on a table-of-contents page or a document map, but information can also be displayed within the block itself. A slight bending of the manual on its vertical axis displays the corresponding pages marked by the tab on the document map. This method can be used with a variety of formats and is fairly simple to implement.

Variations in Font and Text Color

Another method to assist in navigation through a manual is to use variations in font or text color. Variations in text color for any quantity of text is not recommended for a hard copy manual because depending on the color of the text it can prove difficult to read. Variations in font can be used, but in order to produce a readable document, it is highly recommended to use a professional graphic designer to assist in the layout of the text and selection of fonts. One last option is to vary the left-hand margin on language variants within a stacked-format document. Figure 10.19 demonstrates the use of this method on a stacked-format page which contains three different languages. Of course this method cannot be

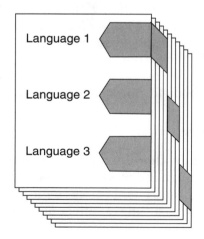

FIGURE 10.18   Color-block tabs.

FIGURE 10.19   Use of varied margins.

used within a document that either contains a great number of languages or languages with different writing directions.

Options for navigational aids for electronic documents are not explored in this chapter. Due to the availability of windowing and hypertext in electronic documents, the searching for information and language is greatly simplified and there is no need for multilingual electronic documents. There is a great deal of information on the topic of designing on-line documentation (e.g., Harris 1990; Horton 1990; *The Windows Interface: An Application Design Guide*, 1991). Some of the methods discussed in this chapter can be applied to electronic documents, particularly those that use windowing techniques. For example, colored pages or text, tabs, and symbols or icons are all very effective methods for locating and arranging information on-line.

LANGUAGE ORDER

To date there has been no significant research on the effect of language order within a document on the usability of the material. It is probable that the location of text in a stack, first, middle, or last, has an effect on use. It is also possible that language order may be perceived negatively by those who always find their language last in the list, or possibly in the middle as it may be more difficult to locate and read depending on the format.

What is known to be important is that languages should always appear in the same order throughout the manual, even when changing layout formats for different sections of the manual (e.g., from collated to stacked in different sections).

Normally, the original language in which the product is produced, sometimes referred to as the base language, appears first, with other languages following alphabetically based on ISO codes (e.g., DE for German, FR for French, IT for Italian, NL for Dutch). Although this scheme may not be completely obvious to the user as to how order was selected, it is an easy method for deciding language order. When including several languages which use a variety of character sets, those languages with similar character sets can be alternated with languages that use grossly different character sets (e.g., Latin, Greek, and Arabic). This may assist users in locating their languages as each language always appears relative to a more easily distinguishable language. For example, the language order of English, Chinese, Spanish, Arabic within a stacked document would help to separate languages that, at a glance, appear similar (e.g., English and Spanish) because they use similar character sets. Another method for choosing language order is by market share. Place the language in which the product sells most, first, then other languages after it in descending order of sales. This may not be a particularly scientific method of selecting language order, but it is an easy option.

CHARACTER SETS AND LANGUAGE DIRECTION

When producing multilingual manuals with languages which use different character sets or are normally written in different directions, certain benefits and also some obstacles arise. As mentioned above, juxtaposing languages which use different character sets makes those languages within the publication easier to identify. Another added benefit is that some languages which have historically been written in a different direction to English are now acceptable in a top-down, left-to-right format, for example, Korean and Japanese (Nakanishi 1992). This makes it easier to combine these languages with Western languages on a single page.

When using different character sets, note that if you are

using any numbering within the document, some languages do not use Arabic numbers. In addition, the size of characters may differ greatly, thus creating problems when preparing the layout of a document. Some of the more difficult aspects of producing documents which contain more than one character set arise in the production of the manual. If the manual is produced electronically, the software must be able to cope with multiple character sets and multiple writing directions.

INDEXES

Creating indexes for multilingual documentation is not just a matter of translating the original version. Page numbers will most likely be different (no matter what format is used) and collating sequences vary among languages. Use a professional indexer and create a separate index for each language.

The index occupies the final pages of a document and, because of its complexity, it is best to provide this kind of information in a collated format. If the format of the book itself is not collated, the format of the index will not be consistent with the rest of the publication. The change in formats within a single manual may not be a problem, if navigational aids are used to convey to the user the manual organization.

USE OF COLOR

The perception of color is universal across international borders. However, be aware that colors have different *connotations* in different countries. The symbolism of a particular color may vary from culture to culture as well as the preference. Where the use of color may affect the manual most is in the production of front covers. The styling of book covers can change dramatically depending on the intended market (Fernandes 1995) as well as packaging of consumer goods. When producing book covers for multilingual manuals, attention must be paid to what styling and colors are most appropriate for all the intended markets.

SELECTING THE MULTILINGUAL FORMAT

When making the decision between the production of unilingual or multilingual documents, there are several factors to be considered. These factors, compared with the cost of multilingual production, can help to determine the cost effectiveness of your decision. In many cases, providing multilingual documentation can actually be money saving and, logistically, make it easier for distribution. Below is a list of some of these factors which should be taken into consideration in order to determine if the production of a multilingual version of your documentation is an efficient and effective way to deal with providing information to an international market.

- Market profile (locale, languages, culture, number of sales per language)
- Document size (number of pages or words)
- Amount of illustrations, figures, or graphics within the document
- Document content (technical versus layperson)
- Document function (training, installation, user guide, reference)
- Frequency of document use
- Profit margin on product
- Local legislation or legal requirements
- Distribution logistics
- User demographics

SUMMARY

To successfully implement a multilingual publishing program, the designer of the document must ensure that this is actually the best solution to what may be a variety of problems. This chapter gives readers a basic understanding of the options when it comes to producing a multilingual document and some of the issues that must be addressed in order to produce a usable document. This chapter is not meant to provide definitive guidelines for producing multilingual documentation, as there are many issues concerning the selection of multilingual documentation for a product, the use of electronic tools, and the production of this type of documentation that are not covered in detail. A major factor that must be addressed by the producers is the management and coordination of the translations and manual production. As one can imagine, for very large documents, complicated documents, complicated formats, or a large number of languages, these tasks require tremendous organization.

As publishing technologies advance, many new design alternatives will become possible and physically producing multilingual documents should become easier and less expensive. One final note is to stress the importance of the quality of the original documents. The final multilingual version of a document can only be as good as the original version. Therefore, it is essential to follow guidelines for producing international documentation. This will facilitate the translation of the original document such that it can become a quality multilingual document.

ACKNOWLEDGMENTS

Much of my knowledge and experience on the design of multilingual documentation comes from the time I spent working at Digital Equipment Corporation with a group of four exceptional people: Alan Brown, Ireland; Anna Hayward, Switzerland; Robert Pariseau, Canada; and Jeanita Snowdon, England. During that period, we had an opportunity to exchange ideas, develop theories, and work on a variety of issues pertaining to the design and production of multilingual documentation.

REFERENCES

BSI 7649. 1993. *British Standard Guide to the Design and Preparation of Documentation for Users of Application Software*. London, England: BSI.

del Galdo, Elisa M. 1990a. Internationalization and translation: Some guidelines for the design of human-computer interfaces. In Nielsen, J. (ed.), *Designing User Interfaces for International Use*. Amsterdam: Elsevier Science Publishers B.V., 1–10

del Galdo, Elisa M. 1990b. A European evaluation of three document formats for hardware installation guides. In Nielsen, J. (ed.), *Designing User Interfaces for International Use*. Amsterdam: Elsevier Science Publishers B.V., 45–69

Fernandes, Tony. 1995. *Global Interface Design*. Chestnut Hill, MA: AP Professional.

Harris, R. Allen. 1990. Linguistic guidelines for graphic interfaces. *IEEE Transactions on Professional Communication*. **33**, 1 (March 1990).

Hoft, Nancy L. 1995. *International Technical Communication*. New York: Wiley.

Horton, William K. 1990. *Designing and Writing On-line Documentation*. New York: Wiley.

Jones, S., C. Kennelly, C. Mueller, M. Sweezy, B. Thomas, and L. Velez. 1991. *Developing International User Information*. Bedford, MA: Digital Press.

Nakanishi, Akira. 1992. *Writing Systems of the World*. Rutland, VT: Charles E. Tuttle.

Sanderlin, Stacey. 1988. Preparing instruction manuals for non-English readers. *Technical Communication, Second Quarter*, 96–100.

The Windows Interface: An Application Design Guide. 1991. Redmond, WA: Microsoft Press.

ABOUT THE AUTHOR

Elisa del Galdo is a native American who has been living and working in Europe since 1986. Ms. del Galdo currently resides in France where she is an independent human factors consultant specializing in the design and evaluation of software, hardware, and documentation for internationalization.

Prior to setting up as an independent, Ms. del Galdo was employed in the UK by Digital Equipment Corporation, where she was responsible for the design and evaluation of software and hardware user interfaces, documentation, and icons and symbols for ten European countries. She also participated in UK National and International Standards.

In the area of internationalization, Ms. del Galdo has performed research on the design of products for localization, translation, and multilingual markets and has been responsible for or contributed to several publications, standards, and guidelines, either in the public or corporate domain, concerning the design and development of international products.

Ms. del Galdo can be reached at: del Galdo Consulting Ltd., 1 chemin du bois d'Opio, les Tomieres, 06650 OPIO France. Telephone and Fax: +33 93.77.72.59. Internet: delgaldo@riviera.fr.

CHAPTER 11

An Intelligent Lexical Management System for Multilingual Machine Translation

INTRODUCTION

An essential component of a machine translation (MT) system is its lexicon or dictionary. The lexicon contains the words and phrases of the source language against which the input text must be matched, as well as their transfers in the target language. Given the state of the art of MT, it is currently not feasible to build, ahead of time, a large lexicon that contains all the lexical information needed during the translation of documents in various domains. Thus, critical to the success of an MT system is an interactive tool that enables users to update the lexical database so that it reflects their specific translation needs.

This chapter presents ALEX (Automatic LEXicographer), an intelligent lexical management system for the Logos Multilingual MT System. Currently, the Logos system supports automatic document translation for seven language pairs. ALEX provides a graphical user interface that allows the user to browse through the lexicon, look up, delete or modify existing lexical information, and add new lexical entries. Large numbers of entries can also be imported from an existing glossary. The design goal of ALEX is to create a user interface that is easy to learn and use. Given the complexity of the lexical information required by the translation system, the major challenge in the design of ALEX is to transform this complexity in such a way that the process in which the user manages the lexical database becomes intuitive and simple. We achieve this goal by combining user modeling techniques, lexical acquisition strategies, and principles of user interface design.

The rest of this chapter is organized as follows: The background section provides information about the Logos machine translation system. In particular, the essentials of lexical representation in Logos are presented. The next section outlines the overall structure of ALEX and shows how the system works using examples. The focus of the following section is the analysis of the key issues involved in the design of the ALEX system. The final section summarizes our current development and outlines the direction of future work.

Terminology

In this chapter, we use some terminology that is specific to the ALEX system or the machine translation field and is not otherwise explained in the chapter. We present it here. Other concepts will be introduced when appropriate.

- A *source language* is the language of a source document to be translated.
- A *target language* is the language into which a document is translated.
- A *transfer* is the target equivalent for a source word or phrase.
- An *alternate* for a transfer is the alternative translation when the target language requires the source word to be translated into a different part of speech. For example, the English sentence "Building the house took one year" is translated into German as "Der Bau des Hauses dauerte ein Jahr." Notice the verb *building* is translated into the noun *Bau*.
- An *entry* is the total information of a source word and its transfer together with their lexical features, such as entry type, number or gender. The term *source entry* (or *target entry*) is also used to denote the lexical information about the source word (or target word) in an entry.

- The *entry type* of an entry can be word or phrase, acronym, or abbreviation.
- The *number* of a noun indicates whether a dictionary entry for the source or target is applicable when it is used as a singular, plural, or both.
- *Inflection* is the morphological information of a word, such as plural endings or case.
- The *category* of a source word is its semantico-syntactic classification.

BACKGROUND

Logos is a general-purpose MT system that is currently employed by many translation service bureaus, in-house translation departments of large corporations, and government agencies. The system supports translation directions from English to French, German, Italian, and Spanish, and from German to English, French, and Italian. The rest of this section briefly describes the architecture of the Logos system and its approach to knowledge representation. A more detailed description of the system and other issues involved can be found in Scott (1989) and Gdaniec and Schmid (1995).

The Logos Multilingual Machine Translation System

The Logos MT system may be considered as an incremental pipeline analyzer-generator. This means that analysis of the source text and the generation of the target text are performed by passing the input stream through a series of modules, each of which conducts a particular incremental task. The system architecture is shown in Figure 11.1. The major components of the system include: Formatting, Dictionary Lookup, Resolution, Transfer, and Generation. Given an input document, the first Format module separates the text from the formatting information and graphics of the source document before submitting the text to the following translation process. Then the Dictionary Lookup module looks up each word or phrase in the input text and represents it in an internal representation language known as SAL (Semantico-Syntactic Abstraction Language). There-

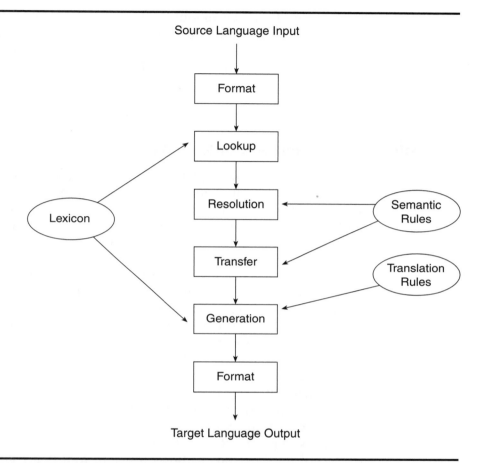

FIGURE 11.1   The architecture of the Logos MT system.

after, the input sentence is processed through the following modules as a SAL string. The Resolution module identifies the major constituents (clause, noun phrase, verb phrase) of a sentence and, during the process, resolves any syntactically ambiguous element. This module accesses semantic rules in the semantic rule base. The Transfer component of the system consists of four modules, each of which performs a certain syntactic and semantic analysis, such as identifying modifiers, coordination, and verb-argument structure. In addition to the Semantic tables, the Transfer modules also utilize a set of *translation rules*. Generation module generates output in the target language based on the result of the Resolution and Transfer. The formatting information is assembled by the last Format module so that the translated text is presented to the user in the format of the original input.

Semantico-Syntactic Representation in Logos

The essence of knowledge representation in the Logos system is SAL, in which words and phrases are represented at a level where semantics and syntax intersect. SAL can be considered both as a classification scheme and a representation language. As a classification scheme, it provides hundreds of hierarchically organized categories that capture the essential syntactic and semantic properties of a natural language. As a representation language, SAL is used to represent lexical information in the dictionary, various rules in the system, and also the intermediate result of the Resolution and Transfer modules. Currently, there are four levels in the SAL hierarchy: *word class, superset, set,* and *subset*. For example, the English word *battery* can be represented as (*noun, concrete, agent, machine*). Internally, each category is denoted by a numeric value so that the translation process actually operates on a sequence of numbers. Thus, the dictionary entry for *battery* is internally represented by the sequence *01 8 35 750 01*. The advantage of this numeric representation is that it allows efficient and fast content-sensitive matching of the rule bases.

In addition to the categories, SAL also utilizes numeric notations to represent other morphological and syntactic features such as *gender* and *number*. More information on SAL will be given in the section Design Issues of ALEX, where the issue of lexical acquisition in ALEX is discussed.

ALEX: LEXICON MANAGEMENT FOR LOGOS

The lexical information in the dictionary plays a very important role in the Logos system. To a large extent, the quality of the translation output using Logos depends heavily on the words and terms available in the dictionary (L'Homme 1994). As indicated earlier in this chapter, a lexicon management system that allows the user to manipulate the lexical entries to meet the specific needs for translating various documents is essential to the success of an MT system. Many words are ambiguous and their transfers in a target language depend on various factors that may not be possible to determine when the MT system is developed. In many technical fields, new terms and their transfers are often invented. To show the ambiguity of words, let's take the English word *file* as an example:

- *File* can be a noun or a verb. It can also function as a prenominal modifier in phrases like *file manipulation*.
- There are also several possible noun transfers for *file* depending on context. For example, French transfers for *file* include *fichier, dossier,* and *lime.* In German, one can use *Datei, Akte,* or *Feile.* In Italian the choices are *archivio, schedario,* and *lima.* In Spanish, possible transfers are *archivo (fichero), carpeta,* and *lima.*
- If *file* is used as a verb, the possibilities in French include *classer* (for filing in an office), *limer* (for filing in a woodworking shop), and *déposer* (for filing a patent). Similar equivalents such as *ablegen, feilen,* and *anmelden* for German, *achiviare, limare,* and *registrare* for Italian, and *clasificar, limar,* and *registrar* for Spanish also exist.
- If the word appears in uppercase characters (as in the phrase *FILE command*) it may be desirable to leave it untranslated.

The original ALEX system was developed in the mid-1980s when the need for a user-friendly interface for lexicon management in Logos was identified. The current ALEX system is the result of a several-year effort in research and development since then. This chapter mainly focuses on a client/server version of the system that runs in the Microsoft Windows environment. In the following sections, we first describe the organization of the lexical database in Logos; then we present the architecture of the ALEX system, as well as examples of how the system is used.

The Organization of the Lexical Database

Lexical database in Logos is a collection of bilingual dictionaries. There are two types of dictionaries: the *core dictionary* and *user dictionaries*. The core dictionary stores most of the commonly used words and phrases in a source language together with their most common transfers. This dictionary is delivered with the Logos translation system. Usually residing on the server machine, it cannot be modified by the user. A user dictionary usually resides on a client machine, storing entries in one language pair entered by the user. The user may create as many user dictionaries as needed. However, ALEX provides a facility that allows the user to organize the entries in a user dictionary into *company dictionaries* and *subject matter dictionaries*. *Company code* is part of an entry, indicating an ownership preference. When translating a document for company ABC (this is a typical situation for translation services), the dictionary entries with company code ABC, for example, will be matched first. Dictionary entries are also characterized by *subject matters*, which are the domain fields to which the entries pertain. This enables the translation system to select alternative transfers applicable in specific contexts. For example, the user may specify that the French transfer for the English word *plate* is *assiette* under the subject matter General, and *plaque* under the subject matter Photography. When translating a document in photography, the system automatically selects *plaque* as the transfer for *plate*. Subject matters are organized as a taxonomy. The Logos system provides more than 200 subject matters. In addition, users of a Logos system can also define their own subject matters.

Overview of ALEX

The purpose of the ALEX system is to provide a suite of functionalities that enable users of the Logos system to easily manage their user dictionaries. These include the facilities that allow users to browse, search, view, delete, modify existing dictionary entries, and add new entries to the dictionary. The core dictionary can be browsed; and it is also used to aid the system in determining lexical features of existing entries in the core dictionary. The user can also import terms to a user dictionary from a glossary. Another important component of the system is a knowledge base that stores information for lexical acquisition. Figure 11.2 shows the overall organization of ALEX.

Browsing the Lexicon   The user starts an ALEX session by opening or creating a user dictionary for a given language pair. Once a dictionary is open, the system automatically starts the browser that displays all the existing entries in a scrollable window. Figure 11.3 shows the Browser Window for an English-French dictionary.

The browser provides a convenient starting point for the user to perform other ALEX functions. Note that only the source word, target word, company code, and subject matter of the dictionary entries are shown in the browser. As shown in Figure 11.4, detailed information of the dictionary entries are displayed in the Entry Window, when the user selects an entry and invokes the View function.

In addition to those already shown in the Browser Window, the Entry Window displays the main features of a dictionary entry. These include entry type, part of speech, category, alter-

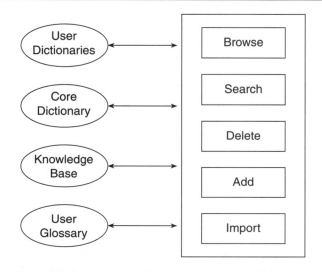

FIGURE 11.2   The architecture of ALEX.

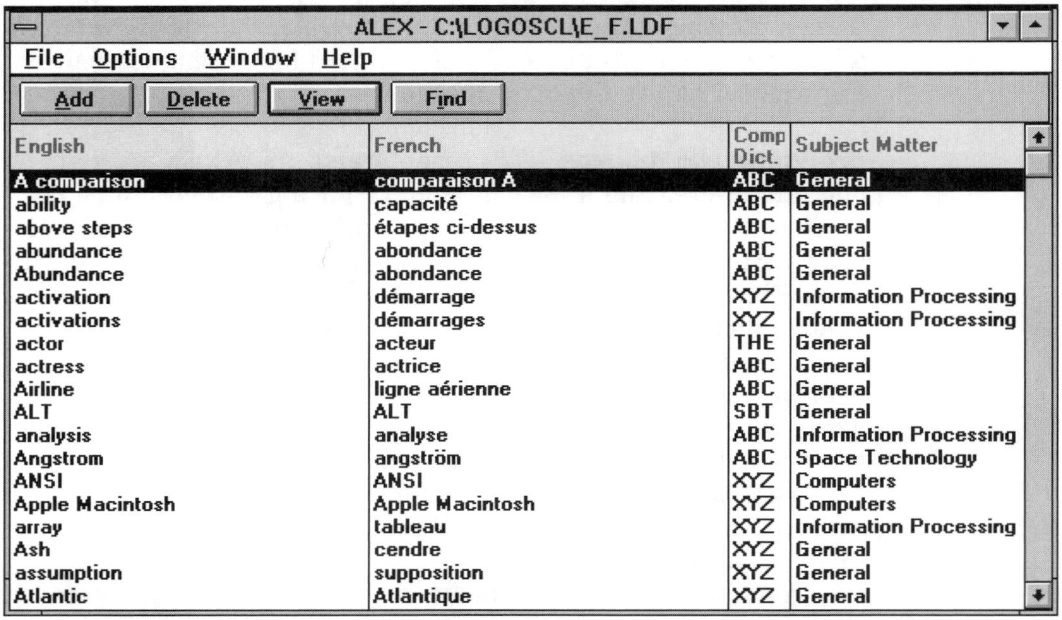

ALEX - C:\LOGOSCL\E_F.LDF				▼ ▲

File   Options   Window   Help

Add	Delete	View	Find

English	French	Comp Dict.	Subject Matter	↑
A comparison	comparaison A	ABC	General	
ability	capacité	ABC	General	
above steps	étapes ci-dessus	ABC	General	
abundance	abondance	ABC	General	
Abundance	abondance	ABC	General	
activation	démarrage	XYZ	Information Processing	
activations	démarrages	XYZ	Information Processing	
actor	acteur	THE	General	
actress	actrice	ABC	General	
Airline	ligne aérienne	ABC	General	
ALT	ALT	SBT	General	
analysis	analyse	ABC	Information Processing	
Angstrom	angström	ABC	Space Technology	
ANSI	ANSI	XYZ	Computers	
Apple Macintosh	Apple Macintosh	XYZ	Computers	
array	tableau	XYZ	Information Processing	
Ash	cendre	XYZ	General	
assumption	supposition	XYZ	General	
Atlantic	Atlantique	XYZ	General	↓

FIGURE 11.3   The Browser Window.

nate, and features pertaining to a particular part of speech and language, such as number for nouns in any language, and gender for Romance languages.

Adding and Modifying Entries   The major functionality of ALEX is its facility that allows the user to enter new lexical entries or modify existing ones. To add a new entry, the user selects the *Add* button in either the Main Window or Entry Window. An existing entry may be modified when it is being viewed. The logic for adding or modifying an entry is essentially the same.

Recall that a dictionary entry consists of the source and target words or phrase, features for the whole entry such as subject matter and company code, as well as features pertaining to the source or target. Normally, the user adds an entry by first entering the source and target words, then specifying values of their features. Some features are simple in the sense that their possible values can be simply listed. For example, the values of the

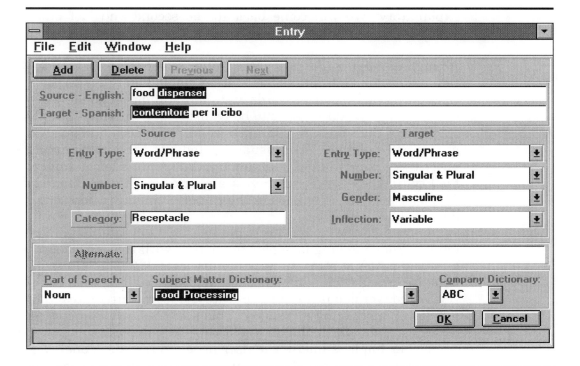

FIGURE 11.4   The Entry Window.

feature *gender* for a German noun can only be *masculine, feminine* or *neuter*. These types of features are presented to the user as a pair of label and list box. For complex features, such as *category*, there is not a simple list of straightforward values available for the user to select. For these, ALEX provides a push-button that starts another acquisition process for a particular feature, if it is invoked. The whole process of entering an entry can be roughly characterized into the following steps: (1) The source and target words are entered (manually or by importing from a glossary). (2) The system searches the input words in the dictionaries to determine if some of the features can be derived from the existing entries. If so, the system sets the values for these features. (3) Values for simple features are specified by clicking on the list boxes. (4) Complex features are acquired through additional acquisition process. The first and third steps are self-explanatory. We will come back to the second and last steps when the design issues are discussed, in the next section.

Importing from a Glossary   Very often, especially in a translation service or an internationalization department of a corporation, glossaries of source words and their standard transfers are prepared for the documents to be translated. Sometimes simple features of the source words, such as part of speech and gender, are already defined. It is usually a tedious task to manually enter these words into the dictionary. ALEX provides an import facility that loads the entire glossary into the _Import Window_. The user may select entries in the Import Window to add to the dictionary.

To reduce the amount of time needed to create dictionary entries from one language pair to another with the same source language, ALEX also offers a feature called _Import Glossary with Matching Dictionary_ that uses a glossary along with a dictionary conversion utility to duplicate the stored attributes from entries in an existing dictionary. This amounts to a tremendous saving in time, particularly in selecting the categories.

For example, suppose the user needs to translate one English document into both French and Spanish and is given a glossary file for each target language. The user may create the French dictionary by importing the French glossary. Then the user uses the completed French dictionary in combination with the Spanish glossary to provide input for the Spanish dictionary. Every French dictionary source entry that matched a Spanish glossary source entry is automatically loaded into the Spanish dictionary by using the _Import Glossary with Matching Dictionary_ function.

DESIGN ISSUES OF ALEX

As shown above, an extensive variety of lexical information is required by the Logos system in order to cope with the linguistic complexity of the seven language pairs it supports. Sophisticated linguistic techniques and conventions have been developed over the years to represent the lexical information. For example, lexical entries are classified into about 1,000 hierarchically organized semantic-syntactic categories. However, it is not realistic to expect users of the Logos system to be knowledgeable of all these techniques and conventions. There exists a considerable gap between the complicated lexical information to be acquired from users and their linguistic knowledge of the source and target languages. The major challenge for the design of ALEX is to bridge this gap. In other words, the system must be simple to use, easy to learn, but still provide all the necessary functionalities for managing the comprehensive lexical information needed by the translation system.

To achieve this goal, we adopted the established principles in the fields of computational linguistics, user interface design, and software engineering in the design of ALEX. In particular, ALEX employs a combination of user modeling techniques and learning strategies. These design principles, techniques, and strategies are the topic of the rest of this section.

User Modeling and Incremental View of Complex Lexical Data

Users of ALEX are characterized into novice users, knowledgeable users, and expert users according to their levels of linguistic competence, which in turn are determined by the complexity of the lexical information involved. For example, novice users usually understand basic linguistic terms such as part of speech and gender; knowledgeable users know more advanced linguistic concepts such as morphology; and expert users are trained linguists who understand deeper issues such as the category hierarchy.

Accordingly, the ALEX system presents the user a triple-tiered incremental view of the lexical information, both when the user is browsing a dictionary and when the user is adding new entries. A lexical feature is classified into *primary feature, composite* (or *complex*) *feature*, or *additional feature*. This classification is basically a mapping from the internal dictionary structure required by machine translation to a lexical representation that reflects the users' view.

As discussed in the previous section, a simple lexical feature such as *gender* is a primary feature. The values of a primary feature can be easily enumerated and thus are displayed using a list box. The user can simply choose a value from the list. Composite features correspond to several features in the underlying internal dictionary structure. For example, the feature *category* actually represents the triplet *superset, set,* and *subset* in the SAL structure. An additional feature such as the *gender* of a prepositional object in a target noun phrase is not as critical as the gender of the whole phrase. A primary feature is displayed to the user as a label. A composite feature is displayed as a push-button. They are both presented in the Entry Window. Additional features are displayed in separate windows when the user finishes with viewing or entering the features in the Entry Window and clicks on the OK button. For example, Figure 11.5 shows the part of speech, gender, and number for the word *rouleau* in the French noun phrase *enduit de rouleau.*

This triple-tiered presentation of lexical features has two advantages. First and most importantly, it gives the user an incremental view of the dictionary information. Second, it allows a novice user to skip less important or more complicated features. Of course, doing so may introduce less perfect lexical

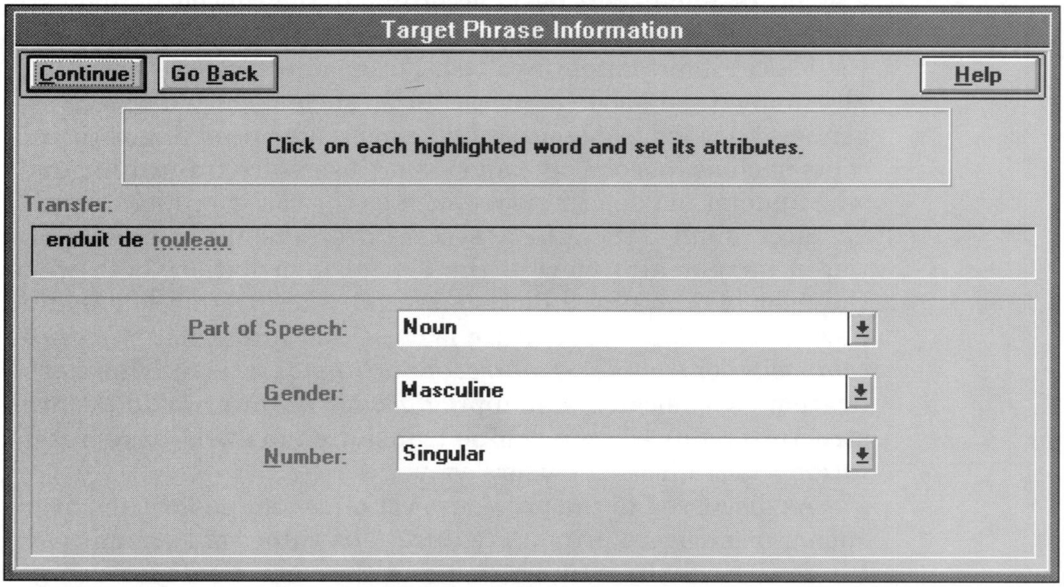

Target Phrase Information

Continue	Go Back		Help

Click on each highlighted word and set its attributes.

Transfer:

enduit de rouleau

Part of Speech:	**Noun**	±
Gender:	**Masculine**	±
Number:	**Singular**	±

FIGURE 11.5   An example of additional features.

entries into the dictionary, thus the translation quality may be affected. However, this is justified when the user needs to enter a great amount of entries into the dictionary in a short period of time. Moreover, the ALEX system always tries to determine the best default value, which will be discussed later.

Lexical Acquisition

One of the main components of ALEX is its Add module, which allows the user to enter new dictionary entries. In a simplistic view of this module, the system just performs a data entry task that can be accomplished by asking the user to specify all the required features of an entry. However, since the lexical structure of the Logos system is complex, the data entry approach will put too much of a burden on the user and make the system very cumbersome. Our goal is to make the system easy to use and learn by (1) reducing the number of questions to a minimum, and (2) asking questions intelligently. To achieve this goal, the Add component of ALEX is designed as a lexical acquisition system that actively and intelligently learns from the user. This intelligence is embodied in a set of learning strategies that are based on the incremental view of the lexical features.

In the previous section, we described the steps by which new entries are entered into the dictionary from the user's point of view. In the following, we discuss this procedure from the aspect of lexical acquisition. When a new source or target word or phrase is entered by the user, ALEX processes the input according to the following algorithm: The first step is *tokenization* where the input word or phrase is validated and normalized. Then the system tries to *look up* the input in the dictionary and fills the internal entry structure with the existing information of the entry and the individual words in the phrase. If the lookup is not successful, the system *hypothesizes* as many linguistic features as possible, based on the known information such as the lexical features of the individual words in a phrase or compound. The hypothesization process relies on the heuristic rules stored in the knowledge base, as well as the dictionary itself. For example, the entry type of an all-capitalized English word, such as IBM, will be hypothesized as an acronym; an English noun ending with a period will be an abbreviation. Another example is the hypothesization of the *head* word or element of a phrase or a compound word. As will be explained in the Learning by Analogy section, the identification of the head word is very important because the main lexical characteristics of a phrase or compound can usually be derived from its head element. Before asking the user to select the head word, ALEX applies the head hypothesization rules to make an intelligent guess. For example, the head word of the Italian phrase *contenitore per il cibo (food dispenser)* will be identified as *contenitore* by the following heuristic rule: The head word in a Romance language noun phrase is very likely to be the word before the preposition (*per*), as shown in Figure 11.4.

Based on the retrieved and/or hypothesized information, ALEX initializes and displays the primary features on the Entry Window.

Learning Strategies

The lexical acquisition process in ALEX employs a combination of three learning strategies: *learning by analogy, learning from feature hierarchy,* and *learning by being told.* A particular strategy is applied to the acquisition of a lexical feature mainly based on the nature and complexity of the feature.

Learning by Analogy   Analogy is a powerful inference tool. It allows similarities between objects to be stated succinctly. However, at the same time, it does not require the similarities to be stated precisely. Therefore, humans often solve problems by making analogies to the things they are more familiar with (Rich 1991; Winston 1980). An example is the use of synonyms in language teaching and learning. For this reason, analogical reasoning is considered a nexus for many issues in artificial intelligence (Hoffman 1995).

Learning by analogy is the major acquisition approach in ALEX. With this approach, the system infers lexical features for a new entry based on its knowledge of the existing entries and their relationship with the new entry being acquired. An advantage of this approach lies in that it may not be necessary to ask users tedious questions about the new entry. Therefore, this technique requires the least linguistic competence from the user.

This approach can be best explained with the acquisition of category in ALEX. Recall that the category is the most important lexical feature in the Logos system. The correct selection of the categories of the dictionary entries is critical to the translation quality. However, category is a composite feature in that it represents the entire SAL structure of an entry. Most users will not have the linguistic competence to make a selection from the three-level SAL hierarchy. Therefore, ALEX takes an incremental approach to the acquisition of the category, in which the following methods are applied in the sequence given: *learning from the source input, learning from the head word, learning from synonyms* and *learning from the SAL hierarchy*. When the user starts the category definition process, the system first determines if the dictionary already contains a body of semantic information about the source word or phrase. If so, a list of generated category selection is displayed. This is the first learning method. In the next two steps, ALEX makes analogies between the input word or phrase with the head word and synonyms, by generating a list of category selections that bear semantic-syntactic similarities between the source word or phrase and its head word or a synonym. Figure 11.6 shows an example of learning from the head word. The input source entry is *parallel port*. Since this phrase is not defined in the dictionary (the option *source entry* is disabled), ALEX presents to the user all the defined categories for the head word *port*, which are *Mass Liquid, Place, Entrance,* and *Thresholds or Boundaries.*

The window shown in Figure 11.6 is called the Category Window. The four option buttons in the upper portion of the window indicate the methods of acquiring the category. The available categories are shown in the *Categories* frame, also as option buttons. Only the available methods are enabled so, for example, if the source entry has no head element or the head word is the whole source entry itself, the *Head Word* option is disabled. The user may always select a currently available method.

Another learning by analogy method is learning from synonym. ALEX allows the user to enter a word semantically similar to the source entry or head word, then retrieves and displays the available category definitions of the synonym for the user to select. This process can be repeated until the user is satisfied

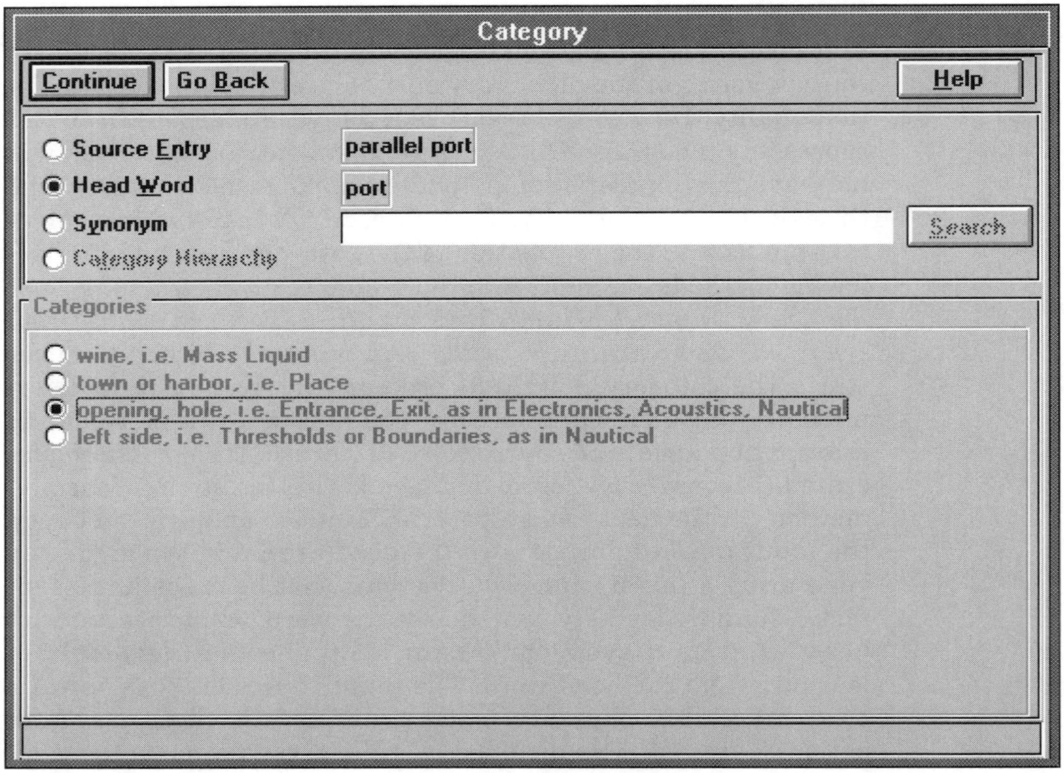

FIGURE 11.6   An example of learning from the head word.

with one of the categories. In Figure 11.7, neither the source entry *modus operandi* nor its hypothesized head word *operandi* are in the dictionary, and the user supplies a synonym *procedure*. ALEX discovered that the categories *Way of Doing Something* and *Instructional Information* are defined for this synonym.

The Categories frame displays *prompts* for the entry, head word, or synonym. Prompts are structured in such a way that nuances of a given word are presented to the user most intuitively. Each prompt consists of one or more *example words*, the category following *i.e.*, and one or more *field of knowledge*. In the

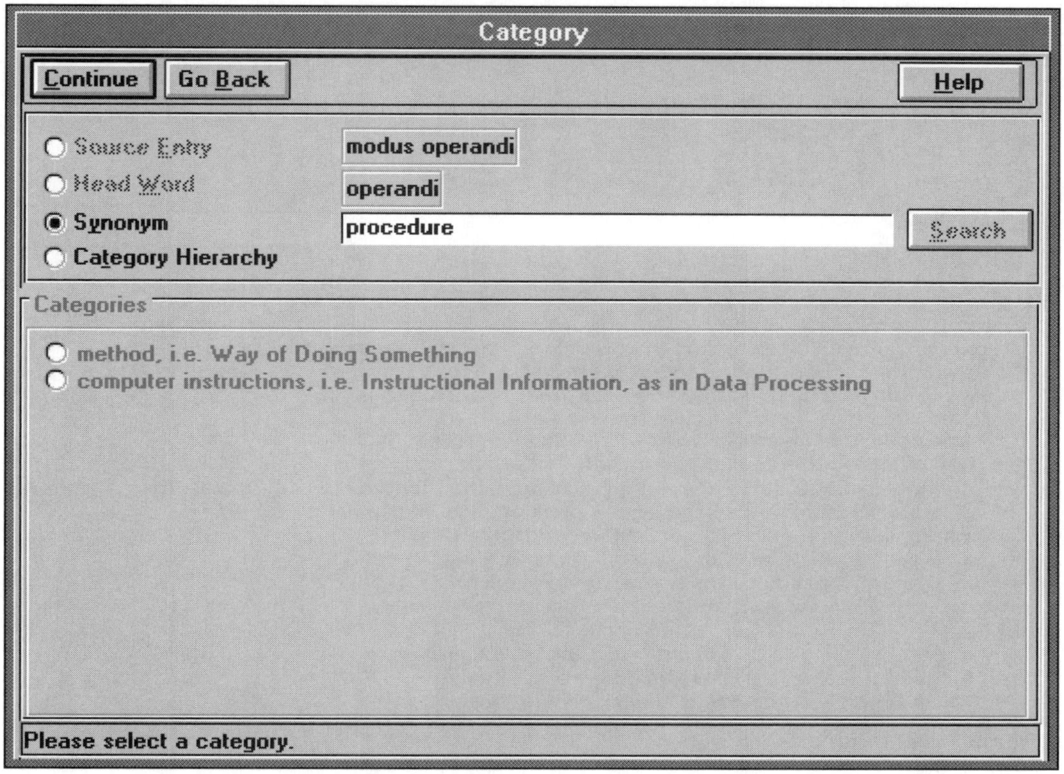

Category
Continue **Go Back**   **Help**
○ Source Entry   modus operandi
○ Head Word   operandi
⦿ Synonym   procedure   Search
○ Category Hierarchy
Categories
○ method, i.e. Way of Doing Something
○ computer instructions, i.e. Instructional Information, as in Data Processing
Please select a category.

FIGURE 11.7   Learning from a synonym.

last prompt in Figure 11.7, the example word is *computer instructions*, the category is *Instructional Information*, and the field of knowledge is *Data Processing*.

Learning from Feature Hierarchy   In ALEX, several types of complex lexical features are hierarchically organized and can be visually presented to users as treelike structures. The system allows the user to walk through the hierarchies to select the proper feature for a dictionary entry. We call this method *learning from the feature hierarchy*. This approach provides the user with a clear and overall picture of the lexical information involved. An example of this approach is learning from the SAL

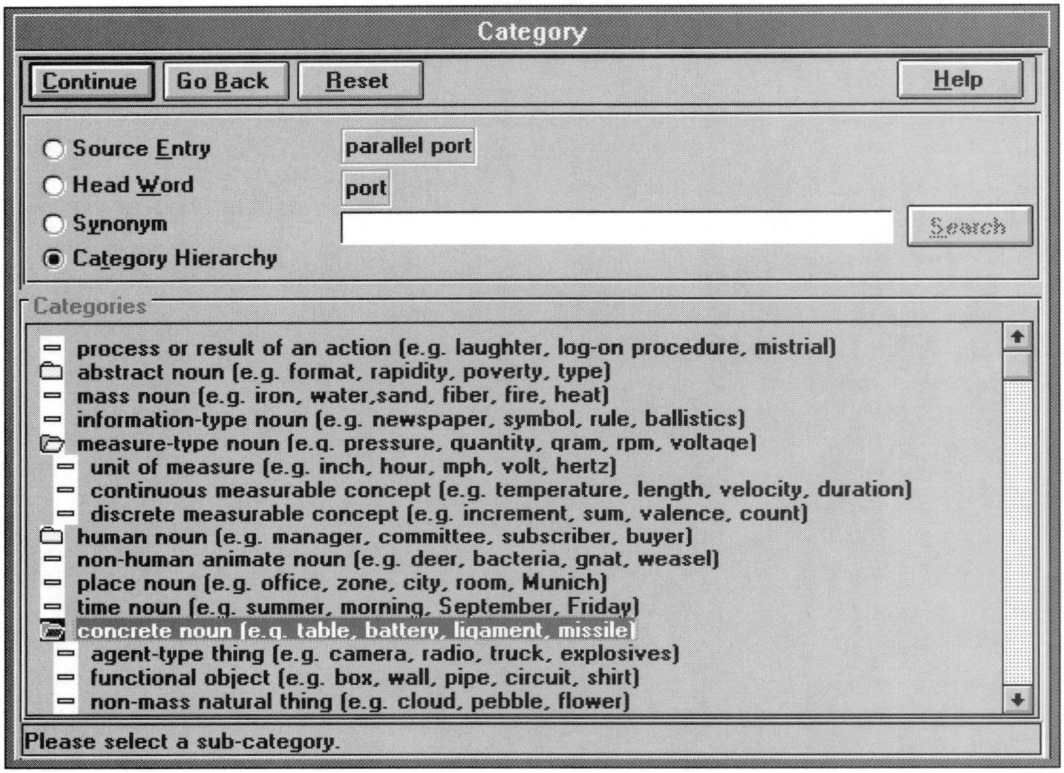

FIGURE 11.8   The category hierarchy.

hierarchy, a method for the acquisition of categories, as discussed in the section Learning by Analogy. Figure 11.8 shows a partial hierarchy of the noun categories.

Learning by Being Told   Learning by being told is a simple method that has been used in artificial intelligence for knowledge acquisition (Hass and Hendrix 1983). This is the basic technique with which ALEX asks for information directly from the user. Whenever the system cannot make a decision based on the previously acquired information or the knowledge base, it elicits an answer from the user by presenting either a list of options or a question. The system is carefully designed so that it only asks relevant questions, which are grouped together to reduce the number of screens in the user interface.

User in Control

ALEX is designed mainly from the perspective of lexical acquisition. However, to the users, the system is always an interface tool that facilitates their task. ALEX gives the user as much control as possible. Whenever appropriate, the system does not force the user to enter the lexical features in any particular order. For example, in the Entry Window, the user may specify the features in any sequence. The consequence is that the user interface design is more difficult because there exist logical relations among the lexical features. In German, for example, the inflection of a noun depends on both its gender and number. We solve this problem by resetting feature values and disabling and enabling feature labels.

CONCLUSIONS

We have presented the ALEX lexical management system, both from the user interface and lexical acquisition perspectives. In particular, we discussed the design principles and learning methods adopted in the system. Due to the limitation of space, other important issues, such as product internationalization, project management, and the roles of end users and marketing staff, while essential to the successful design of ALEX, were not discussed in this chapter.

Future research and development in the following areas may prove to enhance and increase the intelligence of the current system.

- Currently, the user has to provide a synonym for the acquisition of category. The core dictionary and the knowledge base may be restructured so that synonyms of a given word can be suggested by ALEX automatically.
- Currently, the *learning from a synonym* approach only applies to the acquisition of nouns. This is because, in the SAL classifications, while the noun taxonomy is truly

semantico-syntactic, the taxonomies for other word classes are more or less syntactic only. Therefore, semantically synonymous words should not necessarily be placed at the same location in the SAL hierarchy. Semantic nuances of words in these word classes need to be analyzed and made available to ALEX.

- In general, verbs are syntactically more complex than other parts of speech. Therefore, the acquisitions of verbs, especially new verbs, are more difficult than others. ALEX needs a more intuitive way to describe the verb SAL structures to the user.

REFERENCES

Gdaniec, Claudia and Patricia Schmid. 1995. Constituent shifts in the Logos English-German system. In *Proceedings of The Sixth International Conference on Theoretical and Methodological Issues in Machine Translation*, Leuven, Belgium.

Hass, N., and G. G. Hendrix. 1983. Learning by being told: Acquiring knowledge for information management. In Michalski, R. S. et al. (eds.), *Machine Learning: An AI Approach*. Palo Alto, CA: Tiog Press, 405–427.

Hoffman, Robert R. 1995. Monster analogies. *AI magazine*, **16**, 3 (Fall 1995).

L'Homme, Marie-Claude. 1994. Management of terminology in a machine-translation environment. *Terminology* **1**, 1:121–135.

Rich, E. A. 1991. *Artificial Intelligence*. New York: McGraw-Hill.

Scott, Bernard E. 1989. *The Logos System*. Presented at the MT SUMMIT II Conference, Munich, 1989.

Winston, P.H. 1980. Learning and reasoning by analogy. *Communications of the ACM* **23**, 12 (December): 689–703.

ABOUT THE AUTHOR

Yong Gao is currently an architect of core technology in the Intelligent Agents Group at FTP Software, Inc. in Massachusetts. He also teaches a course in Expert Systems at Boston University. Previously, he was a senior computational linguist and project leader at Logos Corporation, where he was responsible for the design, development, and production release of ALEX. He received a Ph.D. in computer science in 1993 at Boston University, where his research centered on natural language processing and artificial intelligence. Before entering Boston University, he was a lecturer at the Institute of Linguisitics in Huazhong University of Science and Technology, China. He also holds an M.A. in linguistics from Wuhan University, China. Yong Gao can be contacted at: Intelligent Agents Group, FTP Software, Inc., 2 High Street, N. Andover, MA 01845, USA.

CHAPTER 12

A Day in the Life: Studying Context Across Cultures

BACKGROUND

The Challenge of a New Market

Historically, information technology has been used primarily by businesses. Originally, early technology was expensive to purchase and so only businesses that had a "true business need" could justify the purchase and use of computers. As a result, many manufacturers like Hewlett-Packard (HP) have spent years becoming very familiar with the needs and characteristics of this business marketplace.

However, with the dropping prices of computers and peripherals, and with the maturation of the business market, manufacturers have looked for other potential markets to tap. There is a growing awareness that one largely untapped market is the home. As a result, the past year has seen an explosion of new products and services aimed at the home market.

A new market requires new information for product developers and marketers. It is important that they understand not only what is similar to other markets but, more critically, what is different and even unique about the new market. Therefore, to meet the needs of this target audience of home users, primarily families, both designers and engineers require information about how families currently use or want to use technology.

Gathering and maintaining this information demands a major research effort. This chapter will focus on how a division of one company, Hewlett-Packard's Inkjet Printer Division, conducted one piece of this research effort into a new market.

The Challenge of Understanding the Family

Doing research into how a family uses computers is similar in some ways to doing research in a business setting. Some of the same questions apply: When was the computer purchased and where is it set up? When gathering this type of information from adults, some of the same methods as are used in understanding business needs, such as Contextual Inquiry (Wixon et al. 1990) and Artifact Walkthroughs (Raven and Flanders, in press) can be used to elicit information.

However, in many respects, trying to do research in a home is extremely different from research in a business setting (Copeland and White 1991). In the family, the context of use is more varied than in businesses. Rapport is even more critical and must be developed with individuals of all ages. Getting the desired information from children is a significant challenge and requires a totally different approach in order to maintain focus in what can be a very chaotic and confusing setting. Research methods in ethnography (Fetterman 1989), such as ethnographic interviews (Spradley 1979) and participant observation (Jorgensen 1989), are a good adjunct to more traditional verbal protocols used with adults.

These types of qualitative data methods create heaps and piles of data. The magnitude and variety of data types collected using these methods require different approaches to analysis and reporting as well. This aspect of the study will not be addressed in this chapter due to the proprietary nature of the findings.

The Challenge of a Global Market

Manufacturers are also increasingly recognizing that the family market is global. Simply understanding the family setting and potential needs for one culture is no longer sufficient in planning products for worldwide distribution.

Understanding the global family is a significant challenge. Not only do families differ considerably within a given culture, they also embody the basic cultural differences of their country. Finding ways to do contextual research cross-culturally is a major challenge.

Therefore this chapter will focus on how HP did contextual research to gather data for new global product development by visiting and observing families working with their computers in six different locations in three countries. The particular emphasis will be on the international aspects of this study.

As mentioned before, due to the proprietary nature of the data collected, the process used to collect the data will be discussed rather than the data which resulted.

PREPARATION FOR THE RESEARCH

Building on previous work by HP's Market Research department, the Human Factors team, led by the project champion (Deborah Mrazek) and aided by the project consultant (Susan Dray), set about designing a contextual study of families.

The basic question which guided this research was: How do families use computers and printers in their home?

To answer this question, we visited twenty families and collected volumes of data on each visit. Of course, the answer to such a broad question is never complete. We were limited by time and resources and therefore focused on the United States and Europe, since these regions represent a large proportion of HP's inkjet printer market. We would like to extend this research, as time, funding, and priorities allow.

Family Characteristics

Technology   In both the United States and Europe, the families each had a PC (IBM or IBM clone) with Microsoft Windows 3.1, and a printer of any variety. Some families had more than one printer and/or computer.

Family Structure   We recruited families with at least two children. In the United States, families had as many as eight children. In Europe, the families had two children.

Children in these families ranged in age from two months to twenty-five years. All children over two years old participated in the study. In the United States, some families were joined by relatives, friends, or neighbors who we then included as active participants in the visit. In Europe, only one family was joined by a neighbor child who also actively participated in our visit.

Other Factors The families we recruited met a variety of criteria. Some of the criteria included income levels, geographic location, proficiency with the computer, and interest in participating in this type of research. Specifically excluded from this study were families who had one or more members involved in market research, or in a business relationship with an HP competitor.

Recruiting the Families

American Families We visited twelve families in the United States. We chose four cities representative of HP's typical markets: Minneapolis, Memphis, Phoenix, and Salt Lake. A market research firm based in Portland located and scheduled three families in each city. They handled all details including payment, directions on how to reach the home, and confirming the visits. The project consultant (Susan Dray) coordinated the study. She spoke with each family immediately before the visit to confirm the visit, clarify directions if necessary, and get meal preferences. This direct contact with the family helped establish the legitimacy of the visit. It also seemed to ease the initial discomfort of the first few minutes of the visit.

European Locations The project champion (Deborah Mrazek) would have liked to include visits to more countries and more families within each country, but resources only permitted us to visit two locations. Both Germany and France are large markets for consumer computer equipment so we chose to visit families in the cities of Dusseldorf, Germany and Paris, France.

We recognize that such a small sample of European cities limits the generalizability of the data, but we were time and resource limited. Even with these limitations we were encouraged by the large consistencies we found in the data.

Recruiting European Families   In Germany, a German market research firm made all of the arrangements. Due to the very strict privacy laws in Germany, they were not able to "cold call" the way the American firm did, which made the recruit particularly difficult. Therefore, the German firm used a number of creative ways to find families including posting advertisements on electronic bulletin boards, placing ads in the personals section of the local paper, and getting referrals for possible leads. Although this approach worked very well it was predictably much slower, more expensive, and tedious.

In France, a French market research firm arranged for two families in the Paris region. These families were previous participants in focus groups who had indicated a willingness to be contacted in the future.

Observation Teams

American Teams   Since the findings of this study would be used throughout the design organization, it was very important that this entire study have organizational ownership beyond the Human Factors group. The key disciplines that needed to be involved were Marketing and Engineering. As we designed the study, one design consideration was that each visit team of three to four people include representation from each of these disciplines. The only visit team member consistent across all visits was the project consultant (Susan Dray). The visit team members varied in their familiarity with each other and this type of research prior to these visits.

The project consultant (Susan Dray) worked with the teams of HP people to coordinate all of the communication, and to make sure that teams were briefed ahead of time as to the structure and format of the visits. Each team had one person assigned to camera duty, who was responsible for learning how to use the video equipment. Another team member typically brought along all of the release forms and the HP logo gifts, known at HP as "spiffs." Prior to a visit team's first family visit, the project consultant (Susan Dray) briefed the team on the protocol in detail to assure a commonly shared focus and answered any specific questions about the visits.

European Team The visit team in Europe consisted of the project consultant, the project champion and a native-speaking translator. We also had an HP Marketing manager join us on one visit in Germany.

The translator in each country was hired by the local market research firm. In both countries we were joined by very gifted women translators who contributed to the success of the visits. Most of the visits in Germany were conducted in a combination of English, German, and a hybrid of both languages. There was at least one person in each German family that we visited who spoke English. In France, the visits were conducted primarily in French, therefore the use of translators was essential.

CONDUCTING THE RESEARCH

The visits progressed similarly in all cities, even though each one was slightly different in logistics and dynamics. The following is an overview of the process used.

Preliminary Rapport-Building

Rapport-building began before the visit during the recruiting process. Through the professionalism of the recruiting process, we established the legitimacy of the process.

The rapport-building process started at the time of the initial phone contact. The recruiter explained the visit program in detail to the family member contacted. The recruiter also answered any questions about the visit before the family was asked to make a commitment. The market research company then followed the initial phone contact with a letter of confirmation. The project consultant (Susan Dray) then personally contacted each family immediately before the visit to confirm plans and answer any last-minute questions.

Initial Visit Activities to Build Rapport

In a visit such as this, the first fifteen minutes will set the tone for the entire visit. Therefore, it was important to quickly build rapport in order to set the atmosphere for the next four hours. Knowing this, we planned a number of rapport-building activities to increase the likelihood for a successful visit.

The first ten minutes was the most awkward part of the evening. We began with a brief introduction of the visit team. We tried to coordinate the food to be delivered when we arrived or shortly after our arrival. We found that eating a meal with the family soon after the initial introductions helped build rapport.

The food turned out to be an excellent icebreaker and allowed us to have a natural conversation with the family. In Europe especially, the families were often quite curious about us and we found that bringing a meal was a particularly effective way to put the family at ease. We had had some initial concerns about whether bringing food would be acceptable in Europe since it is not a common practice, but it turned out to be very effective.

During the meal we talked about the study including why we were visiting them, the goals of the study, and where else we were going. Then the parents and any children over 18 signed a confidentiality statement and limited release form to allow us to videotape. Because all families had been told about the study in advance including that we would be videotaping, this was pro forma.

Formal Data Collection

The next challenge was to transition from the informal unstructured dinner conversation to data collection which was more formal and more structured. This was a potentially tricky transition but we identified ways to manage it. We wanted to keep the children involved, to see their use of the computer and to indicate to the parents the sincerity of our request. Therefore, following the meal we moved to the computer and began our inquiry by asking the children to show us what they "did with the computer." This had the very positive dual effects we were hoping for. We asked them to print a sample of their work if they were old enough to do this. All children over the age of two participated in this way. In one family the four-year-old boy did not know how to print before our visit, but he figured it out while we watched. He then proudly shared the printouts with us.

Each family member in turn showed us similar things, starting with each of the children, and then with the adults. The visit became an ongoing conversation with each family member in turn. We used an adaptation of Contextual Inquiry that followed a protocol that was developed jointly by Human Factors, Marketing, and Engineering. We watched especially how each individual used the computer and printer, and how they described its use. We collected print samples whenever possible. For print samples that had been created before our visit, we conducted an Artifact Walkthrough to understand how and why the sample was created and printed. We were careful not to take any confidential or personal information.

To keep the children involved but occupied during the parents' interview, we asked the children to draw a picture of what computers and printers would be like when they were as old as their parents. For this we gave each child his or her own package of Mr. Sketch brand scented markers. These are fruit-scented markers which were a particular hit in Europe where they are not yet available. Having the children work on drawings served two purposes: It provided us with additional information and, perhaps more importantly, it kept the children engaged in the study while we talked with their parents.

Each visit team member took notes to supplement the video-tapes, audiotapes, and photographs. In Europe, we also used checklists to gather the data systematically.

We spent roughly four hours with each family although some sessions, especially in Europe, lasted much longer. The average time for the European visits was five hours, and one of our French families was so interested in showing us what they did that we were there for over six hours.

Wrap-up and Leave-taking

As the evening progressed and we completed our data collection we again engaged in informal interaction as a preface to leaving. To our surprise the families were reluctant to see us leave. This was particularly pronounced in Europe. In Germany, most of the families brought out the special wine, the special Christmas cakes, or even champagne at the end of the visit. They asked more questions and wanted to hear more about us. This is an indication that the rapport-building had been very successful. The German market research firm, who had been privately skeptical that we would be able to get these very formal German families to open up to us, was particularly surprised by this.

Before leaving we took photographs of the location, and of each family member using the computer. We also noted where they kept supplies, what supplies they had, and where the documentation and other equipment such as fax machines and copiers were. We ended our visit by taking a family photograph (pets and all) which we included in our post-visit thank-you note.

Debriefing

After each visit we debriefed as a team discussing the process and key findings. At the end of the final visit for each city we also did a "city debrief," which was very helpful, especially since the volume of data collected was massive. These sessions also identified things that we wanted to change or follow up on with future families. This flexibility allowed us to adapt as needed throughout the course of the study even though the basic focus and protocol did not change during this time.

Shortly after each visit, the project consultant sent a thank-you card to each family with a copy of the family snapshot so they could remember our visit. The families really liked this, and we had several replies saying they had really enjoyed our visit. Also, when we followed up with the German families a month or so later, most of them mentioned this note and were extremely positive about the visit.

The data was analyzed and presented in a variety of formats and models, which are considered proprietary at this time. Therefore, this chapter is focused on how we did our study, not what data was collected.

LEARNING FROM THE RESEARCH

We learned a tremendous amount about how to conduct an international contextual study, in addition to the specific data we collected. We have covered some of the more general process insights elsewhere (Mrazek, Dray, and Dyer 1995; Dray and Mrazek, in press). The remainder of this chapter will therefore focus on the aspects most relevant to success of an international study.

The Following Process Insights Were Particularly Striking

Spend Even More Time Preparing a European Study Than You Would Doing a Study in Your Own Culture Anticipate problems wherever possible. It is difficult to estimate how much time such a study will take. Because of the cross-cultural aspects of this study, we tried to allow more time for things like logistics. It was also important to anticipate problems and to include fixes to these wherever possible. For instance, in the United States we found that we often needed our heavy-duty extension cord because the power supply was a distance away from where we were filming. Therefore, when we went to Europe we included such a cord along with a plug kit. In addition, we found that it was not possible to do more than one visit in a day given the extreme demands on attention.

We did not allow enough "recovery" time between visits since we were conducting usability studies during the day and doing the family visits at night. In retrospect, our schedule of usability testing during the day and visiting families in the evening was a heavy load, which we would not repeat. It is important to allow enough time between visits to debrief and unwind.

A general guideline we recommend for these types of studies is that the visit team should not exceed working an eight- to ten-hour day. In other words, if the combination of travel, visit, and debrief add up to five hours, then two visits could be scheduled in one day. If the combination of travel, visit, and debrief add up to six or more hours, then only one visit should be scheduled for that day.

Cross-cultural Observation Teams Work Very Well Including observers from both the observing and the observed cultures was very successful. By including observations by both the visit team members and the translator, we captured both cultural and cross-cultural data. The visitor team members noticed things that the local translator did not, and could ask questions that a member of the culture being visited would not think to ask. For instance, the American (visitor team) member could ask about where Germans are likely to buy ink cartridges, how the role of persons has changed in Germany in the past ten years, or how much schoolwork the children are getting. Conversely, the local translator could help the visiting team member interpret answers and actions. For instance, the German translator understood the honor in the special holiday cake served at the end of the visit, and noticed the use of the informal pronoun *du* in the family's questions to the visitors. Together, both perspectives were powerfully synergistic.

Similarly, including observers from both the technical and the social or psychological educational backgrounds was very successful. The technical observer noticed things like the version of the driver being used or some unique workaround the person had discovered. The social observer noticed things like the interpersonal actions between members of the family who were computer-lovers and those who were computer-haters. They also noticed how different members in the family reacted nonverbally when one of the family members was having a problem with the computer or printer.

Rely on Local Knowledge to Advise on Cultural Elements, Such as Dress, Holidays, or Greeting Customs   Only someone living in the local culture will know how to advise a visit team on cultural elements. Since it is common for things like holidays, dress, and greeting customs to vary even within a small region in Europe, it is important to have local advice. For this study, we relied on our local translator to coach us about when and how to shake hands, whether to offer to help clear the table, and how to show respect and interest regarding specific local holiday customs and decorations.

Use a Local Recruiter Since They Will Know How to Find People in That Culture   It is very important to have a local recruiter. This was driven home to us in Germany where it is illegal to "cold call" to recruit. Therefore, our recruiter had to understand how to find participants through other means. This would have been impossible had he not been very familiar with the local conditions.

Use a Local Translator Since He or She Will Know How Best to Interact in That Culture   The visit protocol should be developed to accurately meet the goals of the sponsoring organization that plans to use the results of the study. The protocol should also be fine tuned by someone from the culture being visited, such as the translator, to match the local culture.

The protocol for this study was jointly developed by the project consultant (Susan Dray) and the project champion (Deborah Mrazek). The protocol focused on asking both technical questions and questions specifically about the local culture. Our translators then fine-tuned the protocol so that it was localized to fit each specific culture. Our translators helped identify areas or questions that might have been confusing to our visit sites, which caused us to adopt a slightly different approach in different cultures. For example, in France we were warned that some housewives may have negative feelings toward a computer in the home. We were sensitive to that, and in France we explored that topic in more detail.

Focus on Rapport from the First Contact and Throughout the Study   From the very first contact we focused on building rapport. This was extremely critical at the beginning and throughout the study. We found that without our participants' goodwill we would not have been able to gather data for the length of time that we did, or in the significant detail that we needed. We allowed the family to set the pace, altering the specific flow to fit the particular interaction. We used nonjudgmental terms (such as "guest software") and asked about potentially controversial topics (such as refilling pens) in an interested, nonjudgmental manner. The result was a candid, honest picture of the family's behavior with their printer.

Followup Afterward for Additional Feedback and to Build Goodwill   After each visit, we sent each family a copy of one of the family photos and a thank-you note. In addition, we had our recruiter follow up with each of the European families to learn what they thought about our visit. In the United States, we sent photos and notes, but did not do a systematic followup. Still, we received a number of unsolicited faxes and letters, several of which included more print samples. These followup notes and calls had a very positive effect. Most of the families were "still glowing" from our visit. They expressed positive feelings both for the study and for HP for sponsoring such a study.

CONCLUSIONS

The international family study was a success despite the challenges it posed. We were able to gather an enormous amount of data in a very short time and HP has used that data to help guide the direction of new product development. In addition, we learned how to collect such information effectively and efficiently and have used this foundation to extend these studies to other market sectors.

We also exposed HP engineers and marketers to their customers, and allowed them to have a significant interaction with them. This has had a significant, if subtle, effect. Following our study, HP Marketing took our basic design and developed a program to expose even more staff to customers by arranging customer insight visits. Together, these two projects, along with the ongoing usability evaluations and beta testing program, have helped the organization to "put a face on the customer."

As a result of this study and other efforts, engineers and marketers are both aware of the pivotal role they play in designing printers that are "family friendly" and easy to use. The effort has become a team effort, since they recognize that only if they work together are they likely to reach this goal.

Windows is a registered trademark of Microsoft Corporation.
Mr. Sketch is a registered trademark of Sanford Corporation.

REFERENCES

Copeland, A., and K. White. 1991. *Studying Families*. (Volume 17, Applied Social Research Methods Series) Newbury Park, CA: Sage Publications.

Dray, S., and D. Mrazek. In press. A Day in the life of a family: An international ethnographic study. D. Wixon, and J. Ramey, (eds),

Discovering Design: Case Studies of Field Research in Product and System Design. New York: Wiley.

Fetterman, D. 1989. Ethnography: Step-by-Step; Newbury Park, CA: Sage.

Jorgensen, D. 1989. Participant observation: A methodology for human studies. (Volume 15, Applied Social Research Methods Series.) Newbury Park, CA: Sage Publications.

Mrazek, D., S. Dray, and N. Dyer. 1995. Day-in-the-life visits: How to make them happen globally, or Discovering unstated needs in a family environment. *Forty-Eighth European Society for Opinion and Marketing Research Congress*, the Hague, the Netherlands, September 1995, 353–359.

Raven, M., and A. Flanders. In press. Using contextual inquiry to learn about your audiences. *SIGDOC Journal of Computer Documentation*.

Spradley, J. 1979. *The ethnographic interview*. New York: Harcourt Brace Jovanovich College Publishers.

Wixon, D., K. Holtzblatt, and S. Knox. 1990. Contextual design: An emergent view of system design. *Human Factors in Computing Systems, CHI'90 Conference Proceedings*, Seattle, WA, April 1990, 329–336.

ABOUT THE AUTHORS

Deborah Mrazek is a Certified Human Factors Professional who has been practicing for thirteen years. She has performed all aspects of Human Factors Engineering at Rancho Seco Nuclear Generating Station for five years. She was involved in implementing Human Factors programs for HP Computing Systems for four years. She then performed Human Factors Consulting internally for a variety of HP divisions. For the past two years she has been leading the S/W Human Factors Team at the HP Vancouver (InkJet Printer) divisions. She became involved in international usability testing several years ago. Recently she performed several usability studies in Europe.

Dr. Susan Dray, President of Dray & Associates, is nationally and internationally recognized as a leader in the application of human factors to the design of systems. A trainer, speaker, and consultant with over sixteen years experience, she has pioneered the development of usability methods, and is an expert in the organizational management of technological change. An American, she has worked in both the United States and Europe.

Dr. Dray received her doctorate in Psychology from UCLA and is a Certified Human Factors Professional. She has held various positions in Human Factors research and consulting at Honeywell and American Express Financial Advisors in Minneapolis, Minnesota, prior to establishing her consultancy in 1993.

Nationally and internationally, Dr. Dray has played a leadership role in the Human Factors profession. She is a Fellow of the Human Factors and Ergonomics Society and has chaired its Organizational Design and Management Technical Group, as well as the Computers and Communications Scientific and Technical Committee of the International Ergonomics Association. Dr. Dray edits the Business column of the magazine *Interactions*, and is also on the editorial board of the international journal *Behaviour and Information Technology*.

CHAPTER 13

Icon and Symbol Design Issues for Graphical User Interfaces

Graphical user interfaces with icons and symbols make products successful. International cultural differences make designing effective icons and symbols challenging. A noted expert shows how to design them correctly.

Most of today's successful software products rely on icons and symbols in graphical user interfaces (GUIs) to communicate with the user. Icons are signs that are familiar, are easy to understand, and are often concrete representations of objects or people. Symbols are signs that are often more abstract and require specific instruction to learn. Researchers and developers have discovered that GUI paradigms such as Windows, Macintosh, or Motif do not always provide a ready-made sign for a product's data, functions, tasks, or roles.

As a result, programmers and graphic designers are developing sets of signs that in some ways transcend traditional verbal language. In fact, the number of signs may be greater than some natural languages use for simple communication. For

This chapter is an edited version of the author's earlier article "Symbols on the Desktop: Icon Design Issues for GUIs and Workstations," which originally appeared in *Unix World* (now called *Open Computing*), Supplement, Special Report: International, May 1991, pp. 63-67, and is reprinted in its edited form with permission of McGraw-Hill Publishers, New York.

example, typical suites of CAD/CAM applications may use 5,000 to 15,000 "icons" in their repertoire of signs. Compare that to basic Chinese, which uses 3,000 pictograms and ideograms, and you can see where we are headed: we are creating entirely new visible languages.

Even more challenging is designing icons for multi-professional, multi-cultural, and multi-lingual use. What is meaningful and natural for one group may be ambiguous, unintelligible, or arbitrary for another. For example, the desktop trashcan, which more accurately ought to be called the desktop wastebasket (see Figure 13.1), is typical of galvanized steel garbage cans found in North America. A hacker's (programmer's) jargon from the "garbage in/garbage out" days of computing has become, through successful marketing, an archetypical sign for deleting files. Note, by the way, that the desktop wastebasket is placed "on top of" the "desk," rather than "below" it, a location more typical of real-world experience.

Are other users around the world as familiar with this form of trash or garbage can? By now, most users have been exposed to this classic sign, but as more symbols and icons inundate products, designers will have to take international and cross-professional users' familiarity with the the shape and the color of signs into consideration. A special working group of the International Standards Organization (ISO) based in Geneva is now considering standards for signs of the user interface and will eventually publish their recommendations (see Bibliography). Besides dealing with the technical problems of showing signs in very different pixel resolutions and in different media (e.g., on

FIGURE 13.1   The trashcan icon for deleting files has become an archetypical sign recognized throughout the world of computer users.

screens, in paper documentation, and on plastic enclosures), the group is also considering how much variation from the authorized version should be tolerated.

One example of this variability arises in the case of the desktop folder icon (see Figure 13.2). In North American offices, paper documents are often stored in stiff paper folders with tabs for labeling. The folders, in turn, are stored horizontally in desk drawers, filing cabinets, or in storage boxes. In some European countries and in Japan, documents are stored in cardboard box-like containers on shelves, with the vertical paper sheets punched and held in place by rings or unpunched but held in place by spring clips. The containers are pulled off the shelves using a small finger hole located in the vertical face of the box. This bit of trivia has an important consequence: some people think that the international sign for a collection of files should be the vertical container's face (see Figure 13.3), rather than the horizontal tabbed folder familiar to North American users. It is apparent how discussions for and against particular designs might become heated international debates!

Shape is not the only controversial element. Consider the country mailbox familiar to North Americans. This kind of mailbox has become a sign in many applications for electronic message exchange functions (see Figure 13.4). The mailboxes in most North American users' homes do not look like the country mailbox, and most people outside North America have never used nor typically see such mailboxes. What about the color of the mailbox? Some applications use the government's four-footed mailbox as an icon for electronic mail. In the United

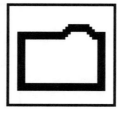

FIGURE 13.2   The typical tabbed paper folder icon represents a collection of document files and is well known in North America.

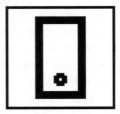

FIGURE 13.3   In some countries, this sign would be familiar as an icon for a collection of documents.

States, the typical federal mailbox on the street is blue, but in London it is red and a completely different shape, in Athens it is yellow, and in some other countries it is green. Obviously, color as well as shape play a role in making icons easily recognized, learned, and remembered.

In a recent project for American Airlines' SABRE Travel Information Network, the world's largest private online network, the author's firm designed an illustrative home window or page that uses several pictorial icons to represent modules of functions, including an electronic mail function. Recognizing that different countries use different kinds of government mail boxes, a customizing function is available to change the shape and color of the icon throughout the system according to the user's preference (see Figure 13.5).

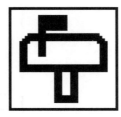

FIGURE 13.4   The country mail box familiar to North Americans is sometimes used as an electronic message/mail icon.

FIGURE 13.5   A portion of the Customizer function of American Airlines' Planet SABRE™ showing variations of the electronic mail icon suitable for different countries.

That recognition brings us to consider how to design icons better. As the industry and international communities sort out what signs to establish as legal standards or approved conventions, there is something you can do: inform yourself about established conventions, already existing good designs that can be adapted, or in some cases are public property, and begin to take more seriously the task of designing effective symbols and icons for cross-professional, cross-cultural user groups.

ADVANTAGES AND DISADVANTAGES

Why are icons and symbols so popular in today's computer graphics systems? What advantages do they offer over words? Part of the answer lies in the realm of marketing. Icons are appealing and can attract a viewer's attention.

Another advantage is that an individual sign may take up fewer pixels and less space than the equivalent in words. This means that more information can be packed into a given window or screen space. The savings of space in menus, maps, and diagrams can be significant.

More importantly, icons and symbols as part of a visible language system can replace national verbal languages and contribute to user interfaces that are international in design and comprehension. By using signs that are recognized internationally, manufacturers have a head start in making their products easier to produce, learn, use, and maintain. The icons and symbols can be an advantage not only on the screen, but also in printed documentation, training, and marketing literature.

If the signs are well conceived, systematically designed, and effectively displayed, the icons and symbols should be easier to recognize quickly in a busy visual context than their verbal counterparts. For example, within a text-filled window, a short phrase at the bottom of the window might explain that there is more to be displayed if the user will scroll the contents. This situation could be represented by a simple arrow that effectively communicates the message and clearly distinguishes itself from alphanumeric text.

Another advantage is the value of icons and symbols in reinforcing and aiding user comprehension of previously delivered verbal information. In tutorial and training materials, a simple question mark inside a round circle can denote a source of help for the user. It can also denote a source of confusion for the computer that it is bringing to the attention of the user. With just a few pixels, an icon or symbol can imply an entire situation.

Icons and symbols are not a panacea for user interface design and information visualization. They can not completely replace words in some complex situations, and there are clear disadvantages to the use of icons and symbols.

An entire repertoire of new icons and symbols must be researched, designed, tested, and introduced into the marketplace. There is no system already in existence that may be readily incorporated, unlike letterforms and typefonts.

Some international sign languages like Blissymbolics and Ota's LoCos provide a starting point (see the Bibliography). These visual sign systems can express any concept that written languages can communicate, but they have no pronunciation. These icon or symbol languages must be re-planned and redesigned for use in computer-mediated communication. As with typefaces, the signs often must appear in different sizes, weights, and styles. An entire "font" of symbols should be designed for each major size. This renovation is a costly and time-consuming task if it is done well. However, the consequences of poor design are confusion and lower productivity for the user.

In other disciplines, there do exist some examples of designing effective graphic sign systems for cross-education level, cross-language, cross-profession, and cross-cultural users. For example, the U.S. Department of Transportation commissioned a study and recommendations for the use of icons and symbols in mass transit environments. Skilled graphic designers created conventions for these signs that have improved the quality of mass transportation signage throughout the United States (see *Symbol Signs* in the Bibliography). Similar professional activities are necessary throughout the software development industry, in which signage systems for conceptual landscapes are now being built into user interfaces.

Because of difficulties in designing, teaching, and comprehending icons and symbols, there is a practical limit to how many different local and global signs one can introduce into a system. Even the pictographic and ideographic Chinese system with its large repertoire of signs has a much smaller number of signs that most people use in practice. Ideally, icons and symbols should be used for what they can do best. At the same time they should retain a clear, consistent approach.

DESIGN ISSUES

Basic principles for designing systems of icons and symbols are similar to those at the larger scale of designing screens and windows. Consistency, clarity, simplicity, and familiarity are key attributes. Sometimes these factors will be at cross purposes, but this is not unusual in design tasks. The skilled professional knows when to weigh one factor more heavily than another. Let's look at a few typical symbols exhibiting these properties.

Figure 13.6 shows a set of signs that demonstrate how graphic design consistency can be established among icons and symbols. The grid indicates the number of pixels used to display the icon. The pixels must be of sufficient quantity and size to establish clear differences of form (i.e., shape, color, texture, line weight, etc.) so that the icons can be identified at normal working distance. On high resolution screens (60-150 dots per inch), squares 16 and 32 pixels on a side are often used. Keep in mind that screen resolutions (e.g., VGA and Super-VGA) are sometimes different and may have differently shaped pixels. Icons and symbols must be designed to appear correctly in each of these screen display standards.

The prototypes in Figure 13.6 demonstrate how typical graphical editing concepts might be shown. Each sign uses a set of visual elements in different ways to build up the image. This approach guarantees some syntactic consistency and also allows the signs and symbols to be easily distinguished. The designer can establish icon and symbol consistency by limiting the variations of angles, line thicknesses, shapes, and amount of empty space.

Figure 13.7 shows how the style of an icon or symbol drawing can be varied to present a corporate identity approach to depicting the basic shape or form. Care must be taken to ensure that such manipulations do not adversely affect legibility.

Figure 13.8 shows how complex even simple icons and symbols can become. One sign from Perq's Accent operating system, which the author's firm also designed, shows an icon with a sub-icon inside of it. These variations of signs show how using a simple set of sign parts can help communicate many different pieces of information. The round symbol shows how the international traffic sign for prohibition (or "cancel") can be adopted for use in

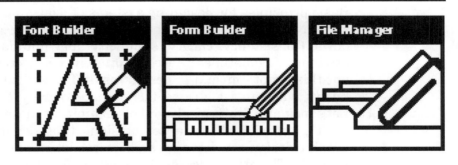

FIGURE 13.6   Signs developed for the Perq Accent operating system.

FIGURE 13.7   Corporate identity reflected in a symbol set.

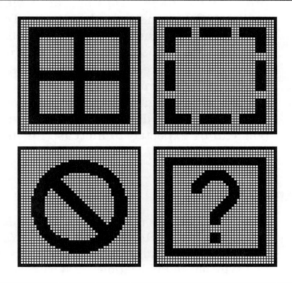

FIGURE 13.8   Complex signs assembled from symbol components.

screen display. This set of well known traffic signs is a good place to start when thinking about an international set of icons.

CONCLUSION

We are seeing an evolution of writing systems in computer-mediated visual communication. Some companies are beginning to devote significant time to the graphic design of these new icons and symbols for international use. Xerox and Apple did pioneering work in developing the use of icons and symbols on the screen. Dicomed, another manufacturer of display equipment, spent considerable time in the 1980s improving the icons and symbols of workstations intended for graphic artists and graphic designers. Interleaf's document layout system introduced in the 1980s also showed a sophisticated, comprehensible approach to icons and symbols. In the early 1990s many more companies invested time and expense to develop significantly larger and better designed icon and symbol sets, not only for CAD/CAM systems and graphic arts systems, but for most office productivity tools, training, multimedia, and more recently online and Internet-based systems. Today's international markets, as well as the rise of the European Economic Community and East Asia's countries as producers of user interfaces, insures that interest in international solutions for icon and symbol design will remain high.

More investigation needs to be done in this important area of user interface design. The design and use of icons and symbols can be expected to increase for most consumer and professional products.

BIBLIOGRAPHY

American Institute of Graphic Arts, *Symbol Signs*, Visual Communication Books, Hastings House, New York, 1981.

Bliss, C. K., *Semantography* (Bliss Symbolics), Semantography (Blissymbolics) Publications, 2 Vicar Street, Coogee, Sydney, Australia, 1965.

Dreyfuss, Henry, *Symbol Sourcebook*, McGraw-Hill, New York, 1972.

Green, Paul, and Burgess, William T., "Debugging a Symbol Set for Identifying Displays," Publication No. PB81-113573, Springfield, VA, 1980.

Horton, William, *The Icon Book*, John Wiley and Sons, New York, 1994.

Marcus, Aaron, "Corporate Identity for Iconic Interface Design: *The Graphic Design Perspective*," *Proc. National Computer Graphics Association Annual Conference* (Anaheim, CA, 13-17 May 1984), Vol. 2, 1984, 468–479.

Marcus, Aaron, Graphic Design for Electronic Documents and User Interfaces, Addison-Wesley, Reading, 1992.

Marcus, Aaron, Smilonich, Nick, and Thompson, Lynne, The Cross-GUI Handbook for Multiplatform User Interface Design, Addison-Wesley, Reading, 1994.

Ota, Yukio, *Pictogram Design*, Kashiwashobo, Tokyo, 1988.

The following recommendations are some general tips for good icon and symbol design.

- **Analyze the verbal contents and the display environment to determine how partial and complete icons or symbols should relate.**

  Existing icons and symbols often have developed in a chaotic manner with elements that may not be relevant, consistent, or useful. Too many different parts may confuse the viewer. The display equipment may have severe limitations in appearance or interaction characteristics (e.g., monochrome CRTs or touch-screen input), which will affect the appearance of the icons or symbols and their use by the viewer.

- **Design the initial signs by creating quick sketches.**

  Once the semantic contents has been organized, create many quick sketches that may vary from logical abstractions to concrete images. Indicate all visual elements, their approximate size, and approximate location. This is a typical stage in the visual design of a complex system of images. At this stage it is easier to manipulate broad differences in the icons or symbols and their hierarchy. It is important not to be too precise or detailed early in the design process. It is more important to explore possible variations. Evaluate which icons or symbols seem to meet the needs of the sender, the receiver, the message, and the medium.

- **Sort the icons or symbols into styles.**

  Consistent stylistic treatment can have a major impact on the perceived complexity of the icons or symbols. Styles should be established in which all the signs are grouped by consistent approach (e.g., part for a whole) or appearance (e.g., curved vs. angular shapes). By sorting the sketches, it is easier to keep track of trade-offs in optimizing the entire set of icons with regard to simplicity, clarity, and consistency.

- **Design a layout grid that organizes all major visual elements.**

  Determine an underlying spatial grid to make consistent all visual components, including point elements, gray patterns, curves, angles, the length and width of ruled lines, etc. It is especially important to use the grid to establish standard horizontal, vertical, and oblique lines and a limited set of sizes for objects.

- **Use large objects, bold lines, and simple areas to distinguish icons.**

  Once a style of presentation is selected, continue to use the same approach as often as possible within the icon or symbol set. Avoid sudden changes in the means of emphasizing or de-emphasizing the importance of certain objects, structures, or processes. Avoid making crucial elements of the sign's significance too small in comparison to the total size of the sign.

- **Simplify appearance.**

  Icons and symbols should be simple and clear. Any extraneous decorative parts should be carefully weighed against the confusion they may cause the viewer. On the other hand, the icons or symbols should not be so simple that they all seem identical; they should be clearly distinguishable. The visual differences in a sign should be as significant as possible from a communication perspective; otherwise, the random or idiosyncratic changes merely add more processing time for the human mind and create a possibility of errors of interpretation.

- **Use color with discretion.**

  Too much variation will confuse the viewer with distracting clutter. In general, for color displays it is reasonable to use five or fewer colors (including black, white, and/or gray) for icons and symbols. Simple color patterns can often be used effectively for background or lowlighted areas that do not need to be examined carefully.

- **Evaluate the designs by showing them to potential viewers.**

After prototypes are available, these should be reviewed and tested using typical viewers. Green and Burgess' report in the Bibliography explains how to set up an evaluation. Evaluations, which can affect all aspects of icon and symbol design, should be repeated if resources and project deadlines permit.

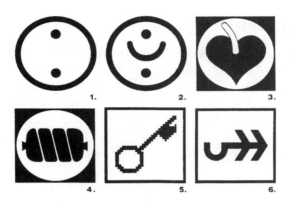

Can you guess what these signs mean? Before you read further, try to determine what they mean, then read on. These examples of signs come from computer-related and general use. If you are confused about them, don't feel bad. They demonstrate the difficulty of designing icons and symbols of user interfaces that can be recognized and remembered by users from many different cultures. All of the images are adapted from figures in Yukio Ota's *Pictogram Design* referred to in the Bibliography.

The first two images are for Telephone and Post Office. They are signs awarded first prize in an International Council of Graphic Design Association (ICOGRADA) competition. The first sign suggests the mouthpiece and earphone of a handset. The second seems to suggest a horn or bugle, which is sometimes used for national post office and telecommunication centers.

The second set of signs represent Plant Quarantine and Meat Quarantine. They are signs in the official New Tokyo Air Terminal Guidance Pictograms set. The heart sign seems to suggest a caring or biological reference rather than a botanical. Not all viewers will immediately recognize a particular kind of tightly wrapped sausage shown in the second sign.

The final two images are icons for Archiver and Back to Initial Screen, propotype signs for general workstation icons proposed for the Ricoh GW200 workstation. The somewhat archaic key shape in the first sign seems to look like a check mark or other device. The second image seems very modern and somewhat ambiguous as to its precise meaning.

ACKNOWLEDGMENTS

The author wishes to thank current and former staff members of Aaron Marcus and Associates, Inc., for their assistance in preparing this article, and American Airlines SABRE Travel Information Network for permission to use the image from Planet SABRE.

ABOUT THE AUTHOR

Aaron Marcus, born in Omaha, Nebraska, USA, has worked on the East and West Coasts USA, and in Hawaii USA, Israel, and Germany. He also has traveled/lectured in Europe, the Middle East, Southeast Asia, and South America.

He received a BA in physics from Princeton (1965) and a BFA and MFA in graphic design from Yale Art School (1968). He is an internationally recognized authority on designing user interfaces, multimedia, documents, and online services. He co-authored HUMAN FACTORS AND TYPOGRAPHY FOR MORE READABLE PROGRAMS (1990) and THE CROSS-GUI HANDBOOK FOR MULTIPLATFORM USER INTERFACE DESIGN (1994), and he authored GRAPHIC DESIGN FOR ELECTRONIC DOCUMENTS AND USER INTERFACES (1992), all published by Addison-Wesley.

Mr. Marcus was the world's first professional graphic designer to work in computer graphics (1967), to program a desktop publishing system (for the AT&T Picturephone, 1969-71), to design virtual realities (1971-73), to establish a computer-based graphic design firm (1982), and to receive the NCGA Industry Achievement Award for his contributions to computer graphics (1992). As President of Aaron Marcus and Associates, Inc., Emeryville, CA, he and his staff work with Fortune 500 companies and startups.

Index